CW01604749

New Testaments

Judith Rice is a freelance writer, living in London. She was born in 1961, and studied Ancient and Modern History at Oxford. Since then, she has worked as a nursing assistant in a psychiatric hospital, a teacher in England and Spain, an editor, a press officer and a journalist.

She is co-author of *Out of a Hop Loft: the story of Toc H*, published by DLT.

New Testaments

People who found purpose talk about their lives

Judith Rice

Fount
An Imprint of HarperCollins*Publishers*

Fount Paperbacks is an Imprint of
HarperCollins*Religious*
Part of HarperCollins*Publishers*
77–85 Fulham Palace Road, London W6 8JB

First published in Great Britain
in 1993 by Fount Paperbacks

1 3 5 7 9 10 8 6 4 2

Copyright © 1993 Judith Rice

Judith Rice asserts the moral right to be
identified as the author of this work

A catalogue record for this book is
available from the British Library

ISBN 0 00 627655 5

Printed and bound in Great Britain by
HarperCollinsManufacturing Glasgow

CONDITIONS OF SALE
This book is sold subject to the condition that it
shall not, by way of trade or otherwise, be lent, re-sold,
hired out or otherwise circulated without the publisher's
prior consent in any form of binding or cover other
than that in which it is published and without a
similar condition including this condition being
imposed on the subsequent purchaser.

All rights reserved. No part of this publication may be
reproduced, stored in a retrieval system, or transmitted,
in any form or by any means, electronic, mechanical,
photocopying, recording or otherwise, without the prior
permission of the publishers.

To my mother and father,
Jeanne and Francis Rice

Acknowledgements

This book is the work of many people. Above all, it belongs to the individuals who told their stories to me. Warm thanks are due to them for taking risks, putting aside embarrassment and speaking with such openness and generosity.

To those many people who put me in contact with potential 'subjects', thank you. In particular, I am indebted to Tom Gulliver, Kerry Brown, Shelagh Livingstone and Kathie Prince.

A lot of people helped along the way, and I would have been lost without them. Louise Burrows unwittingly pointed me towards T. S. Eliot and 'purpose'. Teresa de Bertodano and Kathryn Spink gave invaluable advice and comfort. My agent, John Pawsey, offered patient help. Without my editor, Giles Semper, this book would simply never have been written; it would certainly have been a less rewarding task. I am grateful to my family and friends for their support. Thanks, especially, to Chris Moore, who spent so much time reading the manuscript and was unstinting in encouragement and criticism.

My husband, Tony Nickson, also read the manuscript with a critical eye and helped in countless ways throughout, not least by his enthusiasm. My thanks to him for everything.

Contents

Contents

Introduction

Here is a gathering of people who found purpose.

I went to talk to individuals committed to a way of life out of the ordinary. I expected to meet adopters of discipline, makers of sacrifices, devotees of causes; people who had experienced some sort of conversion (not necessarily religious); escapees from the rat-race.

As I listened to them talk about their lives, other patterns started to emerge. Many were not concerned about commitment, which they either took for granted or considered dangerous. Some, in any case, intended to move on. A few had decided on their way of life so young there was not much to turn their backs on. There were a number who had given up a great deal – the possibility, perhaps of wealth, marriage or comfort – but who did not discuss it in the terminology of sacrifice. Choice, on the grand scale, rarely came into it: just a series of small decisions, or a sense of the inevitable.

Even when stability mattered (and it did not always) the dominant impression was of movement; even if people were at peace, they were undergoing transformation. Very few thought they had arrived.

So the book took on a shape of its own, informed by those I met. I found I was captivated by their life stories, for they all had 'journeys' to recount. I was usually surprised; preconceptions foundered. I became absorbed by the nature of belief, which was often far more fluid than I had understood. It was indefinable, or had altered over years. Even those who shared a faith in God had very different images of him, her, it. . . .

Sometimes I was overwhelmed by the variety of character, experience and outlook as I travelled round. At other times, I felt there was more binding these people together than keeping them apart.

I wanted to talk to a variety of individuals: Christians, Muslims and atheists; monks, nuns and laity; the young and the old. Since I knew little about the people until I met them, I could not slot them carefully into some master plan. It was always clear there would be gaps, and obvious that the selection of 'subjects' was more or less random – that for every individual who appears in these pages, there are hundreds more who could have done. I was not seeking out the exceptional; I wanted to talk to 'ordinary' people.

Certain themes recurred, again and again. It is not surprising: these people range in age from 75 to 21, but all are threading their way through the benefits and crises of the twentieth century, the late industrial age.

Factories and commerce have swept aside traditions and communities. The consequences linger on, generations after the event. Those who talked to me often referred to an unsettled past and a sense of rootlessness or loss. There was also the reverse: excitement at the realization that it was possible to set off alone, in this shrunken world, to make a life elsewhere.

Science and technology were the great hope a hundred years ago. They have been found wanting. Cynicism has set in among the ecologically inclined and those nostalgic for the good old days; but some have found hope in the new technologies, the clean alternatives to smog. The idea of progress had taken some knocks among the individuals I met, but optimism tended to defeat environmental gloom. The young, especially, seemed to be green. Some still had ideas of evolution, believing that the human race would see the errors of its ways; one or two were more impressed by humanity's inexorable decline. Many were working for change. Others were concentrating on living well now.

Of all the barriers to happiness, conflict is the starkest. Total war, grimmest of the achievements of technology and rising wealth, has scarred the psyche of this century. Some of the older people I interviewed had been moulded by the First World War, others by the Second. The nuclear threat hung over everyone, and for some was the guiding issue of their lives. Others were dealing with more conventional violence, or with prejudice.

Inter-dependency – the awareness of *relationship* in every sphere of life – was an almost universal theme. People spoke of being part of the environment, not separate; of the link between the material and the spiritual; of economics as stewardship rather than growth. They were disillusioned with consumerism. They spoke, too, of the impact of different cultures and ideas. It is almost impossible to be self-contained any more; difficult to ignore the myriad different ways of interpreting the world. Technology has created rapid and ubiquitous communication. Everyone is forced into relationship with people they do not know. Even those with a clear notion of absolute truth are compelled to take into account the existence of other perceptions of reality.

Traditional world-views have been shaken in the West, and orthodoxy challenged. God, it has been said, is dead. But it is clear enough that he is not, that belief in some kind of deity is fundamental still to countless thousands. Some of the people I interviewed had no such faith. Of those who did, all had found their own understanding of what 'God' might mean, unable to take on a pattern of belief presented to them in childhood. Many referred to their discovery of the feminine in God. The role of women, and a transformed vision of the female – whether in the world or heaven – has permeated our times. There are those who condemn the change, but all have taken notice.

How far are these themes causes of the way individuals

live their lives, and how far are they merely backdrop? It is difficult to judge. When the people in this book chose to abandon career, convention or the belief-system they were reared in, it was because of a personal imperative. They had experiences, sometimes traumatic, which made them search – although perhaps it was only in retrospect that they discerned a quest. But the personal cannot be separated from the *Zeitgeist*.

These, then, are sketches of people living out their dreams and struggles in the 1990s. I met each individual only once or twice, although telephone conversations, letters and background reading added to the picture. Every chapter is an account of one person's life and beliefs told largely in their own words, interwoven with a description of my encounter with them. All the interviews took place between June 1992 and January 1993. If I had heard their stories a year before or later, they would have been different – for nothing stays still.

ONE

Aisling

In scattered households over Inishmór – the largest of the Aran Islands, off the Galway coast – a group of people share a common *aisling*, or 'vision'. The word is pronounced 'ashling': this is the *Gaeltacht*, a Gaelic speaking area. There are some twelve people on Inishmór, and many more elsewhere, who see themselves as part of Aisling Árann.

'That's why I don't think we're a *community*', explains Tess Harper, who has been there from the start. 'We don't have this notion that we all have to get on. And in fact the more diversified we are, the more rich it seems.' She prefers the word 'network'.

The *aisling* is a way of life, and it is threefold: 'to be rooted in the Celtic, to live in right relationship, to work for transformation'. Any tendency to institutionalize is frowned on. There are committees and shared activities; but households are independent and there is no hierarchy. The people who live in An Charraig, the original household, practise 'Irish hospitality': it is rare for there to be no guests. Many of the visitors return, and in the meantime keep in touch through the newsletter (a fifty-two page booklet) and the quarterly magazine. Some will come to Aran to set up a household of their own, and this is how the network grows.

Tess went to Inishmór straight out of college, seven years ago – inspired by the example of Dara Molloy, a Catholic priest. The two of them have been on the island ever since, and expect to stay for life – although Tess doesn't believe in public commitments, 'making vows for this, this and this

– because who gives a damn really? If you live it you live it, and then everybody's going to know. Intuitively, I could imagine I'm going to be here for the rest of my life, and I feel very much rooted here. I've been planted here and this is where I'm going to grow. That's my experience of it.'

She first met Dara, fleetingly, in a Dublin prayer circle; later she came across him chained to the railings outside the Department of Education, bearing placards. She was impressed; they 'clicked'. At this stage Tess was 'big into Francis of Assisi' – so much so, she had removed the bed from her room in order to sleep on the floor. Her parents said she would grow out of her idealism: she felt humiliated, but what if it were true? Dara, however, was thirty-five – and shared her passion for the saint. He left a comfortable teaching job, and a city lifestyle he felt was cushy, to move to Inishmór and practise what he preached. For Tess, the idea of 'making this idealism the foundation of your life blew my mind, that that was possible – that you could extract yourself from this sticky substance of ordinary day-to-day life and status quo.'

Her parents had expected her to be a teacher, a professional. Like many Dubliners, they barely knew of the existence of the Aran Islands, and were horrified at Tess's plan to go and live there. 'They threw a lot of parental stuff at me . . . it was an incredible experience, but I knew it was me or them. There was a clear sense of, "If I don't do this I'll have lost something very very valuable"; so there really was no option in my mind of compromising.' Her mother said it would kill Tess's father; yet shortly after she had moved to Inishmór he wrote to her to say that everything he had ever wanted, she was living out. Tess laughs as she tells the story now: 'I thought: "If you'd said that three months ago it would have made life a lot easier!" But it was very powerful.' Her father's dreams were sown in her, and she is happy to be living them.

He is, she says, 'an extraordinary man'. Poverty compelled him to leave school early, but all he wanted was to study.

He pored over theology as he grew up, in a conservative Catholic home; and when his mother threw an 'unsuitable' book on the fire, responded by scraping together the cost of eleven more copies. He burned them one by one until ten had been consumed by flames; and told her he would buy as many more again if necessary: 'you won't stop me reading what I want to read'.

Working his way up in a factory, from floor-sweeper to manager, he studied four nights a week and ended up with two diplomas. The price was that his five children saw him rarely, and his health in later life was poor. But the influence of his questioning spirit stayed with Tess, and mingled with her mother's orthodoxy. Catholic tradition was rich, was her conclusion – but the institutions of the Church were flawed.

Every summer the family went on holiday in the Dublin mountains: 'We ran wild; it was brilliant.' As at An Charraig, there was no hot water and no indoor toilet – and she prefers it that way. They made friends with the neighbours, working with their animals and milking cows. The foundations were laid: later, she was eager to abandon the contrivances of city life, and go back to the land.

Encouraged by a teacher, Tess ventured into Dostoevsky and Camus – which excited her far more than school work. At Maynooth College, Ireland's major seminary, she studied Theology 'with all the wee clerics'. Her scepticism was confirmed. Any radical lecturers were forced to leave, she says, and the politics were cutthroat: 'dreadful stuff going on, and all very male'. Theology seemed empty. Many of her contemporaries 'were *utterly* disillusioned, shattered . . . by establishing that there was *no* proof of God, and that a lot of religion was control and a lot of the history of the Church was ol' rubbish'. But Tess, who had never thought any different, survived.

'I kind of call myself Catholic, but I giggle too, I laugh in the same breath. It sounds very ominous! It's not very fashionable, I suppose.' Spirituality, she says, is the bedrock of her existence on Inishmór. Dara's vision of a prayer-filled life attracted her – for without 'a solid foundation of expressed prayer', she was sure she would flounder. In An Charraig there is morning meditation and an evening prayer meeting, which includes 'a whole space for people to say what they want . . . to spiritually nourish each other'. In addition, Dara celebrates daily Mass and some people go to that. Not everyone in the house is Christian; visitors may never talk of their beliefs. But for Tess, to pray is to acknowledge 'that it doesn't all depend on us, there is something benevolent guiding it all'.

She has never doubted that there is a God, 'or another kind of energy – really, I wouldn't give a damn what you call it, you can call it "Joe" for all I care! But it is something other that is powerful.' Her image of this 'other' has altered: 'Oh God, aye! It's changed dramatically . . .' She laughs, remembering that originally she saw him as 'benevolent, but a bit thick and a bit slow at times – which is probably how I perceived my Da to some extent . . . !' Now, she likes to 'play with images', not limiting God to any one of them: 'He could be this little old man, but he also has a wife – who's probably black, who's the goddess . . . And realizing God's much more and nothing of that, and being quite happy to throw it up and say: I haven't got a clue! Who does know what God is, and who needs to?'

The early Irish monks took the Eucharist round their neck and hung it on a tree while they worked in the fields: that tangibility appeals to her. Celtic monasticism was never separate from ordinary Irish life, she explains: the monks often had wives and children and the monastery was a 'spiritual light at the centre of the clan'. After St Enda settled in Aran in 485 AD monasteries sprang up everywhere, and visitors came from other lands, who then took back what they had learned. This is Aisling Árann's model.

'That's why integrating into this local community would be at the heart of what we're at . . .'; as is hospitality, being available 'for people to come and visit and experience it and be moved and maybe changed. And then they can go off and do their own thing. There has to be that link with the world outside.' By living true to themselves they hope, like the Celtic monks, to be 'a kind of spark or flame' for others.

Tess is excited because her Irish is approaching fluency: the fact it has taken her this long is 'a real symbolic struggle that I've had'. The islanders speak English, but their mother tongue is Gaelic, and now that Tess is immersed in local life it has become a necessary tool. The islanders are wary of outsiders, and are generally reserved; so is Tess: 'It doesn't float m' boat, like, to go and chat to people.' But on New Year's Eve, the dawn of 1993, she and the others in An Charraig ran down the road to the local pub to catch the midnight celebrations and 'came in on the countdown. And for me there was a really strong sense – probably the first time it's ever hit me – of *these are now my people*. There they all were jumpin' around and laughin', and a load of them came up and gave me a big hug – and I felt "I *am* in!" '

When Tess first came to Aran it was isolated; the boats which linked it to the mainland were infrequent. Old traditions were still alive, and that was one of the attractions. In the Dublin 'Liberties', where her parents were reared, there had been a strong community; but Tess was brought up in suburbia 'and it was *awful* – just houses and houses and houses . . .' With the advent of tourism, Inishmór is 'doing well', but at some cost. Formerly every hamlet had a tiny shop, 'with a little buzz around each one'; now everyone goes down town. Story-telling in each other's houses has given way to watching television, individually.

Tess wonders if Aisling Árann might bring new colour to the fading atmosphere of Inishmór. 'Like last night, we all went to a party at one of the other households down the road – and the crack was mighty! Somebody played the fiddle, and somebody else the flute and somebody else his guitar, and the night went on . . . recreating the way it would have been . . .

An Charraig has no television: the Sunday atmosphere was quiet, with people reading books and drawing. Tess was making several loaves of soda bread. An English family of six piled in from a rosy-cheeked walk, and filled the tiny cottage with enthusiasm. Their weekend stay was part of a lengthy search for community life, spiritually based. Conversation happily collided with the children's games, and led into a boisterous supper. Everyone gathered for evening prayer; and then hot toddies helped the laughter.

'Western society is running towards a cliff-edge', Tess believes; and 'there's been an absolute collapse of relationship in Ireland'. Aisling Árann is trying to prove that an alternative is possible. As the network grows, and its activities increase, some structures have proved necessary. Because there were so many visitors, a company was formed to buy and run the 'Lodge', a house of welcome. The company is also helping to set up the magazine, which carries no commercial advertising and has received no sponsorship from banks or industry. Tess admits, however, that the computer, fax and printing press they bought for its production sometimes raise eyebrows about their claim to live the simple life. They try to use very little money and members manage their own finances. Tess earns a small income from the magazine, and selling hand-knitted jumpers. Such food as they cannot produce themselves they buy from 'ethical' wholesale producers.

One of the hardest things to learn, Tess says, was that right relationship requires honesty, distance – and certain principles. At the start, in the 'Dark Ages' (she laughs at her own mythologizing of the past), they welcomed everyone. But some difficult characters turned up: 'They'd *do* yer! Like, they'd rob yer or bad name yer, or they'd rob people on the island . . .' Now the welcome is limited to anyone who comes in 'goodwill' to the door of An Charraig. 'So if you have a rip-snortin' alcoholic (and we've had them since) and there's no intention of giving up drink, then they haven't got goodwill towards us or anybody else, so they have to go. The same with anyone who insists on carrying on in a negative way – it just isn't on. And that's not just for us, it's for the island.' Their neighbours' trust has grown as the principle has taken hold.

Tess and Dara came to Inishmór from the city, with no experience of living on the land. Their developing bond with the soil and animals has been their best bridge to the *Árrannaigh* – the people of Aran. Tess remembers 'going down to the fields to sow, with books under our arms on how to do it, and the islanders were roaring laughin' at us – they thought it was the funniest thing.' But then, delighted, they offered help: not for fifty years had they seen a woman plant potatoes in the *Gaeltacht*.

And for Tess, this is *freedom*. She always swore she would not live under anyone's thumb, and 'nobody has power over me now, because I've got what it takes to eat, to live. And there's that really strong connection with the life-source, which in Dublin was lost for me.' Her year is governed by the seasons. Getting the seaweed up to use for fertilizer on the rocky fields means days of labour in the spring. I visited in January, when they were preparing to harvest reeds from the lake for thatch: it would roof the new An Charraig cottage they are preparing to move into.

Tess is responsible for the animals – cats and a dog, fowl, goats and sheep. She can talk for hours about the work, and ruefully describes an early failure when a bad-tempered goat, which refused to be milked, got mastitis as a consequence. Twice a day for a month, Tess had to inject the udder and burst the pus-filled sores which covered it – 'It was *foul*!' – but it had to be done. The very reason for having animals was that 'we wanted to bloody well be in relationship with them! We wanted to see how a goat *worked* – what *was* a goat!' When the animals become too numerous, some are killed and 'that is perfectly all right. Because at the end of the day *we* are going to be culled. We're tuning into the whole natural rhythm that's all around.'

Working with animals, Tess found, made her body agile, her reactions more spontaneous. For a long time, a dichotomy continued in her mind between the mental and the physical. She loved her life on Aran, but hankered after academia. Three years ago, a brief sortie into American university life finally laid that ghost to rest. She realized that her roots were now in Inishmór – yet also that as she lives out her vision there, she is immersed in study that she calls 'engaged'. *The Aisling Magazine* is stimulating work: articles cover economics, Irish lore, justice and religion – and there is always one in Gaelic. Because she is steeped in the Celtic tradition, she reads and learns the Celtic myths; because she has to deal with thousands of people, she is 'motoring through' the collected works of Jung.

The twenty volumes dominate Tess's room – which is a garden shed. She regards it as luxurious. A few hangers take care of her clothes, with a sun-hat lending them a slightly jaunty air; yet she insists she has masses of possessions, and her ascetic days are over. We squeeze in between the bed and the peat-burning stove, and sit on a couple of wooden chairs; she lights a candle for the mood. She has changed: earlier her crinkly hair was loose, now she has put it up and added earrings. She is tall, slim, relaxed; her face is windswept and her smile intelligent and full of charm.

The weather in Aran can be wild: the island hovers on the edge of the Atlantic, and there are no trees to break the storms. An Charraig faces the sea: at night the sky is boundless and the stars hang low. The landscape is famous for its bleakness: a walk across its two-mile width yields only an endless patchwork of dry stone walls. 'But also there's moments of amazing light and colour. A lot of flowers grow in Aran in the springtime, so the fields would just be yellow or purple. And because there's such a contrast with the sky, sea and grey rock, the colour hits you.'

Working outside is her release; the shed her bolt-hole. Tess often wonders 'what I'm doing here, living with all these people'. Community life does not come naturally to her. She analyses her character on the Jungian model – strongly 'introvert, intuitive and feeling'. Which means she finds it difficult 'to draw lines between what's their stuff and what's mine. When I walk into a room, why am I so upset all of a sudden? – it's because somebody *else* is upset and the atmosphere is bloody awful.' Living with a group has often been 'horrific', she says cheerfully.

Jung has helped her cope. His insights clarify what's happening and draw together all the aspects of the *aisling*. 'I'm true to what I'm called to do, and if people can complement that they can live with me, and if they demean that then they have to create their own space. Every household must be living out its own vision, not living off someone else's.' Right relationship starts with the self, extends to other people and to nature, and roots itself in the divine.

The Jungian Self, she says, is the unifying centre of the psyche – constantly calling us to wholeness. And that Self, when once we are in touch with it, connects each one of us to everything around us and compels respect for all we meet. It is the 'divine within'.

TWO

Peace House

The door of Peace House was flung wide in welcome and Ellen Moxley greeted me, with a warm American voice and a Chinese smile, like an old friend. She was short and stocky, decisive and direct. She ushered me into a deep armchair by a crackling log fire, fed me with tea and biscuits and apologized that supper would be late. I leant back in the armchair and sank into ease.

Peace House is a haven, dedicated to activism. When Ellen started it with Helen Steven, in 1987, their object was to help people think about peace and justice – and do something about it. They hope that those who come alone or in small groups, for weekends run by experienced facilitators, will go away filled with good ideas of how to fight for peace without violence. They committed themselves for fifteen years, and 'it's taken off with wings. It's been so successful that we sometimes feel trodden down.'

For them, the most significant issue is the nuclear threat; but this is no longer fashionable. Ellen is exasperated that just when Britain is increasing its nuclear fire-power eightfold by introducing Trident, public protest has been lulled to sleep. Again and again, she and others have asked what Trident is *for*, now that the Cold War is over: 'I'm afraid the answer we get is that it's for Third World countries.' Studies of policy documents, she says, indicate it will be pointed at countries like Iraq, and for her this is a violation of justice as well as peace. The First World and the Third World depend on each other: 'How do we build up the sense of the unity of all of us?'

Since Trident is not a crowd-puller, Peace House also hosts weekends on trendier forms of conflict. 'A tremendous number of women are having problems with their mothers,' Ellen remarks. A lot of them try to work it out at Peace House on special weekends looking at mothers and daughters or women and anger. Men's groups come, self-catering: she doesn't know what they do, but they have a wonderful time. Church groups meet there to talk about the Third World; others focus on subjects such as child abuse, homelessness and South Africa. They have even had a week of painting, which may not have anything to do with peace and justice, Ellen says, but is certainly linked with personal development.

Nevertheless, she is wary of encouraging too many courses of this kind. A lot of people want to come to this quiet homely house in the middle of the Perthshire countryside simply for a retreat. Helen and Ellen only rarely allow this. Peace House, they say, is there to encourage activism.

For though they are pacifists, they are anything but passive. They believe in non-violent resistance, which includes breaking the law. The fence surrounding the naval base at Faslane on the Clyde – where Britain's nuclear submarines lurk – is, Ellen says, 'as violent as the fence round Auschwitz'. Since they think its aggressive six foot diameter rolls and razor sharp wire have no right to be there, they have no qualms about damaging them. When Helen Steven cut through the fence, with other campaigners, to plant potatoes, eat breakfast rolls and sing songs inside (all the things they would have liked to see happening on land which is officially military property), she was sent to gaol. Ellen went to prison for 'snowballing': the simultaneous and symbolic cutting, by peace protestors all over the country, of the perimeter fences of nuclear bases. Each protester cut one wire and wrote three letters explaining the reason. The police watched them cut the wire and then arrested them.

These periods of imprisonment were very brief and Ellen describes them as lessons in solidarity and opportunities for pacifist evangelism, rather than times of hardship. She refused to watch a film she regarded as violent filth and returned to her cell – she was later brought tea and toast by a fellow prisoner who supported her views. Helen dissuaded a woman from breaking the neck of a warder she believed had a grudge against her, and suggested she appeal to the Governor for the warder's transfer instead. She did, and the warder was moved.

Women inside feel powerless. It does not occur to them that anyone will listen to them. 'They say to us, "You're so much more powerful than we are, because you can speak, you're articulate." I think I observed more than I gave. The doctor and the Catholic priest had a really dismissive, patronizing attitude which would never be tolerated by women on the outside. Most of the women inside said, "Yeah, we're with you all the way, but we've been too busy raising the bairns or fighting with our menfolk to come out with you on the demo. But we understand." '

When she traces the story of her pacifist activism, the first thing Ellen mentions is the Quaker meetings she went to at Mt Holyoke, the women's university in Massachusetts. The Society of Friends, since it grew out of the soil of the English Civil War in the seventeenth century, has been non-conformist and fiercely non-violent. From their earliest days, the Quakers have stood against authority and fought for justice – writing letters to people in power, campaigning for liberty, and refusing to fight the State's wars.

After Ellen left university she became involved in CNVA, the equivalent of CND in Britain: 'marches along the Pacific coast for 600 miles, vigils outside nuclear power stations, that sort of thing.' She had majored in zoology and her first job was in the Department of Metallurgy at the General Atomic Division of General Dynamics. A colleague pointed out to her that the company also researched nuclear bomb production, 'and so in the most naïve way possible we paraded outside GA with placards about what the company should be doing.' She was reprimanded but, to her amazement when she thinks about it now, she was not sacked.

'I suppose my lack of ease with the American way of life started to form up then. I kept thinking, here I am bringing in this large salary and having friends round to dinner and quite a comfortable life, but I don't really know anything about what's happening in India and Europe. I'm on the periphery of life.' She discussed this with her mother, who had long felt ill at ease living in a country whose commercialism she despised, and they decided to go to Europe.

'Perhaps it sounds funny that I went with my mother, but we were totally independent. She never batted an eye about the length of time I stayed out at night, and I didn't mind when she had her black coffee and cigarettes. We were real friends.' Her mother was the greatest influence in her life. She was never a pacifist – 'too dymanic and aggressive' – but she always fought for the underdog. After her death in 1967, Ellen took part in a vigil outside the American embassy in London in protest at the Vietnam War, 'and I can remember thinking, this is the sort of thing she would have approved of.'

Ellen's mother was a radical American, who was married and divorced when she was very young. Because of an obsession with China, she took Mandarin lessons in New York in the 1930s, fell in love with her teacher and went out to China to marry him. She taught there, and loved her pupils. They were so enthusiastic to learn that even the poorest managed to find copies of texts such as Shakespeare's *Julius Caesar* in the unlikely setting of Shanghai. But the relationship was not a success, 'because he had very Eastern views on marriage and bank accounts and she was a very independent woman'. He died of pneumonia when Ellen was two, in 1937, and mother and daughter returned to the United States.

They travelled around the country chasing 'impossible jobs'. When Ellen was ten her mother married a third time, and Ellen bears her stepfather's surname, though she also has a Chinese name, Swen Chang Gwa. 'He wasn't as radical as she was, and I remember great long discussions about the Civil Rights movement, and about nuclear power and the nuclear bomb, and I always used to see my mother's side of the story much easier than I saw my stepfather's side.' By the time Ellen and her mother came to live in London in 1963, the marriage was all but over.

Her mother's death was a turning-point in Ellen's life. She was thirty-two, she had lost her closest companion, and though she had an excellent job at an agricultural experimental station, she felt she was sinking into a rut. She was also very anxious to have a child but, since her mother's experiences of marriage had not been encouraging and Ellen's own relationships with men had not worked out, she 'couldn't see it coming about in the normal way'. The Vietnam War was hotting up and she was ashamed of America's involvement. One of her Quaker friends told her the Gordon Barclay UN Fund was starting a project of pre-school playgroups in orphanages, and she jumped at the chance to go out and join them.

'I've always felt wars have no end, and we have to find another way. What I saw in Vietnam confirmed that. We saw terrible things.' One of the things she learned was that violence led to far-reaching corruption. She was invited to stay in the country house of some friends. 'It was in an idyllic setting, and there were these beautiful young girls living there. I went for a walk in the woods on my own and I saw, in a little pile, a packet of pornographic photographs which had been left there by one of the GIs or given to one of the girls. And I realized how this war had trickled through at all levels in the most awful way.'

Ellen was team manager of the new project but, since she was the first person they hired, it was some time before there was a team for her to manage and she spent a year in London learning Vietnamese. The group of six that eventually started work in Saigon was international, and it included Helen Steven, a Scottish woman who was eager to leave her teaching job in a posh Glasgow girls' school and was anxious to work in a developing country. They also took on a lot of young Vietnamese women, who took more and more control – it was they who suggested that rather than shoring up the orphanage system, which was intrinsically corrupt, they should start a day-care centre for the children. They did, and to the best of Ellen's knowledge, it is still there.

'In 1973 I met my daughter Marian in our worst orphanage. I knew she was the child I wanted and I moved heaven and earth to get her.' Marian (her Vietnamese name is Nguyen thi Kim Hoa, 'Golden Flower'), now twenty-one, was a tiny, malnourished two-year-old at the time. She was so ill she could not walk or speak and has never completely lost the disabilities caused by those early years of deprivation; 'but she had this marvellous bubbling spirit and lovingness, which she's kept to this day.' Ellen adores Marian and is intent on helping her to become more independent; the thought of someone attacking her daughter is the only thing which makes her wonder how absolute her pacifism might be. She does not regret not coming by her baby 'in the usual way'.

Ellen went to the States to complete the adoption process, but felt so alien there that she longed to get back to Britain. When she did, in 1975, she could not get a job, and struggled on the dole in a friend's house in Battersea. Helen Steven wrote to her from Scotland, suggesting that unemployment might be more pleasant in a beautiful part of the world. So Ellen and Marian went to join Helen in Scotland and have been there ever since; and since Ellen does not believe in doing things by halves, they have both taken British nationality and call themselves Scottish citizens.

Helen got a job with the Iona Community as Peace and Justice worker, based in Glasgow; Ellen had a miserable job in a factory, periods of unemployment, and a spell as housekeeper at Kilbryde Castle. They had an abiding dream, however, of Peace House.

They eventually established a Trust, but it was many dramas later that they finally acquired the house near Dunblane. Their funding comes jointly from the Iona Community and Quaker Peace and Service (which owns the building). They were asked whether they wanted proper salaries, so that they could buy it and pay off the mortgage, or whether they would prefer to act as wardens and be run by a committee. Without hesitation they chose the latter: not only to be free of a mortgage, but so that they could take a salary below the tax threshold and avoid paying the 12 per cent of taxes which go on defence.

They are happy, but tired: 'I like what I'm doing and it's exciting stuff, but sometimes we feel like pressed ducks.' She is, she says, an introvert and if anybody had told her when they began that over the next six years she would cater for thousands of people, 'I'd have said they were off their nut.' But she does love to cook (Helen does not); and does not like giving lectures (Helen does), so they manage to divide the work up fairly well. They are hoping for a year off in 1994, to take a course to help them with their work, or possibly to go to China – Ellen has never been back. And they are looking forward to retiring and moving to a remote and empty part of Scotland, when their fifteen years are up.

They both run courses on Iona and Ellen is preparing to join the Community, a two-year process. After being so involved for so long, she felt she should 'go the whole hog', and that the Community was a group of strong people who would help her find time and methods of reflecting and praying. She joined the Society of Friends after the death of her mother, because of the support she received from the local Meeting. Her religious views are strong but undogmatic: 'I dislike seeing people really hung up on Christianity. I prefer a more interfaith approach, although Christianity is the path I know best. I believe humanity is our only hope.' She likes the word 'reality', to describe her understanding of God: 'something greater than myself'.

They have not been in prison since they moved to Peace House – just as well, she thinks, as the neighbours might not like it. But they are regularly involved in 'actions': vigils opposing the Gulf War, setting up exhibitions in city squares, chasing a Polaris submarine in an inflatable dinghy, stopping a nuclear convoy and wrapping hazard tape round the lorries. The fellow peace protestors with whom they do this work are her closest friends.

'It's true the police don't take us very seriously; but I think they may be mistaken, because information is a very important weapon.' They collect clippings, they distribute material – in small ways, they alert people to the injustices and threats to peace which trouble them so deeply. 'Even if the darn thing does toddle up the Clyde,' she says of Trident, 'our work may stop it being armed.' She has been disappointed that they have not achieved more, but 'I've kept going because it's not a question of success, but of being faithful to our vision of a world without war. How else can you live? You have to do what you believe in.'

As soon as the tape recorder is switched off, Ellen Moxley leaps to her feet to put on a pan of milk and rustle up some marshmallows: 'I expect you need a drink. I make a mean cup of hot chocolate.' I take my mug and sit by the glowing embers of the fire to browse through the Visitors' Book. It is full of lavish gratitude for Ellen's cooking and both women's hospitality. 'I wish,' said one entry, succinctly, 'that I could welcome friends with the warmth you welcome strangers.'

Postscript: In October 1992, the first Trident submarine arrived in the Gare Loch. Ellen and Helen joined other protestors in canoes in front of it. They continue their campaign against the other three submarines due, and their examination of the links between the expenditure on arms and poverty.

THREE

'Who Dares Swims'

During every conversation, even in the middle of the night, Pamela Banks was listening out for unusual sounds. For the five years she has lived at Faslane Peace Camp she has had to be alert twenty-four hours a day for helicopters or unfamiliar vehicles; ready to report anything untoward to her companions – even though it may mean leaving an evening in front of the television for a wild goose chase through the Scottish countryside. Often the life is tedious; sometimes, she says, it is horrible; but then 'something happens and you forget yourself'.

This time, there was special reason to be vigilant. 'You couldn't have arrived at a worse time', she said, standing at the rickety gate which forms the entrance to the Camp. Her manner was stern; she was preoccupied. Her short hair was pushed back with a band and she wore dangling earrings and a nose-ring. She was pregnant, and carried her two-year-old daughter, Hannah, on her hip. We went into the caravan which is her home, to be near the telephone.

It was July 1992 and peace campaigners in Scotland had been preparing themselves for the arrival of Trident at Clyde Submarine Base. It was expected in September, but nobody knew the date for sure. Nor did they know what the lorries carrying the missiles would look like. A few minutes before I arrived, there was a phone call from one of their supporters, who had seen a convoy of strange vehicles under police escort coming up the motorway from England. It had to be 'it', they thought, two months early.

The next hours were taken up with tracing the progress of the convoy, alerting people in the peace network, raising the press and endless, excited speculation. The Base, with its miles of bleak wire fencing, is a few hundred yards from the Camp. The two other residents had left as I arrived, to find the convoy and tail it. They rang at intervals to tell Pamela where they were. When the lorries were about to arrive, we took up post outside. A police car drew up, and kept a surly watch. Hannah sat in her pram and looked at picture books. Pamela got her camera ready, to snap the vehicles as they lumbered by, green and spikily antennaed. Close on their trail was the Camp car. Pamela's partner Phil waved cheerily and tooted the horn as he passed and Hannah's head shot up with a delighted squeal: 'Daddy!'

It turned out to be a dummy run, but important all the same. The photographs were pored over: how best would peace campaigners tackle the lorries in any future 'actions'? The vehicles seemed to have soft sides: amazing, they could be slashed! Look, it would be easy to climb on this bit of the wheel, to daub the windscreen with paint . . . Actions against nuclear convoys are carefully planned. An accident involving a warhead would be catastrophic.

The Faslane Peace Camp has been a symbol of opposition to nuclear weapons for more than a decade. It began just after the Falklands War, when the government announced its intention to buy the larger D5 Trident 11 missile system from the United States, and base it on the Clyde. When Pamela first came the Camp 'was full of pacifists – you know, weeks and weeks of meetings about cutting the fence because it was an act of violence, whereas me, I'd just go out and cut it! They were hippies.' The Camp is still committed to non-violence in its protests, but is not pacifist. Pamela's attitude is typical: 'I'd like a perfect world but I ain't working towards it 'cause I'm not going to get it. Getting rid of nuclear weapons would be a start.'

If Trident is ever used, Pamela says, 'it would obliterate

the northern hemisphere. And that's just with one warhead – with two, it's bye-bye world.' One warhead, they claim, is the equivalent of ten Hiroshimas. Each missile carries up to eight warheads; each submarine can transport as many as sixteen missiles. The peace campers have organized sit-down blockades of the bases and construction sites. When the mouth of the Gare Loch was being widened for the new submarines, they disrupted the work in inflatable dinghies. They regularly escort submarines in and out of the Base, flying large peace flags. They also keep a daily log of the vessels' movements – partly to monitor accidents, which they say the Ministry of Defence keeps quiet. 'You discover all these things – like the subs are falling to bits, and it's a Chernobyl in a bath-tub.'

Pamela came to the Peace Camp four years ago, when she was eighteen. She and a group of friends decided they were going to spend five years doing 'something outrageous' and raising £2,000 each to put into a cafe-cum-art-shop. One girl went off to India, another to Paris to drink champagne. Pamela decided to live at Faslane. 'I don't know why, I didn't work it out in my head. More and more people said I couldn't and I shouldn't and I'd never get a career if I did, and that just made me more determined to come.'

When she did make an initial visit, 'it was absolutely horrendous. There were all these strange people wearing funny little hats, because one of them was an amazing Tunisian knitter and had knitted everyone these tea-cosies. There was only one woman there and all I saw of her was when she jumped into the common room and said "I'm pregnant!", and at that time, ugh! that was the last thing on my mind. And there was the local copper up on a visit and he kept asking me all these questions, like what my name was and what my mum did. No one really spoke to me, they just gave me all these photograph albums, and they had *a lot* of photos! And I was just thinking, "Oh my Go-od, *really weird*!" ' Next morning she got up as early as she could and caught a bus home, terrified someone might see her.

But she didn't have the courage to admit she was chickening out of her five-year stint. She got involved with CND and met 'this amazing woman on the Hiroshima Tent' at one of their events, who persuaded her to give the Camp a try. She eventually went back after a summer spent as nanny to the family of a senior official at the Bank of Scotland, whose friends included leading politicians. 'High, high, high! And they just thought I was the bees' knees in the nanny department, because their little boys loved me. It was major stink when I left, because I made it clear why I was going.'

She was brought up, she says, to think for herself. Her mother was a nurse in Edinburgh, her father a long-distance lorry-driver. When she was fourteen he died of a heart attack. Her mild rebelliousness took on disruptive force. Her school uniform was strict, but she dyed her hair orange and wore huge earrings. She skipped classes, and despised what she saw as her teachers' narrow-mindedness: 'If you wore a short skirt, you were a secretary. It was sick.' She conformed enough to be a sixth-former and a prefect, but a month before she left she was almost expelled for dressing up as a panda, getting very drunk, and going round the school with a friend disguised as a zoo keeper, peering through the classroom windows. 'The kids were cheering and the teachers loved it!' She liked stardom.

With scorn, Pamela describes the teacher she was sent to for 'guidance' who said she was to stop being silly – the 'problems in her family' shouldn't affect her school work. 'I was like, "Get stuffed, *my Dad's died!*" I went from bad to worse.' She would have gone to art college if it wasn't for her father's death, she says. She would never have gone to the Peace Camp.

The woolly hats had disappeared by the time she returned to Faslane, and it all seemed quite normal. But, like every new arrival in the Camp, she felt they should be doing more. Within a month, she and one of the men of her own age had put together a daring plan. Pamela, who had swum for her county, would swim out to the dry dock and paint a Polaris submarine. Two of the older men would act as decoys.

She swam in the October sea for half an hour, through oily water infested with conger eels and jellyfish 'as big as my body', and arrived at the dry dock at midnight. She painted it with the slogan suggested by a Camp member who had been in the Army: 'Who Dares Swims'. People on the Base still remember that, she says with satisfaction.

Her excitement began to wear off as she sat shivering on the dry dock for several hours, singing songs and waiting to be arrested. She was not going to face the jellyfish again. Meanwhile her decoy colleagues had got through the fence, right through the Base to a Polaris submarine. When they heard the alarm they did not realize it was they who had set it off, and assumed Pamela had been caught. So they went to the gate with a bundle of dry clothes and handed them to the guard, saying they were for the girl on the dry dock. 'And the guard went "*What?*" and walked away!' At about 3 a.m. a police launch came and stared at Pamela, who by this time was singing and shouting for all she was worth although, bizarrely, she had sunk the paint 'to hide the evidence'.

'Are you OK?' said the police. 'I'm *cold*!' she said. They took her on board, wrapped her in blankets and gave her warm drinks. 'And when I got off the boat there were all these armed marines poking guns at me and it was just like *wow*, this amazing buzz!' All around her was astonishment and chaos – the Secretary for Defence was roused from his bed in the early hours, she says with pride, and there were court-martials.

Next day, sitting in a police cell, she was still on a high, but was beginning to feel ill. Phil, in the cell next door, had found a pin-hole and was telling her what she should say to the magistrates. 'In court I challenged the validity of the bye-laws.' She laughs, loving the whole story. 'I mean, what the *hell* is validity of the bye-laws!' When she came out her mother was on the phone, having heard on the early morning news that there had been a major breach of security at Faslane and her daughter had been arrested.

Pamela looks back at the incident as the high spot of her career, and perhaps of Faslane's. 'I'm proud now. Sad, in a way, because it was such an amazing action and we'll never ever be able to do that again. We just happened to pick a section of fence which had the alarms switched off, and the razor wire pulled back because men were working on it. It was just luck . . .' Did it achieve anything? 'We got some publicity, but not enough . . . They improved security; it was a big knuckle-rapper. Publicity is all you can hope for from actions. And when you don't think you're getting anywhere, just to go off and do something is to say, "*I* don't agree and they know that." ' One of her best memories is of the warmth and support she received from the other members of the Camp. Suddenly there were five or six near-strangers cuddling her and throwing an all-night party in her honour. She now gives the same support to others.

Since then the Camp has gone through many changes. Numbers dropped from eleven to two, and stood at three when I visited. A few months later, they were up to fourteen. for a year she held the fort with Phil. People came and went – with some they were too strict, she thinks, with others too soft. She has learned to sus people out and to deal with the manipulative or the 'weird', even when she is scared. There are some things which cannot be tolerated – like drugs, which would give the police an excuse to close the Camp; or a person who will not pull their weight. In the old days decisions were made at weekly meetings: 'It took hours and it was hideous, an open arena for all sorts of under-feelings.' She prefers it when they all get on well enough to make formal meetings unnecessary.

The Camp, she says, has been the make or break of numerous relationships. Phil is not only father of Hannah but of a seven-year-old boy called Sam, who normally lives with them. Sam's mother and her current partner used to live in the Camp; they now live nearby and remain actively involved.

Pamela's second child was born in October, three months after my visit – a girl called Ailsa. The advantage of having children young, she said, was that when she is in her thirties, her children will be old enough and she will still be young enough for her to do what she wants. The Peace Camp has been a great place for a baby. There is never a day when Pamela does not have help, or when Hannah does not have playmates; they are kept well-supplied with clothes, Hannah has the whole Camp to play in and she can have a bath every day. Much better, says Pamela, than trying to bring her up in a flat on her own.

For the first few months of Hannah's life it was different. It was winter and never stopped raining. There was one shower, one toilet and one place for cooking and eating. Phil and Pamela were on their own and were about to close the Camp, but they couldn't bring themselves to do it. Instead, they set about reforming it. They got rid of all but the best caravans and built a path through the middle, to protect them from the Scottish mud. It now has a neat and ordered look. Pictures and slogans in vivid colours decorate the outside walls. There is space for sitting together or for privacy, and there is an office with a computer; there are baths, flush toilets and stoves, and electricity from a generator so they no longer have to work by candlelight.

Pamela has always planned to leave Faslane, one day – possibly to train as a nurse. The plans to set up a cafe-cum-art-shop long ago fell apart. With enthusiasm, she talks about the independence of the last four years and the strength and tolerance she has learned. She is nervous about going back to a 'stable' life and thinks she will be lonely when she leaves. 'I've got no other interests in life. I've got Hannah and the Camp, and there's not many people who want to sit and have conversations about what happened here . . . But it's definitely been worth it. I certainly think it's going to be the best five years of my life. The Camp's going to go down in history, and I've been part of it.'

Postscript: The first Trident submarine arrived in October 1992. Pamela and Phil were planning to leave the Camp in June 1993, for Phil to take up a place at Stirling University.

FOUR

Bruderhof

Everyone looked happy. The dining-room was big and light, and chatter only paused while grace was said before the people ate. They passed the food along the trestle tables: the women dressed in calf-length gingham with polka-dot headscarves; the men all bearded, with black tunic-jackets or shirts under braces. Harry Magee gave me a chair beside his wife, and introduced me to his daughters, his daughter-in-law, his grandchild and the fiancé of his middle daughter. Each one greeted me with uncomplicated smile and outstretched hand.

This was the Darvell Bruderhof in Sussex, the only Hutterian community in Britain. It is housed in an old sanatorium, surrounded by gentle views. Though the 'Brethren' have done some building of their own in the last twenty-two years, most have made their homes in the long, narrow huts where TB patients had their rest-cures. In this unlikely setting, 250 people live according to the model of the early Church; helped along by fax machines and cars.

The buildings are well-spaced, so front doors open onto grass and plenty of fresh air. They make curious family homes, for a corridor dominates each one: presumably it once served as a link between the patients' rooms. In Harry's house, it has become the kitchen; but it is still the only route from the front door to the lounge. Decoration is sparse, and the feel of an institution lingers in the dark green paint. The rooms are homely, with crockery and plants; everything is clean and has its place.

A printed copy of 'The First Law of Sannerz' hangs on

the wall in every house and place of work. 'There is no law but that of love. Love is joy in others. What then is anger at them?' it begins, before expanding into clear instructions: 'There must never be talk, either open or hidden, against a brother or a sister . . . under no circumstances behind their back. Talking in one's own family is no exception either.' Sannerz, in Germany, was the first of the twentieth-century Anabaptist Bruderhofs; and the 'First Law' is taken very seriously by its successors.

The Hutterians are uncompromising in their Christian ethic. They refuse to fight, swear oaths or enter public office. They do not vote. Baptism, they believe, should follow an adult confession of faith: to baptize infants is a nonsense. They insist on lifelong faithfulness in marriage; and they share all their possessions.

The original Anabaptists emerged in Reformation Europe. One group decided to pool their goods and live in 'Christian brotherhood' – they had a leader called Jakob Hutter, and were nicknamed after him. In the sixteenth and seventeenth centuries, the Hutterians were tortured and driven from their homes – first to Russia, eventually across the Atlantic. The Jesuits, Harry remarks sadly, were chief among their persecutors; never wishing to criticize, he tries to understand that they thought they were doing what was right.

In 1920, a new Anabaptist Bruderhof was founded at Sannerz by Eberhard and Emmy Arnold – Harry's eyes shine as he tells the story of their eagerness to live by the Sermon on the Mount. They shared the widespread disillusion with governments and churches which followed the First World War; they wanted an alternative, and a Christian faith worth living for. 'We have been overwhelmed by a certainty,' Eberhard wrote, 'that all life created by God exists in communal form and works towards community.'

The new Bruderhof became part of the Hutterian Church – still thriving in America and Canada – in 1930, although it retained some sense of separate identity and special loyalty to Eberhard and Emmy Arnold. It adopted the dress of the older Hutterian Church: so the 'Brethren' everywhere now wear clothes that recall the sixteenth-century peasants who were forced to flee their European homes because of their beliefs. 'We don't like to call ourselves Hutterites,' said Harry, correcting me kindly. 'We're just brothers and sisters really, but by law we have to have a name. We call ourselves the Hutterian Brethren.'

Becoming a committed Christian is a voluntary thing, says Harry; that is why most of the Brethren are baptized in their twenties – some much later. 'The person has to be mature enough to make the decision in his heart, and really feel that God has called him to this . . . We don't want to force our children to do it because we do.' Children born within the Bruderhof receive their primary education there; then they go to school in the local town and sometimes on to college. During this time 'they can see what the world is like and what the choices are'.

Both of Harry's sons went to live outside. One came back; the other manages a garage in Tulsa, Oklahoma. 'In every other letter he says how grateful he is for what he learned here – but it's not for him.' If teenagers rebel, there are efforts to identify the problem; sometimes they are found a place in a different Hutterian community or fixed up with an apprenticeship. There is an eighteen-year-old girl in the community who has never worn the headscarf – that is fine, Harry says, because she has not yet decided to be part of the life.

Every year a few outsiders come to join the Bruderhof. Generally they spend a year or so as novices before they make a firm commitment. In Harry's day it was different: decisions were made quickly. It was the Second World War and people had to choose for war or peace. 'One woman was on her way through on a bicycle,' he recalls, 'and she asked for a night's lodging and that was it!'

Harry was always a pacifist. Both his parents lost brothers

in the First World War, and he knew from the way they spoke of them that they never wanted him to fight. His father had trench fever and was gassed, 'so when he came out his lungs were more or less finished. He couldn't get a job and my mother had to work. He finished up as an odd job man in a bakery.'

The family lived 'in the deep slums of Manchester, the very poorest part'. Their income was pitiful. But Harry beams: 'We had the happiest time you can imagine, because there was such love between my father and mother, and I think that was one of the biggest influences in my life. They were like an engaged couple until the end.'

His mother was a Methodist, and sent her only son to Sunday School: 'I wasn't aware of what was going on, but the love of Jesus I did feel.' Later, his parents joined the Co-Operative Society and Harry went to the children's circle, where he learned of Robert Owen and the early Socialists. The idea of living in community impressed him. Although he was 'all set for a regular bourgeois life', he was frustrated because he had glimpsed an ideal – in the Co-Op, the comradeship he saw among the local poor, and the New Testament.

At eighteen he was conscripted. He immediately signed up as a Conscientious Objector, refusing even to 'assist' in the medical service: 'I said it's only taking the place of someone else so he can go and do my dirty work.' But pacifism is an active thing, and Harry wanted to do more. He now had a job at the Co-Op Wholesale Society, and heard glowing reports from a colleague of the Bruderhof which then existed in the Cotswolds. 'I pulled my horns in a bit. I was a city boy, I couldn't stick it in the country with all those midges and things.' Nevertheless, he went to visit – and there was no question in his mind that this was what he wanted: 'Here is the spirit of love, of brotherhood; this is the Gospel in actual fact – it's not theory, it's not just reading it in the Bible, it's not doing it just on Sundays, it's the whole life; and I was completely convinced.'

The hard part was writing to his parents to tell them what he planned to do. The wages he had just begun to earn had doubled the family income and promised to ease their lives. But God, they said, would provide for them; they knew he was following his conscience. 'They had more faith than I,' says Harry, 'they were helped in the most amazing ways.'

After a brief spell in prison for his pacifism, Harry settled in the Bruderhof. It was a more vigorous life than he was used to; he had to get accustomed to working on the farm and in the gardens and often sleeping rough, and 'the food was nothing like we had at home – potatoes in their jackets and cabbage soup and occasionally a little bit of meat.' But he always had the conviction he was part of something greater than himself: 'We felt we were working for the Kingdom of God. That joy and enthusiasm, called the "first love", was very strong.' And what exactly, I asked, did the 'Kingdom' *mean* to them? 'God's Kingdom, of peace and justice, love and brotherhood,' he replied, '. . . on earth.'

The Hutterians believe the Church was there before the earth was made. They separate Church and State; and though they generally respect the law, they put their Christian conscience first. The Cotswold Bruderhof was established in 1936 by refugees from Germany, expelled because they refused to give the Hitler salute. It is ironic that when the war began, the local people were frightened that so many people from the enemy country were living up the road, in case they might be spies. Parliament, reluctantly, said the Germans from the Bruderhof would have to be interned 'for their own protection'. The Hutterians asked instead if the whole community could leave the country – and were astonished when the answer was yes.

They ended up in Paraguay, the only country that would take them, making a home in the wilderness. They battled with malaria and severe conjunctivitis, and in the early days a number of their babies died. The first shelter they put up consisted of poles in the ground, with no walls and a grass roof; gradually, they started to build houses with the exquisite local woods. They planted maize, bananas, peanuts and tomatoes, and kept cattle.

They lived there for fifteen years. 'It was highly exciting, often dangerous', says Harry – and he means spiritually as well as physically. They got so absorbed in building their community, he says, that they 'went off the tracks'. They had to spend long hours, talking into the night, to identify what they were doing wrong: 'a certain worldliness . . . There was something about the wild life there that began to get into us.' They grew proud of what they had achieved: 'It led to a sort of communal arrogance – we're the good guys and the others are the also-rans. We recognized it and had to fight it out.'

They had put their community at the centre, he believes, instead of Jesus. What set them right was meeting some of the Brethren from the United States, who were still full of the 'first love'. Movement among the Bruderhofs is valued – it ensures they never forget their roots and helps each one survive. In later years Harry often moved around, to vacate or fill a space, or to contribute his labour. He lived in Uruguay and the United States and says the only difference was the climate – the Bruderhofs are all the same. He has been at Darvell since 1987. It's almost too easy these days, he muses: 'You don't want poverty for the sake of it – that would also be wrong. But we have to have the attitude that we're ready at any time to suffer for what we believe in.'

It was in Paraguay that Harry married Lotti, originally a refugee from the Nazis. He went to the minister to say he liked her, as the custom is. The minister spoke to Lotti, who said she was not averse to Harry. They were then allowed to spend some time together; when they wanted to become engaged, Harry had to ask the whole community. This is still how Bruderhof marriages are made.

The minister has no authority in this or any other matter. He is called a 'servant', and has no training. He is simply somebody who is seen to have a gift for leadership, and for discernment of God's will. Decisions are made by consensus – the Bruderhof is not a democracy. If one person disagrees with a suggestion, it will not be carried out: 'It's quite a courage needed to be that one, but it has happened.' There is an elder, but even he has no particular authority.

Harry is stumped when I ask him if there have ever been serious problems of discipline or disagreement. 'When a thing is forgiven with us it is forgotten and it is as if it never were. Forgiveness is a new beginning. I just can't remember!' If individuals offend the whole community they are advised to spend a week in silence until they have repented. Harry does recall one difficult occasion, when a man who refused to repent was asked to leave. But then it was discovered the entire community had been mistaken and he was in the right. They invited him back – and asked for *him* to forgive *them*.

The community meets, for practical discussion or worship, almost every evening. There is no set pattern of prayer – much of that is done in private. Work, however, is tightly organized, with a regular daily schedule. The Darvell Bruderhof's main income comes from the two businesses it shares with the other communities: one making toys for kindergartens and schools, the other producing equipment for people with disabilities. These occupy most of the men – no one is unemployed, no one retires. The workshops are neat and ordered: the men were sitting in the sunshine, when Harry showed me round, having a break. Not for long. 'Snack over,' called a Tannoy, 'time to go back to work.'

The women do the cooking and the laundry, and care for the children. Even these tasks are organized on a communal basis – every baby is looked after in the 'department' from the age of six weeks. The traditional male and female roles which frame the Hutterians' lives are, they say, 'natural'. The headscarf, one of the women explained to me, is 'a sign that we are not the head of the family, but that we *are* part of a group. It is a sign of modesty, humility.'

All goods are held in common. If a person leaves the Bruderhof they cannot have back the possessions or money they donated when they joined. But 'we wouldn't let them be destitute', says Harry – unless the community itself was too poor to help. More difficult for many than giving up their property, he thinks, is sacrificing their 'inner development': for talents and abilities are also pooled for the common good. If a young person has a taste for music or medicine, it is the community that decides whether it can be pursued. They try to assess how likely it is to secure the individual a livelihood, and to be helpful to the Bruderhof.

The Church, Harry says, must be founded on a rock. Community life depends on the utter, happy commitment of every single 'brother' and 'sister' and on ready forgiveness: without these things the Bruderhof stumbles. And this is why at one point in his story he gradually fell quiet and the air tensed. 'Now comes the calamity,' he said. 'I've got to be honest.'

He and Lotti 'went off the tracks somehow', when they left South America in 1960, and were asked to leave. 'We weren't unfaithful to the life, we *never* were, we were sure of our calling, but certain things occurred, we were unclear . . .' They were not 'sent away', he adds; they were given the chance to think things over at a distance. It took them several years.

The pain the memory caused him filled the room. He mentioned it only, he said, to show that his life in the Bruderhof had not been constant joy, and found it hard to explain exactly what had gone wrong. 'In a quiet way we weren't really honest, we weren't really in agreement with decisions that were being made. We were there physically, but not innerly taking part.'

But 'the thing is, God helped us through . . .' He can still remember the letter he wrote to the Bruderhof when he and Lotti wanted to return: 'We said it was as if Eberhard and Emmy had planted a garden, and we'd come in with hobnailed boots and marched all over it and spoiled it.' His delighted face relives the bliss they felt when they were 'taken straight back and lived happily ever after'.

Harry Magee is a tiny man, filled with joy. At lunch he sat with his family at the communal table, and handed me a hymn book. Two hundred and fifty voices filled the room: 'All things bright and beautiful, all creatures great and small . . .' I had not sung it since I was a child.

FIVE

Daughters of Brahma

Electronic music chimed out of the wall at half past five, interrupting my conversation with Sister Manda. 'It's played around the building for a few minutes of meditation, every few hours,' she explained. 'It gives us the opportunity to calm down and look at everything in a different way.' So we paused and closed our eyes, until the notes faded away.

We were sitting in a small top-floor office in Global Co-Operation House, international centre of the Brahma Kumaris World Spiritual University. The building opened in north-west London in 1991 and cost £4 million; despite its name it is staffed twenty-four hours a day and protected by a video-entry system.

It is a modern conference centre, with underground car-park, air-conditioning and simultaneous translation system. But its function is also symbolic. The windows 'represent our ability to see clearly with our inner eye . . . while the doors of our hearts can open to give of our generosity and love,' the souvenir brochure explains. The white band round the roof, it continues, 'is the building's contribution to the skyline . . . it symbolizes our desire to spread spiritual light and understanding to the world around.' A mandala-like symbol of God as light in the seminar room assists the guided meditation which closes every session; and as you enter the building the first thing to catch your eye is a mural of pastel-coloured angels dancing from darkness into light – giving, as the brochure puts it, 'an ethereal feeling'. Sister Manda took pleasure in showing me round: it was she who liaised with the architect and engineers, and chose the furnishings and equipment; and she who is now responsible for the building's maintenance. She is thirty-three: a white sari gleams against her Indian complexion; but she speaks with the tones and mannerisms of her generation of English women.

The World Spiritual University, she explains, was founded in Karachi by a prosperous diamond merchant called Dada Lekhraj, later known to the students of the University as Brahma Baba. In 1936, when he was sixty and his children were all married, his wife suggested they leave the world behind and go to live in an ashram under a guru, as was the custom for devout Hindus at their stage of life. Brahma Baba refused, but shortly afterwards had a series of visions. In them, he foresaw his own perfection as a spiritual being; and a period of global turmoil, leading to better things.

'He believed he had to be an instrument of God, and surrender himself completely – mind, body, wealth, everything,' Manda says. He wound up his business and 'very naturally he started speaking and teaching spiritual ideas which were not his, which he had not read anywhere. It was like another power had taken over; he would just start speaking and people would gather in front of him. They saw Brahma Baba as a divine being, and they experienced themselves as divine beings.'

Many of these people were women, who in Sind at that time received no education. 'Their role was to stay at home and have children and look after the house and that's it. And here was Brahma Baba teaching celibacy! Women were going back home and telling their husbands they wanted to be celibate. Young girls were saying they didn't want to get married. It was quite a revolution.'

Brahma Baba believed women had to be the new spiritual teachers. Men, Sister Manda explains, tend to assert 'I know, and what I say is right'; but the qualities needed today are love, sacrifice, compassion and mercy, which come more naturally to women. Brahma Baba transferred all his wealth into the name of the Brahma Kumaris, the 'daughters of Brahma', by then nearly 400 strong, and put the administration into the hands of eight young girls. The founding 'daughters' lived in seclusion, studying and meditating. When India was partitioned and Sind became part of Pakistan, they moved to Mount Abu in Rajasthan – and began to expand.

The Brahma Kumaris now have 2,000 centres all round the world. It is twelve years since Manda first came across them in Leicester. They have taught her confidence and self-esteem, she says, and given her a sense of purpose. The independence and idealism which attracted the first daughters of Brahma also drew her half a century later, as she emerged from adolescence in an adopted country.

Mandakini – her full name, shortened later for the sake of her English schoolfriends – was born in 1960 in Dar es Salaam, the capital of Tanzania. When she was eight she and her sister were sent to live with their aunt in a small village in India, to receive a steady education. The aunt was young, with four small children, and it was a difficult two years for Manda: 'It made me very strong, very hard, now I take nothing for granted.'

The economic situation in Tanzania deteriorated and her parents returned to India. Her father tried a number of business ventures. But he had never liked village life; he could not settle, and nothing worked out. When Manda was thirteen the family moved to England, unhappily shifting from Finchley to the Elephant and Castle in South London before they finally came to rest in Leicester.

Manda spoke no English and was not allowed to study for GCEs. In her fifth year she convinced the school that her English was now adequate, and was allowed to do Religious Studies ('not that I was interested, not even slightly!'), Art, Craft and Design. She went on to college to do O levels, including typing and book-keeping, because she was keen to get a good job. She loved studying but 'I was the oldest in the family and I was thinking, "I'm eighteen and I'm not earning any money" '; so she left after her exams to work for an insurance company. 'That was the first time I was properly exposed to Western people. There were a lot of Indian kids in the school I was in, and we were a very close family, so I didn't go out or do anything else. I really enjoyed working.'

It was at about this time that her mother started to go to the meditation classes run by the Brahma Kumaris in Leicester. Manda told her she was being brainwashed, but 'I remember going through this turmoil in my mind – what do I *want*? Do I want what she's doing or to carry on? And I remember the moment when I made that conscious decision – *no*, I'm not interested in this, I'm just fine the way I am.'

But when she was twenty she went back to India for the first time, and loved it. During her eight weeks there she changed: 'I lost interest in things, in a worldly way of life, and I got interested in helping people.' Back in Leicester, her mother started asking her if she wanted to get married, since she was now of age: Manda wasn't sure. Then 'I woke up one day and I said I'd go along with her to her meditation. She said "fine", she was very casual about it. And I remember, the first or second time, I had a nice feeling, a great deal of inner happiness – not excitement but a beautiful feeling internally, of things being just perfect.'

Some months later Manda, by now a regular meditator, visited the Brahma Kumaris in London. It was January, when they were returning from their annual visit to the headquarters at Mount Abu. 'And *everybody* was just blissed out – just talking about this place as if it was heaven on earth.' She enlisted the help of her sister as she pressed her father to let her go back to India, and he finally gave way. She went to Mount Abu for three weeks, 'and my life changed there. Everything became real, all the concepts I had heard here. Their life revealed their experiences of meditation, and just such joy and happiness as I had never experienced before.

I decided that this was what I wanted, this was truth.' She told the senior teachers there of her decision and they tried to put her off – only Dadi Janki, the organization's Co-Administrative Head, one of those founder members who had been determined as a young woman in Sind to abandon social convention and live a life of spirituality, encouraged her. And that was enough.

Manda got her company to transfer her to London. In 1985, she left her job to live and work full-time at the centre, which was her 'heart's desire'. Her father was disappointed that his daughters were not behaving in the traditional Indian way, but he 'couldn't say no, because he wanted his children to do what made them comfortable'. One of Manda's sisters now looks after the Brahma Kumaris' centre in Dubai, the other is 'a chemical engineer, a top oil dealer and very Westernized'. So far, only her brother has shown signs of getting married. Her father has come to terms with it all, she laughs – now he also meditates.

Sister Manda is one of fifteen women at the London centre who serve as administrators, teachers and symbols – their white saris a sign of dedication and simplicity. They take no vows, but there are commitments. They have no income and no possessions, and they are celibate.

'It's not like giving things up, it's not being *demanded* of us', Manda says, shunning any hint of 'negativity'. The choice was hers. Celibacy, she says with delight, is 'a beautiful thing': if she started to feel otherwise, it would be time to leave. They are happy to be supported by voluntary donations from others and, even when they were building Global Co-operation House, to have no money in the bank and no investments. It would *feel* wrong to charge for the lectures, classes and seminars they offer on meditation, stress management and positive thinking, she says. And, she smiles, since she does not smoke, drink or go out, what would she spend money on?

'My life is not mine any more', she says with energy. She

believes all the Brahma Kumaris, who are numbered in thousands, feel the same. Most of them are men and women with jobs, families and homes, who want to make their minds 'fit to receive God', so that when need be God can work through them. All of them follow an unvarying morning regime, rising to meditate alone from 4 a.m. to 4.45, 'because that really is a very special time for silence, the atmosphere is very conducive', and later joining others at the centre for further study and meditation together before breakfast. The idea, Sister Manda explains, is to give four hours a day for spiritual nourishment, at a time when there are no other demands.

'Truth is our nature, it's just that we've forgotten it,' she says. 'Our purpose is to bring people that awareness.' The Brahma Kumaris claim their University's syllabus has a vision and understanding which unites all religions. Their concern is with teaching people 'to think in the correct manner' – to remember that they are spiritual beings, not physical; that peace, love, purity and happiness are their original qualities.

The first lesson in the syllabus is an explanation of the nature of the soul. Sister Manda summarizes by explaining that souls are tiny points of light, and the Supreme, called *Baba*, 'Father', is also a point of light. 'The soul is an eternal being, it exists for ever. I never come to an end – can you imagine me being here today and just disappearing tomorrow?' Our task, to lose our accumulated negativity and become divine beings is now urgent: 'The world can't go on as it is, that's what *my* logic tells me,' Manda says. Time is a cycle, not a line, and 'it's time for the cycle to spin, it's time for change.'

Only individually can we make the change happen, Sister Manda insists – governments can alter nothing. The Brahma Kumaris never take political action, but they are seen on platforms with politicians and have been closely associated with the United Nations since their 'Million Minutes of Peace Appeal' in 1986, when they asked people all round the world to contribute prayers or positive thoughts. Dadi Janki is in demand, in England and abroad, to give lectures and 'offer spiritual insights', and Sister Manda accompanies her as interpreter.

Most of the time, Dadi Janki says the same thing; just as Sister Manda repeats like a mantra the basic themes of her beliefs. When I went to Global Co-Operation House to hear Dadi Janki speaking on the theme of 'Conflict Resolution in an Age of Upheaval and Change' with Lord Ennals, a great friend of the Brahma Kumaris, I began to long for something different. My rising impatience was exacerbated by the fear it would be spotted: 'If an angry person is sitting in a room,' as Sister Manda says, 'it creates an atmosphere.' But the rhythmic repetition of themes and phrases is what it's all about – the message of the Brahma Kumaris is simple: 'It's not that I have to take peace *from* somewhere, I *am* peace, I *am* a being of love, I *am* a spiritual being,' as Sister Manda says. And what she feels, twelve years after accepting that teaching, is that 'every moment of my life is being used in a worthwhile way. Each moment, for me, becomes an eternal moment.'

SIX

On the Line

Four years ago Stewart (not his real name) came out of prison. He had spent a long time there – formative years.

He returned to the Shankill Road, the area he grew up in; one of the poorest and most troubled parts of Belfast. In Longkesh, he had become convinced there were alternatives to violence. By enabling people to talk across divisions, without denying them, he hoped to encourage an end to the killing.

Shankill has an unemployment rate of 67 per cent and over half the youngsters leaving school each year have no qualifications at all. It is on the Peace Line, which 'is unique in Europe now, because it's the only wall that's dividing any city. Along the road, it actually has electronic ramps which the army control when your car drives up – it's all quite sinister and eerie.' Children learn early that the Line is there to protect them from the people on the other side. No wonder, Stewart says, there is sectarianism among the young.

Longkesh released him to take up a job in community work, which focused on the economic problems of the area. Then he moved to a project which was long-established, but looking for a more radical approach. Its members had come to feel that instead of resolving the conflict, their work was merely helping to *manage* it. Organizing holidays away from the ghettos did not suffice: as soon as the children came back, peer pressure to be involved in violence was as strong as ever.

Most community work and all the government initiatives, in Stewart's view, serve merely to contain the Troubles. To end them all sides must co-operate, which will not be easy. When he started work with the project, he insisted he would not discriminate, even against paramilitaries. He would work with anyone who wanted to resolve the conflict. 'There was a lot of danger involved because the money was coming from the government. But they agreed, if I could do it quietly and prove it could work. So that's what's actually happened.'

Stewart accepts that fighting is an option; a valid course of action whenever there are opposing views and interests. But he is also sure that every death in Northern Ireland in the last score years has been in vain. The killing can only stop, he believes, when its motivations are understood. 'People in Northern Ireland will say the paramilitaries are all a gang of psychopaths and monsters. That's not true. If you met me in the street and spoke to me and never knew my background, you'd probably go away and say "Well, isn't he a decent fella . . . !" And then if I phoned you up and said I've done years inside for paramilitary activities, you'd turn round and say "*What?*" You can't just tell. It attracts the best and the worst, the same as the British Army does.'

Stewart was born in 1955, 'here on Shankill, in a two up, two down house with an outside toilet. My family were working-class people, respectable. They hadn't much money, we got by. My father was a socialist, my mother a unionist – which led to a lot of conflict in the house!'

In the strongest and fastest of Northern Irish accents, Stewart recounts memories of Loyalism and Orangeism, of Union Jacks, pictures of the Queen and the annual festivities in memory of the Battle of the Boyne: 'The 11 July was our big night as kids. We'd light this fire, make the effigy of the pope and put up bunting – really great stuff! And all that camaraderie. I mean there was no hatred or anything, you were celebrating something that happened hundreds of years ago.'

It was the days of the Stormont government and Stewart's father criticized the Protestants in power as a 'fur-coat brigade, lining their own pockets'. His mother voted Unionist because her parents had before her. She took it for granted that Britain was their life, its system of justice beyond compare. Later, she changed her mind, when her son was punished for crimes he assured her were not his. Stewart's parents divorced before he reached his teens. As a result he remembers little political debate, only elections – when his mother's women friends discussed the merits of the candidates' families rather than their policies. 'You can't vote for him, his father was an alcoholic!' was a typical remark. The assumption was that anyone from their own class lacked intelligence; that the bright would move to a better street and enter medicine or law.

At sixteen, Stewart started working in an engineering firm on the Springfield Road. A lot of the other apprentices were Catholics. He had a good many debates with them, earning a reputation as a forceful unionist. One morning, he found in his locker some rounds of spent ammunition and a note suggesting the next one might be in his head. 'I didn't really pay much attention to that, but that's what started it off.' He got involved in local gangs. Then the vigilante movement began, in response to the IRA's decision to 'bomb the Brits and the Protestants out of Northern Ireland', and to attack civilian targets. Groups of men recruited on Protestant street corners, and Stewart was easily persuaded to join the Ulster Volunteer Force (UVF).

He was attracted by the ideal of a federal Ireland, and by the policy of hitting back at the Catholic community in order to drive out the IRA. Later he realized it was having the reverse effect: people started to join the IRA in greater numbers out of fear and anger.

For the next two years he was involved in a range of paramilitary activities. The small unit he belonged to carried out specific tasks, not necessarily aware of the overall picture. But 'I went into it with my eyes open. I knew what I was doing, understood the reason and the logic behind it and agreed with it.'

He was often on the run, moving from house to house. The Army would come to the street he had grown up in, and make it so uncomfortable for neighbours that his return would quickly be reported. Then, he says, the soldiers would come and kick the door down in their search. It was a hard time for his mother.

One encounter with the Army left his cheekbone fractured, and he tells the story at some length. Cornered in an alleyway, he was arrested and put in the back of a Land Rover. 'I think there were eight soldiers, and they all sat with their feet on me and my face was pushed into the ground. They took me to this place on the side of a mountain and put this hood over my head, handcuffed my hands at the back and got me to kneel down. All I could hear was water drippin'. I didn't knew where I was. One of them came up behind me and cocked the gun and then hit me in the back of the head and I fell into this stream. Now, I didn't know whether he'd shot me or not, 'cause I had a headache. I heard them all laughing and screaming and yelling. Next thing, they pulled my hood up and said, "Ah, you thought you were dead, you bastard!" – stuff like this, taunting me.'

Later, at the police station, they showed him pictures of a car, with blood stains and bullet holes, in which two Catholics had died the night before. 'And they said to me, "This is something that you've done." ' Two other men from the UVF had been pulled in at the same time, and were made to get on all fours and bark like dogs, 'and these were big lumps of fellas. What they were saying to me was, "These are two of your soldiers." ' Stewart was instructed to stand with his fingertips against the wall for his interrogation; but he refused, determined not to sacrifice his dignity.

The soldiers were only young, like him; they must have found it 'a bit of a challenge', he thinks. He understands their point of view. His paramilitary involvement was well-known, and there was a concern to put him away for *something*. In the end he got a long sentence, for a violent crime. He did not do it, he says, but was involved on the peripheries. 'I've never claimed to be innocent, because I knew what was happening. But the police tampered with the evidence. One policeman actually perjured himself.' Stewart is anxious both to put the record straight and to acknowledge he is not free of guilt. His wife chips in, expressing her frustrated loyalty: 'But you were always innocent!' They have known each other since childhood.

All paramilitaries end up maimed, killed or imprisoned, Stewart says. He thinks he got the best option. In Longkesh he set about improving his education, and acquired a degree in Social Science. It opened his mind: 'I was reading Che Guevara, Marx and stuff. I suppose after you've read these things you're not quite the same.' Though he had thought of himself as left-wing, he had been concerned for his community alone. Now he began to think about Northern Ireland as a whole, and about how it fitted into the world. A 'global perspective' transformed the familiar scene.

More significant still, he had debates with nationalist prisoners. 'Being a paramilitary, you see the republicans as the enemy and totally different. Here you were simply dealing with people who were from the same background, had done the same things as I did as a kid, for different reasons.' Conversations grew frequent as each group's curiosity became aroused. Results could be amusing, he smiles: the miners' strike ranged loyalists and republicans together – on each side of the argument.

They did not persuade each other, on this or any other issue, but agreed to differ. Stewart never lost his desire for the link with Britain to be retained: 'I mean, I'm an atheist. So if there was a United Ireland tomorrow, the first thing I'd be worried about would be somebody imposing their religious beliefs on me. We've seen that recently, when the girl didn't even have the right to travel for an abortion. The other thing is, I don't think I'd be economically better off in an all-Ireland.' In prison he learned to respect the nationalist viewpoint and to grope towards accommodation, but not compromise.

The paramilitaries from both sides had an agreement not to engage in conflict in Longkesh. If they wanted a change in their conditions they negotiated with the Governor and the Board of Visitors. 'We would argue it from a moral point of view, rather than, "Over the wire and get in there!" '

Well, Stewart reasoned, these were the extremes of Loyalism and Republicanism: if they could agree on a way to live together, the ordinary citizens of Belfast could surely do so. He took the analogy further. Inside they *had* to co-operate with each other, because there was a 'common enemy – the people who were locking the gates. So out here . . . Well, I wouldn't describe them as the enemy, but the government can take that place. Because they're the people who are keeping you in poverty or deprivation.'

Poverty does not stop at a person's religion or political ideology. It is the one thing everybody in the Shankill area of Belfast has in common, and he believes it is the cause of many of their ills. It is noticeable, he says, with the women's groups he works with: 'Whenever they have discussions it is always how much money they have to do for the week; how much butcher's meat is in the Shankill and how much it is in the Falls; and about bargains, making ends meet.' The Protestant working class have suffered as much as the Catholics, he says. Unemployment affects everyone: 'Get jobs – and *then* worry about discrimination!'

His argument is that the policy of sectarian violence he supported in the early 1970s was right for the time, but will not work now. Civil rights campaigns and student revolts have given way to consensus politics. 'Ten years ago, people who had been complaining about their houses having rats in them would have set traps and caught the rats. They would have taken them to the local housing office, opened the door and thrown the rats at the secretaries. That's the way the world worked, it was confrontational. Now we're into talking, and that's what I think we need to do.'

In the Shankill he has set up a 'standing conference', a forum where representatives of different community groups can discuss common problems and possible solutions. People must be able, he insists, to say what they think. 'We got it off the ground and nobody was nice to anybody. It was very very hostile, and in fact a lot of people here were shocked and hurt, and just couldn't understand and couldn't believe the gap was as wide as it was. But a week passed, and everybody came back and said, "You know, I'm not gonna run away from this. If that's what they think of me I should be putting them right." '

Even those most battered by the experience felt it was positive, 'because nobody was killed. And we're talking about people living on the Peace Line, who normally don't pull triggers, but either verbally or monetarily support the armed struggle.' Stewart emphasizes that he is not encouraging the seeking of a middle ground: he likes the vigour of separate identity and ideology. 'I'm not into peace and reconciliation. It's not about people kissing each other and hands across the Peace Line. It's about people understanding why is the other person doing what they do.'

His base is a bare office, alleviated by a few photographs. A colleague works from the Whiterock Road, on the other side of the Line. There is a third office on the Springfield Road, accessible to everybody. Stewart and his colleague try to strengthen existing community organizations, such as tenants' groups, and to work through those. He found it hard to itemize a typical week or even month, but most of the time he would be talking: to locals about unemployment, to a university gathering in Eire about the situation in the North, to the British government about the need for economic regeneration, or to paramilitaries about why they should not be shooting youngsters for 'anti-social behaviour'.

He believes his project is unique in Northern Ireland. Most

cross-community work 'tends to be hold hands and pray, that sort of stuff. And to me that's fine, if it's what people want to do, but it doesn't put food in your fridge.' Others try to cross the barriers through sport and socializing but, he says, they play safe: 'If it were a youth group, you'd probably say, "Don't mention Rangers or Celtic!" ' Whereas that is the first thing Stewart would want them to talk about.

There are risks. He did not want his photograph taken. But the dangers, he added, should not be exaggerated. He would never ask his wife to live in Shankill if he thought it would put her under pressure; as for him, 'after coming out of one prison you don't want to put yourself in another one.' A sense of vocation, even mission, fuels him – he compares it to preaching the Gospel. He believes the Northern Irish have a lot to offer, and are destroying themselves. Honest meetings are the only way forward: 'People have to be prepared to get bloody noses. Metaphorically speaking, of course.'

SEVEN

'. . . *Not a Perfect Work, but Infinite Desire*'

A high metal fence, painted green and topped with spikes: this is Belfast's 'Peace Line'. Sister Noreen Christian lives beside it, and is a founding member of a new ecumenical community – Currach.

The fence consists of railings with a gate, which is locked at 10 p.m. It was recently adapted to keep out motorbikes, since that was how the last set of killers had escaped, a few months earlier. They had shot a young woman on the Springfield Road, in the pharmacy where she worked. She was a Catholic, known for taking medicines through the gate to Protestants.

I was woken in the night by Noreen phoning the police. Someone had been trying to force the fence's lock, she said – this sort of thing happened all the time. The police did not turn up: that was usual too. Yes, she nodded, it could sometimes be dangerous living here; but it's where she wants to be.

'Essentially what I think we need to do is help people keep relating, because the powers that want division are always delighted when Catholics move out of a Protestant area or Protestants move out of a Catholic area – or a big barrier like that gate is put up between the two people. That is the winning of negativity.'

The Currach Community got going in August 1992. Sister Noreen had the idea for it three years ago: she got a planning group together, and backing from her order, but had no property. Then she heard that the Methodist church, on the

Springfield Road, wanted to create a route of safety for people crossing to Sunday services from 'the other side'. The church was on a Catholic road, and the wall of its backyard formed part of the Line. Beyond, in a Protestant street, were two derelict houses.

Noreen and the Methodists agreed to work together. The church bought the houses, as a meeting place and 'corridor'; Currach moved in, to make a home of it and offer welcome. Prayer meetings and mother-and-toddler groups take place here, and other interchurch and cross-community gatherings. But there is also privacy for the people living in community: Sister Noreen, a Dominican priest, two young Americans (one Protestant, one Catholic) and an English couple in their twenties, who work as doctors in the city. Renovation is complete – everything is new and tidy. Noreen sometimes worries if it is *too* nice: but there is enough penance in life as it is, she comments, without making things worse. There had been an attempted break-in through the church – 'probably just kids, for a dare'. As a result, the view now from the passageway, which connects the houses at the rear, is of a firmly padlocked gate and a wall surmounted by barbed wire.

Currach is deliberately flexible, and expects a frequent change of members. Everyone must be committed to ecumenism 'in their being', Noreen says, 'and give energy to it if they can. I would hope to give my entire energy.' For some, earning a living may take priority, and the doctors were furiously revising for exams when I was there. What matters is their presence. At Christmas they played carols at the Peace Line gate by candlelight, and invited local residents to join them for mince pies.

Noreen's interest is the needs of women. She has been experimenting with 'conflict resolution' workshops on a model she learned in the United States. 'We kept our role plays to family situations – Oh they were a scream! They were lovely, live women: they came back and said "I tried that out on my man and he laughed his leg off!'' So we focus it on the life experience of the people we're talking to. Eventually . . . the same dynamics occur, of course, politically. So we'd hope to go on to train people in mediation.'

We sat in a room with a window looking out onto the street. It was a Saturday, and mothers bustled to and fro with shopping. Noreen 'walks alongside' women, such as these, whose only relaxations are 'cigarettes and sitting hunched over a fire, watching the television and worrying about their kids'. She brings in people trained in massage and aromatherapy, and has a variety of methods at her own fingertips – most recently the 'Metamorphic Technique . . . I've already offered it to the old lady over there! I've done reflexology with another lady, and I've offered it to Margaret who's just walked past – there she is again! I see my part here as helping to heal people's immediate anxieties.'

This neat, modern nun, with her casual clothes and talk of therapies and auras, has come a long way. But her transformation has brought her back to working-class Belfast, where she began. She offers her past.

* * *

Fleeing the house, in the blackness of an air raid warning; her first book, featuring a giraffe 'with its lovely long neck – I was absolutely enamoured . . . !'; 12 July bonfires outside their home: a party for all the street, including Noreen and her sisters, though it was celebrating a Protestant victory at the Battle of the Boyne.

It was many years before the Troubles. Noreen's playmates in the street were often Protestants, but she remembers feeling guilty when they put on a play for the neighbours to raise funds for the Protestant church. She listened to tales of the bad times in her parents' youth, when the police searched Catholic houses in the middle of the night; and when her uncle was warned by a Protestant friend at work to stay at home that afternoon – and later heard the Catholics had all been beaten up. Noreen found it hard to get a holiday job because of her religion and thinks that she, like other Northern Irish Catholics, acquired a victim's mind. This is one of the themes of her healing work today.

Noreen's school life was disrupted by emotional upheaval. From cleverness she slipped to scraping through, with crushes and confusions eating up her energy. She had no one to discuss her problems with, and so they lingered, well into middle age. But one thing held her together, even through turmoil – music. Haydn, Mozart and Bach nourished her emotions, 'possibly to an extreme'. She sang in choral works, and as a schoolgirl had the leading part in countless plays: 'I have dramatic tendencies . . . !' This she inherits from her father; from her mother, a desire to make a home. Currach's domesticity is largely hers; and though she thinks she might have married unwisely, carried away by romance, she is sure she would have made a devoted wife and mother.

After passing her final school exams, she remembers going to the seaside with her friends. Cigarette ash burned a hole in her 'gorgeous taffeta dress' – she now finds it hilarious that she was wearing such an outfit on the beach at all. At the summer's end she was entering the Dominican novitiate. The cost of kitting her out with postulant's habit, towels and sheets was so enormous that her mother said her bathing suit would have to last: she would not need one 'inside'. It was far too small, Noreen laughs; she kept pulling it up, then down, in vain adjustment . . .

'A nun or a film star!' she had replied, when asked what she would be when she grew up. Her piety was not unusual; it was common among her friends to go to daily Mass. But spirituality was in her bones, she says: she never doubted her vocation. She may take mischievous pleasure in listing the deprivations of her three years as a novice, but she remembers them as happy. 'Horrible, horrible!' she says, describing the way her weaknesses were probed to discipline her soul: the novice mistress, knowing Noreen hated to be wrongly accused, deliberately blamed her for things she had not done. But at the time she welcomed it. Even as a child she had saved her sweets for penance. In the novitiate, just south of Dublin, the only light in her room came from the corridor. Hot water was provided for her ewer once a week and she was allowed to have a termly bath. She loved the chant in chapel; other than that she relied on the wind-up gramophone and the convent's only record, which she could play on feast days. It was Bach's Toccata and Fugue: 'I just gulped it up . . .'

These novices were teenage girls, but all emotion was suppressed. Few letters or visits were permitted. 'You learned that your feelings didn't count, that you were there to become the perfect religious, and nothing was to be standing in the way. Personal relationships were not encouraged, so you usually went out in threes and fours for recreation.' Even when her fellow novices left, as many of them did, she only found out after they had gone.

Noreen felt drawn to Africa. Heart pumping, she told the novice mistress, who said nothing. Then, weeks later, in July, a list was read aloud to the gathered sisters: the names of those who were to sail for the Cape in three months' time. Her name was one of them.

They were to emigrate for life. Noreen could not go home for her farewells, but stayed in the Belfast convent for some weeks. Her mother visited her there each day, and her father taught her to drive. She remembers, with a giggle, the ritual of reaching the convent gate – and climbing out of the car, while her father turned it round and brought it back within the grounds for her to get back in. Such was the sisters' separation from the outside world.

The young Noreen had a distant and perfectionist God. Her parents' adage was 'If a thing's worth doing, it's worth doing well'. Noreen, the eldest of five girls, was always keen to gain approval and accept responsibility. In religious life, she tried to please authority for more than twenty years. The *rules* had to be obeyed, whether they came from the Bible or the Church. To the sisters it was all 'God's law'.

In the early 1960s, the Second Vatican Council 'loosened up perceptions' and a long process of change began. Religious orders dropped many of their regulations: for the South African Dominicans, the 1970s saw the gradual exchange of habit and veil for 'civvies' and the purchase of a holiday home beside the sea, as well as structural reform. What had been forbidden was encouraged: visits back to Ireland, friendships, a more flexible routine of prayer. Religious resigned in droves from orders everywhere. But Noreen Christian was one of many who felt liberated. She embarked on an exploration of herself and her convictions. The God she believes in now does not expect impeccability. She understands why she always loved the words of Catherine of Siena: 'God wants not a perfect work, but infinite desire.'

When she first arrived in Cape Town, the old regime was still in force. She sweltered in the heat in obligatory black cloak and white serge habit. With no experience or training, she was thrown into teaching. Loneliness overpowered her. In compensation she formed a close attachment to one of the other sisters, but there was little opportunity for private talk: 'It *led* you into extremity!' A few months after her arrival in South Africa, Noreen was confined to bed for several months by a mysterious disease. She says now – no hesitation – it was psychosomatic. Cut off from her family, she had then been moved another 1,000 miles from the sister she had befriended, to Johannesburg.

Noreen stayed in Africa for twenty-six years. She loved it – but with reservations. The career she sketches in is of a teacher and headmistress, accepting organizational roles reluctantly but using them to steer through change. The work was exhausting: raising funds, managing people and institutions. She felt the pressure. On holiday, 'I would want to run along the beach or the rocks, screaming and shouting; to get into my bathing costume as soon as possible and *live* in it if I could . . .'

Later, she realized the problem went deeper than strain. 'Psychically I had been looking over my shoulder for a quarter of a century.' To live alongside black people, and do pastoral work with individuals, was what her 'whole being' yearned for. But there had been no opportunities: the little she could do was crammed into the gaps left by her duties running schools for whites. Even the thrill she felt, when finally allowed to open her school to every race, could not assuage her self-reproach.

There was another guilt as well. Her friendship with the sister she had become close to, in that first loneliness in Cape Town, had waxed and waned in its intensity. Now, in her forties, Noreen felt suffocated. She had idealized relationships: the loyalty she had demanded, from herself and others, was taken 'to the nth degree'. Now she wanted to withdraw a little, but her friend found this very difficult: it was agonizing.

Noreen could not cope. Ten years ago she returned to Ireland for a break. Immediately, the tension started 'coming off in layers' – she acts out the relief, exhaling deeply and melting into the settee. Then savage questions fell upon her, about the meaning of existence and her own psychology. She became depressed. 'It was real mid-life crisis stuff.'

Psychosynthesis counselling, and several training courses later, she was almost 'well'. And when it suddenly hit her that there was no need to return to Africa, it was – '*Aaaaaahhhhhhhhh*': a diminuendo of a sigh. But what now?

She got a part-time job in a Kensington hotel, where no one would know she was a nun, to see what that was like. She was beginning to put together the different pieces of her life. For a year she did a course with the Richmond Fellowship: 'real supportive stuff to help you process what was going on in yourself'. Theory and practice, the material and spiritual, the sacred and profane, began to intertwine. She had had enough of dualism.

Christ had always been a reminder that God included both the human and divine: he had been the focus of her prayer.

But her education had instilled in her a hierarchical image of the universe, with a big boss patriarch in charge, and this she started to discard. God is 'in everything', she now believes (but still only 'in my head'). All things are interconnected: trees and rocks no 'lower' than human beings. She sees God as 'the almighty one, who allows and invites everything that's created to participate in the flow of giving and taking of life . . .'

Impressed by the ecology of Buddhists, among others, Noreen at first felt angry and betrayed because the Church had jettisoned this part of its theology. Now she is moving past rebellion, trying to blend what was good in her youthful training with what she has recently learned. She sometimes prays with the help of essential oils, and has reacted against the discipline of early morning Office. A rose quartz crystal she has just been given draws her close to nature: 'One of the things I'm trying to absorb is that everything that has matter has energy . . .'

The memory of Jesus' closeness to the elements, she believes, was held by women and then suppressed by a Church afraid of losing power. Now, the tide has turned. Noreen has set up a women's theology group, and is searching for a spirituality which will recognize the feminine in God. The Church, she protests, attributed it all to Mary, 'who kept being presented as *perfection* . . . I couldn't relate to her, this virgin mother.' But now 'I've just come across a prayer addressed to God as Woman. Oh, when I read it I thought, "*Aahh*". It was just gorgeous!'

To 'find herself', Noreen felt she had to stay in Northern Ireland, working deep among its troubles, as she had never done in Africa. She persuaded her order to send her to the Falls Road convent and for a twelve-month period involved herself with Cornerstone, a small ecumenical community nearby. Then she was elected Prioress. For four years she grounded herself in the Dominican community of Belfast; it was her first real experience of being a member of the order in Northern Ireland. After that, she moved to Currach.

The symbolism of the name expresses 'where we're at' – though she gleefully admits it is just a touch contrived. The word is Celtic, the boat an ancient Christian symbol. A currach is made of hide and wood: 'the fruits of the *earth*. And they're put together by tar, which is brought about by *fire*. It floats in the *water* . . . and the *air* blows it along!' She bursts out laughing, 'We squeezed that in! And we felt it was quite an open, womb-like symbol, so we felt it had a feminine element!' Leaning back she laughed and laughed, and drew her story to a close.

* * *

Leave the door of Currach and go through the spiky gate to the Springfield Road. Facing you are two new houses, especially designed for their location. There are no windows at the front, just a fancy pattern in the brickwork. The entrances and windows at the side are protected by high walls. And the reason why is clear, if you stay in the gate and look to either side at the houses on the Peace Line. Almost every one is burned and boarded up. Threat and dereliction daub their brownish signatures across the walls.

Yet there is one still occupied. An elderly couple have remained and tend their garden, neatly. Outside their door is an ornamental watering can, sparkling with paint of vivid colours.

EIGHT

Priestess of Isis

'To start with facts: I was born on Friday the thirteenth 1917, in London, but I became totally aware of myself and reality at three months old in Cicester (they call it Cirencester now) when I woke up in full consciousness.'

The Hon. Olivia Robertson, co-founder of the Fellowship of Isis, lives in the family castle in the south of Ireland. She lists her ancestors, to show that her background was 'unpsychic'; though she has wondered whether connections with the Freemasons, centuries back, may indicate her interest in the occult was inherited. There was also Robert Graves, author of *The White Goddess* – a second cousin once removed.

'Now, how did life develop . . . ? I seemed to be an absolutely normal girl who liked *Just William*, and wasn't a bit "trailing clouds of glory from whence I came" at *all.*' Olivia divided her youth between England and Ireland. She became an artist and a writer. Her books sold well and scoffed at the spiritual. Life was easygoing: she would drift around Dublin – meeting friends in town, eating a boiled egg for tea and penning a few words in the afternoons.

No comparison with her workload now! It is Olivia who deals with the enormous correspondence of the Fellowship of Isis. Letters come in regularly from the members (11,600 in seventy-three countries), and enquiries flood in from the curious or needy. Was it true that the Fellowship, as I had heard, was the main organization honouring the goddess? 'Well, people have said that, they have *said* that, but I don't want to boast. Say "*one* of" . . . !'

There were hints, even in her early years, of uncommon powers: 'I used to know if people were going to die. I'd have a dream, I'd know. But I never thought anything of it. It was as if I cut it off. It was hardly a thing you're going to tell people anyway: "You're going to leave this earth in two months!" '

Her 'awakening', when it came, was 'an expansion of consciousness. I didn't lose my personality, Olivia; I'm still very down-to-earth, myself. But I extended, if I can put it that way, into the other world. I suddenly was aware that this life was a dream. It was a shadow of reality.'

The transformation began in 1946. Surrounded by a golden light, she became aware of 'eternal reality, of being an eternal being'. Her influences were still conventional enough, she says: Jane Austen and Lord Chesterfield's letters. She was writing in *Tribune* about children's singing games, and contributed to the Girl Guide magazine. But 'I became aware that there were Beings who belonged to another world, who were more advanced than we are, Beings of light. I didn't know what to call them. I thought "gods, goddesses" – it amazed me that women could be like that! "*They*": I called them "*Them*". "Fairies" seemed a bit too tittupy. "Spirits" – well, if you like. "*Beings!*" – I used the word with a capital "B". "Deities". I suppose now I'd use the word "*Pantheon*".'

Olivia did not altogether welcome these experiences. She liked to get on with everybody and did not want to be associated with 'a lot of *nutters*, barmy people wandering around with placards saying "The end of the world is nigh!" ' It was the *last straw* to come across an artist's impression of a giant spaceship, apparently seen by an astronomer, in a magazine left in a railway carriage. What was worse, 'I recognized it. I knew this, out of my body as it were; I'd been in this spaceship, I knew it travelled beyond the speed of light. So I thought "O my God, this is too much!" '

Thus began her 'time of seeking'. She went to listen to

the speeches in the House of Lords, to lectures by people famous for their acumen, to symphony orchestras; all seemed 'fast asleep'. Perhaps the occultists had the answer, she thought. 'So I went round to all these societies, and I found they were all true, I didn't find they were all bosh. But it was only a part, it wasn't my experience – it *was*, but it wasn't quite. I couldn't *jam* all my experiences into a place over the Himalayas called Shangri La; I couldn't turn my Beings into Tibetans, when they were star people.'

She felt very conscious of the vast scale of the universe. 'And the language of this new world I was discovering was telepathy. So I spent hours in meditation trying to learn telepathy, and I was getting guidance through to an extent.' People generally dismissed as charlatans, if not insane, seemed to her the only ones who were awake. She started to read magazines she would have scorned before, with titles like *Prediction*.

The next stage was 'what they call the Kundalini Power or the Vital Force. It began in my heart in 1948, like a steady glow occasionally. Then it began to move up to my throat. I thought, "My goodness, what's going to happen when it gets to my head?" It didn't *worry* me, it was like a silvery shower. But I didn't know what it was – I called it "electricity" – until I read books and saw diagrams of people's auras and all this carry-on. Anyway, now we get to when we founded the Fellowship . . . My real work starts.'

Her brother Lawrence, an Anglican clergyman, had turned to the goddess and left the Church. Olivia was happy enough in Christianity, for eclecticism suits her. Nevertheless, the Church of England's God had started to seem 'so tiny', and squeezing her spirituality into dogma was 'like pouring the Ganges into a jam jar'. Her brother's conviction that God was a woman persuaded her the time had come for change.

Olivia and Lawrence, with his wife Pamela, founded the Fellowship of Isis in 1976. Each brought something different: Pamela, a love of nature; Lawrence, a studious theology;

Olivia, an interest in the mystical. A new age was beginning, they believed. 'The old age was that of the linealogical mind, analysis, proof. The new age was creative, more related to the supernatural.'

The mysticism of human nature, Olivia explains, was being killed by the rational male mind. Facts, 'the boots of fate, the sandal feet of truth', are useful, but not to be relied on. Obsession with scientific thought was damaging the psychic faculties. People were losing touch with fairies, angels and goddesses. But simultaneously, there were signs that a new humanity was being born. People seemed to be remembering previous incarnations, and glimpsing future lives; some were learning to communicate with nature spirits. 'Our aim was to be in touch with people who could spread this rainbow knowledge to others.'

Olivia's concern was to present the Fellowship 'in a way that would be agreeable to a person that could read and write properly. And not come out with pseudo-science of a dippy sort, taking any psychic messages as being true – you know, everything I say is true, which is *nonsense*. Accepting I knew practically nothing, but then, nobody else did either.' Mystery plays and dramas, fairy tales and parables, were her particular contribution.

The Fellowship produced a duplicated manifesto, but made no attempt to publicize itself. And what an extraordinary response there was! Some thought they were the answer to prayer, others laughed them off. Their family and friends thought they had gone mad, but were impressed to see them on the television. Local villagers absorbed the eccentricities of 'Miss Olivia' and became accustomed to film crews at the castle. It was good for the bed-and-breakfast trade and the shop. Not all who come are searching for the goddess, Olivia remarks: someone recently wanted advice about the decline of the Swedish aristocracy. They come for healing, guidance, counselling; to talk things over with a priestess, that they would not touch on with a priest.

'It's a new awakening and it's coming through the Goddess, through the feminine side, simply because that's been neglected. We accept the male God, but we feel he's got plenty of attention anyway.' He, or she, is 'life itself . . . reality, all love, beauty and truth'.

The Fellowship of Isis has no secrets. There are no vows: 'I'm absolutely against commitment!' Anyone can join. Membership aims to promote 'closer communion between the Goddess and each member', according to the manifesto. People join as individuals, or go along to their local Iseum; they receive a newsletter. It is especially popular in Nigeria. Writers like it ('We had the famous Borges: he joined just before he passed on.'). It is not exclusivist, and other allegiances can be retained. They have all sorts, Olivia says, although no Muslims spring to mind. Some members prefer to be anonymous – such as the members of Christian religious orders.

'What we do is, we have seminars here and people come and practise the rituals and we really enter into another dimension . . . During a weekend or a few days, we go twice to the Temple of Isis. We tune in, and it produces an extraordinary happiness.' Their year is an 'eight-pointed star': The solstices and traditional Celtic festivals are observed, along with the Panathenaia and Eleusinian Mysteries, Norse ceremonies of the tree of life, Wesak (a Buddhist festival) and the Druid Order of Tara Ceremony, which works for the environment. There are also weddings, ordinations and rites of rebirth, many written by Olivia. 'Whatever it is, we make the *whole* time part of it, so we examine our dreams as well. We have very beautiful robes we wear and we use incense and beauty down in the Temple, and prayer, so that we make all of our lives more magical.'

For the rest of the time Olivia and her brother meditate daily in the Temple and keep the Fellowship ticking over. They send out certificates of ordination (there is now a priesthood of 400) and manage the College of Isis, which confers Magi degrees after a correspondence course. Doctrine is confirmed by reference to ancient sources, Olivia explains, but comes initially 'through oracles. That is, I get inspired. I enter into a slight degree of trance and receive oracles from the Goddess directly.' If, say, she wants to plan a ritual, she gives a minimum of 24 hours' notice. 'And then you sit and receive it. You feel this strong electric-like power which the Pythoness seemed to get at Delphi. There, I'm afraid, they killed a goat, which is ridiculous and quite unnecessary.' Only priestesses receive oracles.

Some rituals take place in the ground of Clonegal Castle, which is over 300 years old. Especially popular are the older ruins at the castle's edge, known as 'the abbey': two small cells, strewn with ivy, crumbling and open to the sky. Across the lawn there is a cloister walk of ancient yew trees – planted by monks, tradition says – their gnarled and massy branches arching to the ground.

A dragon, left over from a film, flares its nostrils near the back door to the castle. Inside, Olivia throws off her cloak and hangs it near the crocodile. The rooms are choked with bric-a-brac from 'the far-flung empire': a Chinese dragon screen to ward off evil spirits, four-poster beds, a breastplate grazed by a bullet. The furniture is dark, the drapery worn. Wooden carvings by Olivia's nephew rest exquisitely in gloomy corners. Most graceful of them is the halcyon bird. It stands beside the Temple door.

Down a short flight of steps the Temple begins, and ambles through the basement. Pottery, hangings and carpet ease the granite floor and walls. Small rooms open into each other, mini altars for ceremony or private prayer. A blue and gold heat of Tutankhamen is accompanied by wooden busts of Masai female figures. Brightly coloured pictures illuminate a Hindu corner. Virgo, Cancer, Sagittarius and all the zodiac are represented. A Druid well, coverd by a grille, is dedicated to the goddess Brighid and reputed to have healing powers.

Olivia covers her long red woollen skirt with a spangly robe and sets a circlet on her long brown hair. She wants to be properly dressed for her photographs, although she is a little shy. Her staff is topped with the *Ankh*, symbol of the origin of life. She stands before the altar of Isis, which gleams with candles, gilt and feathers. In the centre is a statue of the goddess.

The connection with the ancient Egyptian civilization is important to the Fellowship: that was 'before we went mad'. The Greeks concentrated far too much on the intellect, Olivia explains, and went 'very peculiar' as a result. The name Isis was 'given' to her in her first vision of the goddess: a woman 'made of pure white light, with lightning, as it were, out of her head'.

The goddess is 'coming through' today, Olivia says, because this is the time when 'we're changing from being *physical* beings, bound by the five senses, into being *cosmic* awareness. We're moving into the space age. And that involves outer and inner space.' As eternal beings, she believes, we are immortal, and one of the Fellowship's 'strong points' is its belief that the afterlife can be experienced *now*. 'So you've no fear of death. You can go right out of your body.' Could she describe that? 'It varies according to what you're like! I think why some people don't want to explore it is that they'd probably find themselves in hell!'

Our life on earth, Olivia explains, is a sort of television film: 'a video nasty in some ways, very beautiful in others'. Each of us has a greater self, a spirit being, living in 'harmonious and happy circumstances. You look at this film and you get more and more absorbed into it, hypnotized by it. You start identifying with one particular character – as a baby. You *become* that person. You forget you've got a soul which lives in all time-space.' The work of the Fellowship is to help 'awaken' people, so that they realize again their true spirit selves.

The Priestess Olivia, at seventy-five, is full of zest and curiosity. 'A person who has no focus is a bored person, trying to do this awful thing, kill time. Members of the Fellowship of Isis need to waken *every* morning with tremendous expectation. You create a day and it's unique, one more bead on the necklace of your life.' Are there regrets? 'None. Because my true spiritual affinities are in the inner spheres. When the time comes for me to leave this earth, I feel the Goddess will come and say, "It's time to leave that television now and come out into the sun." That's a nice wrap-up, isn't it?'

NINE

The Lifeboat

When Jim Lutomski was five years old he fell ill with a high fever and lost the will to live. 'I kept turning my face to the wall as little kids do – the death instinct that Freud talks about: "To hang with it all, give me peace, I can't be bothered." '

His father stayed at home, trying to encourage him. When a spark of energy returned, 'we spent two days together, day and night, building this model of a lifeboat. And of course, *bang!*, back came the instinct to live . . . I can still remember putting this bit on and that bit on: "That's where you put the people"; and "Where do the children go?" – "Oh, they go in here" . . . working it all out.'

When they had built the boat his father said, 'Do you want to say a prayer? It makes you *strong*!' (Jim does a Tarzan gesture with his arm, grinning.) What little boy could resist such a promise? Jim prayed, 'and I found it actually worked . . . I felt myself getting stronger and stronger and stronger.'

Father James Lutomski is one of the Society of Jesus – known as Jesuits. He was ordained as a priest in 1992, after ten years' training. The Society was founded for 'the help of souls'; a Jesuit hopes to gain salvation through saving others. This sort of language has always baffled me. Jim, in his exuberant Scottish accent, laughingly attempts to clear up the mystery: 'It's something to do with an invitation to an intimate relation with God: in so far as you run away from that, you create problems for yourself and those around you.'

The afterlife interests him little, 'because we are not

immortal, but we believe in the resurrection. Big difference. We have faith that somehow God will raise up the poor and all this kind of thing. But we are nothing but dust and ashes; we can never forget that.' What happens at death is in God's hands, and Jim trusts it will be all right. But 'the resurrection life starts *now*'. Ever since his father helped him build the lifeboat, he explains, he has had 'a little hope machine inside. Somehow, bringing folk back to life has always been important to me.'

His father taught him how 'to suffer constructively; and there's all the difference in the world between that and the senseless suffering a lot of people go through.' It's no good complaining because God doesn't give you a new bike, Jim says wryly: 'You've got to let go of that kind of magical thing.' And as for plane crashes and earthquakes – they 'take away completely an intellectual understanding of God, because it's obviously ridiculous: come *on*, who's running this show?' When a jet was blown up over Lockerbie Jim was one of many young religious who hurried to the scene to counsel relatives. Utter devastation met him: bodies everywhere, parents shattered by the loss of children, fragments of people who could never be identified because too much was missing. Yet there was 'resurrection', even so; God was there: 'It's not that there's some plan God has, but that no matter what happened, there's hope in this situation.'

Down-to-earth resurrection of this kind depends on facing up to truth; emotions being tackled, not suppressed. Strong men know how to cry, Jim's father said; those who do not weep are dangerous. 'That was his own experience – he went on about the Nazis: omnipotent, god-like thugs.' As a soldier in the war he had seen the concentration camps, and later the blues would descend on him when he thought about that evil. Like many others in the Polish corps, he married a British wife and stayed, for there was nothing to go back to when his home had been destroyed. But unlike others, he immersed himself in Scottish life and loathed the

Polish nationalism which lingered on in Glasgow streets.

He was radical, imaginative – a cartoonist in the Army; Jim's mother was 'always around the house, a typical west of Scotland mum'. They lived in Renfrewshire, part of the Glasgow overspill, in a community whose focus was the church. Jim's earliest memories are of the Sunday pilgrimage to Mass, 'the safari with the pram'. Protestants went to separate schools, and were a great unknown. The divide could be aggressive: it was one of the things which upset Jim as he grew up. He was always preoccupied by the world beyond the family and distressed by people's failure to be 'pals'.

Jim's father was an architect, who only took on work that would improve the future – he believed environment made people good or bad. Housing rehabilitation, student seminars and building churches took his time, and ensured his family was always poor. He prayed 'for *hours*'; and Jim remembers the night and morning children's stories, accompanied by prayers. A strong impression formed that God was *real*: 'Daddy, what *size* is God?' he used to ask. 'Is he bigger than *you*? Can he go on your bike?'

Jim was always talking to God. But the first time church became important was when he was ten. At Mass one day he suddenly became completely lost in an experience of 'the whole world, and everybody in the world being present and people coming out of concentration camps, coming into life. Tremendous! And the sense of God just smiling down on all this and bringing life to it.'

The torment of adolescence was exacerbated by the 'crazy carry-on' of his relationship with God, and the question of what it meant for his future. He was told he should do science, but wanted to study literature. To express his disapproval of the system he made deliberate mistakes in homework. A careers adviser 'almost fell off his chair' when Jim said he was considering the priesthood, and told him to wait till he was older.

At Stirling University he read Philosophy and English

Literature, throwing himself with frenzy into study and activities. The great thinkers and literary giants left him bored: 'So what?' Marx he studied inside out, and reckoned was 'pretty Old Testament'. Poetry appealed: the Celtic songs and – well, Gerard Manley Hopkins, the Jesuit poet (for a moment he is *slightly* embarrassed). He also wrote.

Philosophy, he decided, was 'avoiding doing anything about anything: sitting and understanding and not changing'. Linguistic speculation was all the fashion; his diagnosis of it now is: 'vaguely schizoid; a radical splitting until your world is totally disintegrated into hundreds of mathematical bits that have no connection with anything. A hallucinatory world – a good sign of a failure to face reality.' Meanwhile, his picture of God moved further still from other-worldliness. Jesus fascinated, and 'God was starting to become Man for me – or, what was important was *being human*.' He grew active in student politics, disappointed that other Christians kept out.

In his final year his father died of a heart attack, without warning. 'And that took the carpet out from under me com*plete*ly.' The loss was devastating. And for Jim, as the eldest son, what hurt most 'was the sudden sense that "everything now lands on me. I've got to somehow take up the torch." Because we *had* a torch, you know; some things we believed in – a better world . . . And I thought, "I can't do this, I'm not up to it", I suddenly felt absolutely tiny, useless.' He had been worried he was arrogant; now he almost fell to bits.

His brothers suffered even more. One of them ('popular, handsome, extrovert': the description is wistful) slid so far he started making farewell speeches. Jim watched, powerless. One night Conrad didn't come home and Jim went looking, knowing something was wrong: 'Have you seen my brother? You know, the daft one . . . ?' He was nowhere to be found.

Later, the police blundered in – to ask them to identify the body. Jim went to the morgue, with its giant fridges.

'I can't say why, I can't say why, but God was present there. The thought going through my head was "one of his little ones has gone home . . ." ' His brother had died in an acid house, overdosed on drugs and medication for depression. 'Psychologically speaking it was suicide, whether it was accidental or not. It would have happened sooner or later.' And what made Jim boil was that the neighbours moralized about it: the family was made to feel ashamed.

After these two tragedies, he would read the Book of Job and rail: 'What the *heck's* going on?' Nobody could help, it was just him and God. Did he doubt that God was there? 'Oh, he was there all right, he was just being a bastard. There wasn't a day when I didn't think, "This isn't *fair* . . ." I used to go to the church and sit there and just *defy* him: "Come on, you big ba*lloon*, why don't you come up with something decent for a change?" '

Two days after his brother's death, Jim started training as a psychiatric nurse. That was difficult; but gradually, over many months, dealing with shattered psyches helped him reorder his own. He lost some of his brashness; became less selfish and more sensitive. And as he 'saw the lifeboat coming back', he grew absorbed in studying the flux of personality: 'I've got this thing about life as a process of being absolutely shattered and disintegrated, and then reintegrated. Whether you succeed or not depends on whether you've got this integrative faculty – the ability to reintegrate.'

Jesus himself, he reflected, had collapsed in disillusion several times; and then reconstituted his ideas, with deeper understanding. As he mulled this over, he listened to the patients' fascinating stories of religion. He was never quite sure what was going on; but it was clear that 'people's ideas of God generally tie in with their character structure and how they get on with people. A psychotic has a tremendously persecutory image of God and a depressive has a big, sad God.'

When anyone relates to God the image they have is a projection from within themselves, he says – as it is when they talk to their granny. 'The secret is, are you prepared to find that the other person is actually a person distinct from what you think they are?'

Jim's God is not omnipotent; 'if he is, he hides it very well.' He is not super-good. 'Neither do I think he's bad and cruel and perverse – setting things up so we have to jump through various hoops. That kind of rubbishing of God means a kind of idealization of self. We have to fight through that tendency to split our perceptions into absolutely good and absolutely bad.' The psychologist Winnicott wrote about 'good-enough mums' (less damaging than the perfect ones); similarly 'I think God is good *enough*, and that's better than being too good.'

Even if someone's idea of deity sounds loopy, Jim takes it seriously. And this, he says, is typical of Jesuits: they trust the individual. The spirituality of the Society of Jesus fitted in entirely with the psychological insights he had gained. So when he reluctantly left the nursing that he loved to pursue his troublesome vocation to the priesthood, the change was not as radical as he expected. Entering the novitiate was 'the biggest leap of faith I've ever taken'. But soon 'the penny dropped that, well, "They don't really have a lot to teach me, because I've been doing this for years, intuitively." '

The language was different, but the insights were the same. St Ignatius, who founded the order in 1540, taught his followers to practise the 'discernment of spirits' – that is, to find out which impulses drew them towards God and which ones dragged them away. The principal method he used was the 'Spiritual Exercises', a programme of guided meditations.

The urge towards God is the most primitive impulse of all, Jim believes; more basic, even, than to suck the breast. And that, he thinks, is what Ignatius was getting at in the very first Exercise; 'that when you make contact with your Creator, everything else suddenly starts ordering itself and becoming creative within you'. After that, the individual is helped to examine, week by week, what distances them from God and what reconciles them to him.

Depth Psychology is 'rediscovering what Ignatius already had under his belt', Jim thinks. Just as Ignatius said the human being must follow the Lord – get to know Jesus – even if the implications seemed unwelcome, so psychology defines the person as a process: 'You're not "now enlightened" – it continues, continues, continues. A lot of things have to be brought up from the unconscious, so you have to keep asking for them even though you don't want to.'

Jim thinks Ignatius' approach is especially relevant to an industrial society, where faith in God is complex, no longer automatic. Sixteenth-century Spain was in a similar condition, he suggests: people needed to be helped to find their own God. When Jim was in Barcelona, for the two years prior to his ordination, he came to understand the cultural grounding of his order. He is sure that if Ignatius had been German, the Society of Jesus would never have been founded. It was a 'happy accident' that he inherited Hispanic mysticism and plurality; and also that he was a soldier, skilled in organization. 'If he'd been a John of the Cross, a bit like my personality, he'd have written a poem about it and nobody would have known what the hell he was talking about!'

Britons interpret Ignatian spirituality in an individualistic fashion – but in Catalonia Jim realized that 'it's very, very communal; it's about conquering the narcissistic impulses and developing the loving man's. The Exercises are about creating community. That was a great revelation!' As was the realization that to be a Jesuit was to be *dynamic*: 'It's about getting down to life among the poor; all the time looking where to go next. The big enemy of Ignatian spirituality is rusting, getting stuck.'

A Jesuit must be prepared to go anywhere, any time. When Jim was sent from Glasgow to Spain it felt like a forced transplant to an alien culture. Once there, he had the time of his life. Now his is working in a Brixton parish, and hoping to train with the Institute of Group Analysis. He has fought hard to carry on his psychiatric work, but his priesthood comes first: 'If my Provincial [head of the Jesuits in Britain] told me to go and do a PhD in rubber technology because that's what we need in Bolivia, I'd go and do that.'

So perhaps it's just as well that Jesuits can't marry: it is impossible to put down roots, Jim says. But he has found it hard to do without personal intimacy. He keeps in touch with an old flame, whom he often mentions; and likes to see her children grow. Feeling called to the priesthood was like being on a speedboat, he says; family life was a sailing boat, struggling to keep up, but falling further and further behind. Nevertheless, he is *always* meeting women he's attracted to: 'You say, bloody hell, well . . . Another wonderful opportunity missed! You meet these couples, and I don't know if it's true or my projection – but you feel, "Stand aside you *wimp* – this woman's *far* too good for you!" ' He laughs, dismissing an imaginary rival with a sweep of the arm.

As a young celibate priest, he is himself the subject of 'in*cred*ible idealizations', assumed to be all-powerful, all-knowing. 'There is a big danger we buy into that, making ourselves out to be more dangerous than we are. There's nothing worse than all this guru carry-on.' He is often cast in the role of 'Dad' – which he finds tempting. But 'the dynamic of Christianity is that we're brothers and sisters and friends . . .'

The Jesuits take a vow of poverty, which they interpret in relation to the expectations of the society they live in. They also, nowadays, talk a lot about their 'option for the poor', and Jim is sure that working with the marginalized is 'where the Holy Spirit is leading us'. But poverty can be emotional. Much of his energy is canalized at present into counselling and spiritual direction.

And the Church itself needs some of that, he thinks. 'It's

a *pain* sometimes, being identified as a Catholic priest, because you're really ashamed at times of stupid Mother Church – she gets over-anxious about her children and doesn't trust them.' The Church's ethics and anthropology are a mess, he argues: philosophically-based and couched in the language of the Middle Ages. Worst of all, it has been canonizing neurotics; making saints of narcissists: 'It makes no *sense* . . .' But if there is a crisis, the answer is not to pull out; priests like him, trained in Depth Psychology, have work to do, he thinks.

Lights blazed in a crowded Glasgow church, awash with flowers: James Lutomski was being ordained, and was bedecked in priestly robes. When next we met it was three months later, in a dreary room in the Brixton house he shares with three other Jesuits. A black shirt and dog collar, his normal working garb, lends his boyish face authority. Over thirty years ago this priest's father rescued him – by telling him that big boys cry, and that prayer makes you strong.

TEN

Heaven and Hell

Captain David Arnott's wife is very small: light-boned and well under five foot tall. 'She got battered about something bad', the Captain says. 'I used to wake up in the morning and the house was smashed up, and at that time I couldn't have minded what was happening. She took this for years and years.' Those were in his alcoholic days. Once, she left him, but he 'made such a stink' she never tried again. 'She loved me so much that she didna' want to leave me, but she was scared to leave me because she knew how violent I was.'

Now the Captain and his wife are officers in the Salvation Army. Together they run Laurieston, a Glasgow day-centre for the homeless, destitute and unemployed: 'anyone in need'. It is closed only once a year, on Boxing Day. The couple work for twelve to fourteen hours at a time, and days off are rare. That's 'no problem'. If there is a train crash, fire or other disaster they will be there, with a canteen for the emergency services. They are on twenty-four hour call.

Laurieston is in the Gorbals, an area notorious for slums and crime. 'It's got a worse name than it deserves. It's like everywhere else, you've got your bad folk and your good folk. A lot of the folk are good.' The area's infamy goes back to the tenements, demolished in the 1960s to get rid of the violence. But when the slums vanished, the Captain says, so did the sense of community. Massive blocks of flats were built, which brought new problems. Grey and dismal, they glower above the barren streets. 'A lot of the folk up the tower blocks have got beautiful houses, but some canna' leave them empty or they get broken into.' There is high unemployment; drug and alcohol abuse is common.

I understand you've won awards for your work?, I venture. He grows a little cagey. Just the Glaswegian Citizen of the Year, he says, 'and that's of no interest outside Glasgow'. He doesn't like publicity. 'If you give people a new suit or a cup o' tea they'll say, "You're a great guy, I don't know what I'd do wi'out you!" And if you believe that, you're in trouble. If you're ever tempted to, there's always something happens to bring you back down and say, "Well, it's no' me. Everything I do is through him, anything I do is to glorify Jesus. I don't do anything out o' the ordinary, I do what he's allowing me to do and that's it." '

We sat in Captain Arnott's office, and his wife busied in and out at intervals with cups of coffee and bites to eat. The 'Cap'n' is in his early fifties: stout, straightforward. He is immaculate in Army uniform. When he was a drinker he sometimes didn't change his clothes for days, he says. He has told his story many times and does so briskly, sparing nothing and attentive in response to questions. Does it bother him? 'To a certain extent it is painful, but I don't mind if it helps someone to get over a wee bit o' problems. If I tell someone my story it's to say "It's happened to me, and it can happen to you." '

Captain Arnott was one of five children. His father was a baker, his mother a housewife and seamstress. He grew up in an area not dissimilar to the Gorbals. They always had a decent place to live, he says, and his father was never out of work. 'We had quite a good life, and lots of things which maybe other kids didna' have.'

In his early teens, already drinking, he had his first significant encounter with religion. Although he'd been to Sunday School and was in the Boys' Brigade, Christianity 'was above me, as pie in the sky'. Right up till the time of his conversion he believed 'that man himself was God and that if someone writes something down they have invented it, and that as man wrote the Bible down then he invented it'. At fourteen he went to hear Billy Graham with a friend. They sat at the back of the hall and drank a half bottle of black rum his friend had stolen from his workplace. 'It was vile, you know, it was terrible. But that was my first real connection with what you could call an evangelical campaign.'

He worked as an apprentice butcher by day and on an ice cream van at night. 'The ice cream salesman I worked with, he was what you might call a bevy merchant. I had a good relationship with him but he liked to drink, so I drank with him. It wasna' hard for me to get involved and to get deeper and deeper into it, because I was on a right ego trip. I was drinkin' wi' men, and I was only a boy.' Soon all his money was going on alcohol and on the cigarettes he had smoked since he was nine. He began to steal to get more cash, 'and being in the butcher's trade at that time, there wasna' a better trade in the world for having a fiddle, you could make a fortune at it. So that was the way my life went from then on.'

He would have drunk himself into the grave, he says, without his wife. They met when he was eighteen and married two years later. At twenty-two he nearly died from kidney disease. They moved to Cumbernauld, a new town not far away; there they fell further and further into debt. His drinking grew heavier. He started losing friends because he was violent. A job with the fire brigade came to an end because he was always late for duty. There was a period in hospital, drying out, but straight after discharge he called into the pub on the corner of the road. For his wife's sake he attended Alcoholics Anonymous, but got tanked up on the way. After a spell in psychiatric hospital he managed to keep sober for nine months, helped by group therapy; then he got over-confident and blew it all.

'After another two years on it, I came home one night and I just collapsed straight onto the floor. I was as clear as a bell from the neck up, but my body would not move. That was the start of the problems with my legs.' A doctor told him he would end up in a wheelchair. But he went to the pub on his crutches. He would sell a car or a camera for the price of a drink. There was so little money around by the time they had their fourth child that they could afford one nappy only, which his wife continually washed and dried. Years, he says, of degradation for them both.

Then the children started to go to the Salvation Army's Sunday School, and loved it. An officer came to visit the family at home. When Captain Sewell saw the state of the house she realized something must be done. She helped out with food and clothes, and got the electricity reconnected. She helped set David up in a taxi business. On occasional Sundays he went along to the services, but made so much drunken fuss he was asked to leave. Then he started to call in regularly, without a prior visit to the pub. He was grateful to them and tried to accept their God, but couldn't.

A captain in the Army came to the Arnotts' house to have a talk. 'I went and got drunk first, before he came, and made life pure hell for him. It must have been the most uncomfortable three or four hours of his life.' Shortly afterwards he heard the captain's wife had had a baby. 'While he was out with me, his wife, who was forty-two and ten days overdue . . .' Well, David thought, there's no way *he* would have made a sacrifice like that: the captain must have something he did not. 'And that started me thinking. I wanted to get what that man had, and what Captain Sewell and all the rest of them had . . .'

One Sunday evening a talk was given which seemed almost designed for him, as if the visiting speaker knew all about his life. It was uncanny, he says, still with awe. He was so moved he was tempted to go up to the 'mercy seat' where converts made their 'decisions for Christ'. But he held out. Suddenly, his daughter went forward. When she came back, her commitment made, she sat on her father's lap in tears. To his bemusement, he was crying too.

One of the officers came up to him: wasn't it about

time . . . ? 'No, no, another night' – David shook his head. But, the officer said, there may not be another time. 'After a couple of moments I went forward and accepted Christ into my life. While I was kneeling there I felt the presence of somebody beside me. It was my wife – she came and made a decision as well. I'll never forget that night. It was the most uplifting experience I've ever felt. It was like being out in the rain in a big overcoat and then coming in and taking it off, feeling the weight being taken off. It was fantastic. Captain Sewell stood there and she sang verse after verse of 'Just as I am'. And I don't think there was a dry eye in the hall that night, because it was an answer to everybody's prayer.'

It was a new start. 'I felt something like I did the day I was married. I was united with somebody, it was a joining together. I was so filled with joy and happiness and light-heartedness, that I knew I'd met somebody I wanted to spend the rest of my life with.' The week after his conversion he sought out his creditors. Slowly, he paid off his debts. In 1976 he left his last drink abandoned at a bar.

Three years after that, he and his wife started working at Laurieston as 'envoys', non-commissioned officers. The Salvation Army's military terminology dates from the jingoistic 1860s, when its founder William Booth set out to wage war against the devil. The authoritarian command structure is designed to speed up decisions and improve efficiency. The Army today is both a Christian denomination, stressing evangelism, and an enormous social work agency. It works in ninety-five countries. In Britain it provides accommodation for some 4,000 homeless people – more than any other single organization.

Salvation Army officers are generally shifted to a different post every three years. For some reason Captain Arnott doesn't understand, he and his wife have been left at Laurieston. He'll happily move on, he says, when Jesus indicates that they have served their purpose there. 'The reason that I *know* this is what he wants us to do, is that when I'm not here I just don't feel right.'

When they started Laurieston was only open in the mornings. They extended the hours and started a 'Sober Club' in the afternoons. Another charity ran a midnight soup run, which they eventually took over. It is only since the Captain had a couple of heart attacks that he has stopped doing the soup run personally, after a full day's work.

Their time was full. But to become commissioned Army officers they also had to study. Most of their course was correspondence, supplemented by a month at the training college every year. Very difficult, the Captain comments, especially when 'you're not that way inclined. I've always been a worker and a doer and I've always done college and night school and things for the butchers and the fire brigade, but it wasn't the same as just sittin' and doin' studying.' Theology, he adds, is not the easiest subject. Both he and his wife lacked confidence. But there was pleasure in seeing the marks they could achieve, so many years out of school.

Sundays, when he preaches and does the 'platform work', are his most tiring day. About sixty people come to the afternoon service, and are given tea and a sandwich afterwards. He has no qualms about this combination, though it is often criticized. 'If they come to be physically fed on a Sunday, they also get spiritually fed. They listen to every word you say and they're fantastic singers. We'll bring 'em in, we'll feed 'em, we'll clean 'em up and then we'll tell 'em God loves 'em. Because there's no point telling a man God loves him if he's hungry and he's wet.'

The weekday work focuses on practical help. Everybody gets something to eat and drink; most are also given a change of clothing and a shower. The majority are men but there are a few women, and an increasing number of single-parent families in need of furnishings and other help. Captain Arnott's particular concern is for the countless people sleeping rough. In London they congregate in 'cardboard cities'; in

Glasgow, he says, they're on their own in terrible conditions. If anything happens there is no one to help.

He tells of a middle-aged man he came across on the soup run, every night for a month, sitting on a toilet behind the old casino. He said it was his get-out – if the police came he would tell them he was there to use the toilet. One night, the Captain found him lying down. 'His trousers were down at his knees. He had his back to us. I shone my torch on him and it looked like behind him there was a big red balloon. And it took me a wee while, just a couple of minutes, to see what it was. It was his testicles. They were cancerous . . . the size of a kiddy's football, they were enormous. This was the reason he was sitting in the toilet – he was comfortable. Do you know, he'd never moved from the place in four weeks? The only thing he was getting to eat was what we were bringing him at night.' They got him to the hospital. Some time later the Captain saw him walking down the road, in good health.

The characters who use the centre vary, he says, but 90 per cent are alcoholics. Many are very young and 'there's an awful lot of heartache in it'. Occasionally, if one of them abuses another user or the female members of staff, the Captain loses his temper. This he regards as a great failing, the 'old self coming out'. Whenever it happens 'my conscience, namely my wife, is at me saying, "Do you remember who you are?" And that upsets me. I stop to think that Jesus lost his temper in the Temple, but I shouldna' give myself that consolation at all. He's working on it, he's worked miracles at it, but . . .'

Over the years, there have been about fifteen converts among the users of the centre. There may be others; people move on and only a few come back, well-dressed, to tell them they 'found the Lord' at Laurieston. Most, at least, 'respect our beliefs and know that we mean business'.

So what does 'Salvation' mean? 'That you totally accept and love Jesus Christ as your saviour. And that was our purpose, what the Salvation Army was brought into being for, to save the souls of men.' Jesus, says Captain Arnott, is a personal friend, the best he's ever had. 'It's like, my wife is away from me at the moment, but she's still here. And to me, the Lord is maybe in another room, but he's still here and he's watching over us all the time. When the time comes I'm goin' t' die, I'll just step through that door into another room and I'll be with him.'

Those who cannot accept Jesus go to hell, he says, adding that most of them are there already. 'To me, hell's not a big bad fire. What some folk need to do is look at their lives and ask, "What if this lasted for eternity?" Heaven begins here as well, it begins on earth. I don't believe we wait till we die. I was living in hell until I was converted. Afterwards, I was living in heaven. I'm still living in heaven.'

ELEVEN

The Rabbi

'Eternity for Men' seemed a suitable aftershave to find in the bathroom of a rabbi. I made my way through the bungalow – each wall lined high with books, labels neatly indicating politics or novels – to a sitting room stacked with chaos. 'Put your feet on anything! Sit on anything! Put the plate of biscuits anywhere!' I knocked over the phone, precariously balanced on half a dozen daily papers and a pile of letters. 'Ah yes,' said Willy Wolff sadly, 'that tends to happen.'

My armchair was next to an array of dictionaries: Polish, Hebrew, Russian, Chinese and more. Rabbi William Wolff sat facing me, a small and dapper man with crisply laundered cuffs, tidy waistcoat, a tie knotted to perfection and highly polished shoes. His skull cap perched on hair that he beamingly acknowledged was grey, 'but certainly not white!'

Conversation turned to the afterlife. 'Oh, I'm a firm believer in an existence after death, but Judaism is far less clear on that than Christianity.' Moses Maimonides, the great Jewish thinker of the twelfth century, said that just as a fish cannot know about fire, so we cannot know about the world to come. Judaism has no clear doctrines of heaven and hell. 'Both Church and Synagogue say we shall meet any loved ones in that next world . . . I'm willing to find out in time. The only thing that worries me about that is what happens to the people you *didn't* like on this earth? It seems too cosy to meet one and not the other!', and he explodes with laughter.

At a conference on bereavement, the day before, he had

been given a group of committed Christians for 'what's nowadays called a *workshop*, whatever that may mean. They sat round in a circle and wanted to know about Judaism. And one of the things that needed a fair bit of explaining was that when I go to see a dying person, whether I say prayers *with* him or *over* him, doctrinally doesn't really matter. It won't give him an easier passage into the next world, as far as I know.'

As a rabbi, his main concern is giving comfort to the families. If he is on his own with someone who's unconscious he says no prayers at all – in case the person opens their eyes and gets a shock. 'I was explaining this and one of the ladies said to me, "But what do you do for them *spiritually*?" and that totally threw me . . .' No such rigid distinctions can be made, he thinks. He was once summoned to the bedside of a man with terminal cancer whom he did not know. Four hours later the man died, and his widow said that from the moment the rabbi had been at her husband's bedside, he had been calm. 'What I did spiritually I know not . . .'

Rabbis have no sacramental role, and great weight is put on formal teaching – but these, in Willy's view, are the only differences between the functions of a rabbi and a priest. 'I believe you're a minister first and everything else second.' When he worked in Newcastle his closest friend was an Anglican vicar, and they found most of the issues they had to deal with were the same. Last time Willy was grappling with a marital crisis in his congregation they had a chat, 'and after that I knew exactly what I had to do'.

He enjoys working with his congregation: running the religious side of the synagogue and school, making decisions, giving religious instruction, counselling. 'This is a far more fulfilling job – or whatever it is – than my previous ones, because you operate at a much deeper level. And sometimes you do make a difference to people that can be quite humbling.' The phone ran constantly while I was there and his voice, a little formal for the interview, swung into enthusiasm when he picked it up. He is always on call: 'Yes, and that I accept. It's not difficult, quite the reverse. I think one's availability must be more or less total.' For years he was a Fleet Street journalist and it was much the same: 'They wanted to know, what theatre are you going to?; what seat are you sitting in?; if you're going out to dinner, what's the phone number? It's been a feature of my life!'

Conducting ceremonial is one of his greatest pleasures: 'It has to be well done and I'm told' (this with a cascade of laughter) 'that on the *bimah*, the platform where it all takes place, I sometimes have a bit of a reign of terror!' Between Friday night and Saturday morning he may take three services; more at festivals. He has always had 'a great interest, an emotional attachment' to worship. Never thinking he could be a rabbi, he made mental notes as he watched others leading liturgy. 'When I actually came to doing it I had no problem with it. I'd known for decades how I would handle certain ceremonies.' He was sometimes nervous, he admits: 'The first time I took a funeral I was shaking, and I said to myself, "You'd better get on with it, these people are depending on you" . . . I used to die a thousand deaths before every sermon, but now I take it in my stride.'

Despite his commitments he does not lack a social life: Willy Wolff is a gregarious soul. He had been at a dinner party the night before, 'with people you might describe as very county. Very lively conversation, but partly about the kids playing cricket at Marlborough.' He told the story as an illustration of the ease with which he carries his 'two cultures'.

Willy's family left Germany in the earliest days of the Nazi regime, as refugees. They lived in Holland for some years but were again forced to flee; this second move was hardest for Willy, who was old enough by then to have put down roots. But in London he adapted and quickly felt both Jewish and English – never German.

It was a lonely and unhappy family: his parents' marriage was not good, and their uncles and aunts had not escaped

Berlin. There were few relatives around when Willy was a child: 'quite a large deprivation'. The experience of being exiled 'destroyed my family . . . yes, I think undoubtedly . . .' His father was deeply hurt by what had happened, and died early on. Willy had a great 'affinity of taste' with his mother – who shocked his friends in later years, he grins, by declaring roundly that she did not relish his entry to the rabbinate.

In the early days in London, as a refugee, Willy felt conscious of being 'different'; but he sings the praises of his grammar school headmaster, who took a special interest in him and helped him integrate. He found he enjoyed politics and loved debates. At the London School of Economics he was considering a career as an academic, or a diplomat with the new state of Israel. But a severe illness stopped him getting his degree and he got a job on a Slough paper.

Willy stayed in journalism for a quarter of a century. 'Yes, I loved it, there's no two ways about it.' On the *Yorkshire Post*, the *Evening News* and others he worked as a reporter, feature writer and leader writer. For years he was a parliamentary and diplomatic correspondent for the *Daily Mirror*, and ended his time there as diary editor ('which means gossip columnist'). He describes the 'enormous joy' of leaping out of bed at 6 a.m. to get to the office and write a leader. He's not sure what he liked so much: it was fun, it was serious, there was great camaraderie. He remembers the pride of belonging to the *Daily Mirror*, and the £25 bonus they all got when the circulation hit five million. MPs and ambassadors would always give him interviews, knowing the paper reached so many people.

He was not strictly observant in his Judaism at this time. At times of crisis he might slip into Evensong at a cathedral as well as go to synagogue. But he has always been, he says, 'a religious person'. By this he means his stand on ethical issues starts 'from an enormous respect for the sanctity of life, born and unborn. On abortion, I don't take the totally rigid Catholic line; I certainly take a line that most lady members of my congregation strongly disapprove of, being all secular ladies!'

As a journalist, he thinks his 'religious' attitude came out in his relationships rather than in any tendency to 'write uplifting stuff', a notiion which amuses him. When a colleague died – long-serving rather than a shining light – it was Willy who made sure the paper sent a representative to the funeral. They had to be seen, he insisted. In the end he went himself, with a reluctant literary editor. On the way back the editor fell pensive 'and suddenly asked me, did I believe in life after death? I said, "Well, I started life as an Orthodox Jew . . ." '

The middle-of-the-road Orthodoxy that Willy was born into was disinherited, he says, 'chased from the main synagogal bodies of this country, and overtaken by ultra-Orthodoxy' in the 50s and 60s. He found ultra-Orthodoxy's 'fundamentalist' approach to the rabbinic interpretations of 2,000 years ago unacceptable. But since he had no acquaintance with the Liberal and Reform traditions in Britain he was not sure where to turn.

It was not a loss of faith, he says: 'Judaism isn't quite like that.' Emphasis is placed on practice and behaviour more than on belief. He felt a need, however, to move gradually towards 'a more workable idea about God than the grandpa-in-the-sky idea.' The Torah, the Five Books of Moses, make it clear that God is a mystery that can never be known, 'and I've come to accept that. Contradictions that other people perceive, between their idea of God and the way life works – in the end I may be too easily content to say this is beyond explanation.' He totally accepts that there exists 'another force, another being, call it what you like – I prefer to use the words "another dimension".' Judaism's greatest gift, he thinks, was its recognition of an *invisible* God.

How that 'dimension' intervenes into our lives 'I do not know'. But he does know that acceptance of God inspires an attitude of *awe*; and the implication, he believes, is that human beings too must be treated 'not only with respect but with awe, and in one sense untouchability. Take care – but more than care.' And what is the role of institutional religion? People need a reminder that the invisible exists, he thinks, and an outlet for the wonder it inspires.

While he was working at the *Evening News* he went to a Bar Mitzvah, at the invitation of some friends, where he met a rabbi from the Liberal tradition whom he got on very well with. Before long he was helping the rabbi out by editing a newsletter, and was getting more involved. He had always dreamed of being a rabbi but had assumed there was no niche for him; now he began to feel there might be a contribution he could make. Today he works with both Reform and Liberal congregations. Reform services are more traditional, he says, but many of the differences – on intermarriage, for example – cut across the two.

Rabbinic training takes five years. He went to Leo Baeck College in 1979. At first he combined his studies with newspaper work and gleefully recalls dashing out of the office with a Bible tucked under his arm, hurling himself into a taxi, and coming back three hours later to see if there were any holes in the letters page.

After a year he went freelance and was better off than he had ever been – but that soon changed. He is very conscious now that working as a rabbi is financially a strain; it would have been a difficult choice to make had he been married. But he suspects he is more a family man, by nature, than a bachelor, and so might never have entered the rabbinate at all if he had had a wife. Looking after a congregation 'does give scope for whatever there is in me of the paternal. That was undoubtedly a factor in the decision.'

Every year on Yom Kippur, the Day of Atonement, 'one of the sins I confess is that I have not produced any children!' It is compulsory for *everybody* to get married, he laughs: the first commandment in the Pentateuch is 'Be frutiful and multiply'. It is possible that his marital status has hindered his rabbinic career, but he is not sure. Some congregations, when choosing their next rabbi, look for a rabbi's wife as well – others may have had a bad experience, he jokes, which makes them glad to have a bachelor.

Becoming a rabbi has involved a dramatic change of life for William Wolff. He sometimes misses being in the journalistic thick of things: his roots are in London. But he has no regrets for he enjoys the life; as a journalist he felt he was an observer, now he is taking part. And he does feel stimulated by the wider vistas of his work: the life of Anglo-Jewry, the 'immensely challenging position of being in two cultures'.

He talks a lot about his faith to non-Jewish audiences, but 'I don't feel I've got to defend Judaism all the time as the greatest thing since . . . er . . . *before* sliced bread!' Judaism is not a proselytizing religion, but Rabbi Wolff always seeks to be helpful to would-be converts and does make time for them. If there were too many – he hoots with laughter – it would only add to his workload.

He had a lot to do. Could we draw the interview to a close? My taxi came while he was on the telephone, discussing politics and practicalities, and emitting loud guffaws.

TWELVE

For My Sake and My Sisters'

'It isn't even a matter of choice. I wouldn't be able to do it, I would be out of a job in six months, I'd go daft!' Maria Gibbons has a doctorate in Biology, and six years ago was managing a fish farm. But she was not satisfied. She threw it up and went to stay with a friend on the outskirts of Galway City. There she has remained, struggling with little money in order to live by her beliefs.

A feminist and political activist, she describes herself as 'a video worker, not an *artist* at all'. A lot of people think she is mad, she smiles. They wonder why she isn't making 'progress' – why they have not seen her films on television yet or heard her name around. She admits it would be 'nice' to have a steady income and to be well-known, but she would fear the loss of her integrity.

'If you're working for television you're *totally* restrained on what you can produce. You'd be talking about spending £15,000 on making a half-hour documentary. Whoever's giving you that £15,000 would control the programme.' It can take as little as £100, she maintains, to get the truth across. But to enough people? There are other ways: she had just returned from a Dublin meeting about setting up a video network, to distribute films made by co-ops and community groups around the country.

The work she does with women, the Galway unemployed and others is about empowerment: she is working *with* them to make films, enabling not teaching. 'And the whole thing is ultimately political, in the sense that it's all about causing change . . . so that there's less oppression – less *oppression*!' She elaborates: The media buttress the status quo, but if the people learn to use the instruments of media they can exercise their power for themselves. 'All the work of my life is committed to the process of women taking control of their lives and taking a much more active part in the world. Maybe my sense of myself is tied up with that, as a woman, I don't know. But it hurts me, it *hurts* me, to see what happens to us and the way we're treated. And I just want to do something about it, both for my own sake and my sisters'!' She does not work with women's groups alone, though that would be her preference. Her feminism has heightened her awareness of issues such as racism, of minorities like travellers.

It is 'fiercely important' to her to know what she is talking about. She prefers a local base, with issues she can comprehend: she too is a woman, she too is often unemployed. Occasional contracts and the dole keep her going. 'I think part of me yearns towards life without any of the trappings of civilization at all. I don't want money – I think it does corrupt and it will corrupt me as well.' She is happy, but sometimes feels peripheral and wonders what she's doing. There is no 'master – or mistress – plan'; she is very simple, she insists, living on her instincts. She regrets her tendency to analyse in black and white. Yet contradictions jostle as she explains what makes her tick. She also speaks of over-intellectualizing, of a slow development because she rationalized emotions.

Her story is told by a blazing fire, which occasionally she feeds with coal while searching for a word. Rapid sentences spill over grins and interrupt each other; rumpling her hair, she clarifies a point. It was an overwhelming need to integrate her personal life, political activity and work, she says, which made her finally abandon a conventional career.

Maria was born thirty-eight years ago, on an isolated farm. Her early memories are very happy: playing with her brothers and sisters and friends, wandering in fields and helping with the animals. But a sense of suffocation developed in her teenage years, and the convent where she boarded makes her shudder even now. Her parents had left school early to help out at home: the emphasis they put later on their own children's education was typical of the times. The 50s and 60s saw Ireland's tranformation: free schooling, indoor plumbing, cars, television, 'and *money*' suddenly became the norm. Maria's younger brothers take these things for granted, but she has never lost the flavour 'of what life was like for probably hundreds of years'.

There was a travelling library: 'You'd be allowed to take out three books and there'd be a *dive* in to get them. I used to love reading. I just wanted to know about everything, I think. I still have a bit of that.' Her father's subscription to *Time* opened windows to a distant world. There was one photograph of chatting girls 'and they had *blue denims* on, bell-bottoms! And I can remember looking at them and thinking, *I* want to wear those! But it was so far away.' Most vivid of all, she remembers Kate Millett on the magazine's cover and 'drinking up' the article about her. The radical feminist became her hero.

It was some years before Maria could get hold of Millet's *Sexual Politics*; when she did she knew 'that's it!, that's it!' Vague feelings she had always had were written there, articulated. What use was the passive creature in a long dress who made brief appearances in films? It was the Cisco Kid that she identified with – he *did* things. She had long said she would never get married: she was an active person, not 'a housewife, where you did what you were told'. It was joked that her father was exasperated at her birth ('*another* girl!') because he already had two daughters and wanted a son to work the farm. Maria laughs, for there were five boys after her – 'It served them right!' – but at the time it hurt. And she remembers that though the girls brought in the cows and washed the churns when they were small, the boys took over as soon as they had grown; 'we were made redundant.'

Millett gave direction to Maria's discontent, but she was too shy to join a women's group until her third year at Trinity College, Dublin. All the time she longed to be part of the demos and sit-ins disrupting the capital. Trinity had drawn her because it promised to be 'different': this was only the second year the Catholic Church had allowed its members to attend the Protestant establishment. But she was swamped. It was as much as she could do to cope with living in a city. She survived by sticking to her books.

After she finished her degree she put her rucksack on her back 'and headed off to London on my own. It was just something I had to do – "I'll sink or I'll swim". And I swam. That's when I began to grow up.' She got involved with people 'active in various anarchisty-type things', went on 'marches and whatnot' and moved in with a self-taught painter from Bradford, a working-class communist who was 'fierce contrary'.

Back in Ireland she did a Ph.D. in frogs and toads – working mostly in the Burren, County Clare, but based in Galway. It was one of the happiest times of her life. She loved being outside in the country and having the freedom to work as she chose. Through camogie (women's hurling, the traditional Irish game) she met the local people. She was involved in anti-nuclear activity and began to throw herself heart and soul into the Women's Movement. She still remembers her delight when she met an old schoolfriend at a meeting about violence against women – the first time her politics were linked with her past.

Ireland's first referendum on abortion, in 1983, was an attempt by pro-life groups to change the constitution, so that abortion could never be legalized in Eire. The Women's movement, keen for broad support, took the line that change was unnecessary. Maria wanted to go further and argued for 'women's right to choose'. Though involved in the campaign from the beginning she became increasingly cut off from it, 'but obviously I was getting confident enough to argue my own point of view'. The referendum was lost, the constitution changed. Ironically, Maria says, that has now opened the way for legal abortion in limited circumstances, but at the time the feminists felt 'a fierce sense of defeat'. Maria, who was also in a state of anti-climax at the end of her research, fell into depression.

Part of her struggle was confusion about her own sexuality. It took her a long time to work it out, she laughs – she was over thirty, 'better late than never!' Again, the answer came to her through a feminist writer, this time Mary Daly. One of her books had a description of what it was like to be a lesbian. 'And I remember reading it and thinking, "But that's me! So I must be a lesbian!" ' It was an intellectual recognition, nothing to do with 'fancying women'; neither physical nor emotional. 'I was so out of touch, I think, with that part of myself by that stage . . . I just knew she was describing me, or an aspect of me anyway.'

It took Maria months to work the discovery through. In Ireland, she says, 'lesbians don't exist' – they are hidden away. Eventually 'I met somebody, a woman, and I sorted it out from there.' But she also got in touch with lesbian groups in Dublin, where she had gone to live. She was elated by self-discovery and 'suddenly I'd found a community. For the first time, I think, I had a feeling of being at home.'

Her commitment to the lesbian cause is absolute – almost greater than her feminism, except the two are intricately linked for her. In Galway, for the past few years, she has been involved with an abortion helpline (technically illegal) and a new women's resource centre. As part of her video work she records activities she is involved in, to ensure there is archive footage. She is also part of a growing group of lesbians who are 'out'. This is not always easy, and she feels vulnerable – for in Maria's view the town's trendiness conceals 'a certain hypocrisy'.

She took a long time to tell her parents she was lesbian, fearing another row such as the one when she told them she had given up Catholicism. She had stumbled on her atheism when at Trinity. The college did not observe Catholic festivals. On the Feast of the Immaculate Conception ('I remember it well!') she went to lectures as usual and forgot to go to Mass. She realized too late: ' "*Shit*!" . . . And then, "But I'm still alive!" And I never went to Mass again. I've never had a qualm, I've never given it a moment's thought since and that's twenty years ago. Out the window, rubbish!' The Church has not even been an issue in her political campaigning: 'It's an enemy, yes; but it's an enemy among many.'

Despite finding her 'anchor' in the Dublin lesbian community, Maria left – to manage the fish farm in Donegal. Whenever she is tempted to give up her precarious lifestyle now, she remembers how much she hated the two years she spent there. It toughened her up, she says, but it was sexist, lonely and out of kilter with her politics. The farm was owned by a multinational and she was cut off from her radical friends. When she got away to an international women's conference in Dublin, she decided on the spot to quit.

She went back to Galway, and wondered what to do. A friend gave her a careers test: what would she most enjoy, if she could choose? The answer was 'Film'. At the unemployed centre a short course was running on Media: Maria joined. The eight students gelled so well they formed a co-operative after the course had finished. All were learning video from scratch; all were keen on 'helping to give people their voice'. They stayed together, their numbers diminishing, for about three years, until they broke up for lack of earnings. Now Maria works freelance and alone, but not by choice: 'I'm waiting to meet the right people. My motivation isn't as good as when I had a group to work with.'

Collectivity is crucial to her thinking, and it's how she gets her 'buzz'. When I met her she was working on a project with women from the rape crisis centre, around the theme of sexual violence. They are the experts, and she helps them script and edit a video they will eventually use. They are interested in the content, not the technicalities; whereas the people who go to Maria's courses for the unemployed are interested in the filming itself: the process of making video dramas on their own experiences matters just as much, she thinks, as the final product.

Maria's workshops try to boost the confidence of people intimidated by the technology of videos and the mystique surrounding the figure of the artist, 'the creative genius and all this sort of stuff'. She dislikes being labelled a 'community artist': she does not want to 'help the underprivileged', she says, but to transfer skills. And, in so doing, not only to encourage people to develop their own creativity, but 'to go on from there to a collective exploration, that eventually will lead to the revolution!'

But despite her love of the collective, her way is solitary. She has only recently started to vote, in recognition that occasionally 'the system' can effect change: she has had to admit that Mary Robinson, the first female President of Ireland, has helped Irish women walk tall. The 'unhealthy' handing over of responsibility, that she associates with political parties and religious communities, does not appeal to her. 'I believe we're all on our own path, and I've a very strong sense of myself, and I think other people, as being distinct individuals. And that's all we have – a responsibility to live our lives as truthfully to ourselves as we can. And that's one thing I'm doing and obviously compromising hugely . . .' She laughs, self-deprecatingly.

Children would be nice, she says – it is the only sacrifice her choice of life has called for. But she never got as far, she jokes, as 'the gory details' of just how she would have them. She realized she would have to use her education to provide the security they would need, and 'I suppose one thing was more important, more necessary to me than the other. To have children isn't an obsession. But to live my life in some way that has meaning for me, I think is an obsession – maybe!'

THIRTEEN

The Praying Mantis

Feminism was the hardest sacrifice for Saba Khalid (then called Hilary Rawlings) when she became a Muslim. Her commitment to the Women's Movement was part of her identity.

'It was a tremendous struggle, to give up the idea that feminism held the answer to what was going wrong with the world.' Many of her women friends were committing suicide or going slightly mad, so she knew it was time to get out. It was the end of the 1960s: people were picking and mixing their religions, she says, in a spiritual supermarket. The idea was 'to *take* this and *take* that and know all about it and be able to talk about it; and have a few joss sticks burning and do a few mantras and a bit of dressing up'. In Islam, things were different: 'You surrender. You say, "I submit. You will tell me what I need to do; I give up jurisdiction of myself. I place myself in Your hands." '

Islam means 'submission'. If your sacrifice is unconditional, she says, 'you wake up on the other side and you find it's all there again – but transformed.' All that she had sought in feminism she found in Islam. The separation of men and women she had fought for 'was part of the Muslim ecology', as were women's rights. 'It was all there, linked with spirituality and self-knowledge; and the political and social solutions were whole, all-encompassing.'

She did not expect the sex war to end, but now accepted limitations. Sexual experimentation was out. The questioning, uncertain sixties had instilled an 'insidious message', she recalls, that promiscuity led to greater psychological health.

She had worried about being 'repressed'. The clear boundaries of *Shariah* (Islamic Law), with its prohibitions on adultery and homosexuality, came as a great relief.

Saba had always believed that the path to liberation lay through knowledge. If she could understand herself, she thought, the rest would follow. She was born in 1940, 'a child of the Raj'. Her mother 'relied on being a celebrated beauty', and had numerous affairs and marriages. She was asked to leave by Saba's father, who remarried and then died of cancer. Saba was brought up by her stepmother along with six other children, only two of them her own. It was a difficult childhood, Saba says, 'a rough beginning with fractured relationships'; and it left her with a sense of failure.

Searching for 'unity' and community, she could not settle. She had a research job and studied some philosophy; she was an artist and travelled for a while. Attracted by the Peace Movement and politics, she toured Europe and America with the 'celebrated radical theatre group', the Bread and Puppet Theatre, which had grown out of the anti-Vietnam campaign. While she was away she lent her Islington house to the Gingerbread Group for single mothers and then to the Black Panthers.

An 'oracular voice' on the television, one day, echoed her growing conviction that the oppression of women was as great as that of black people. Saba sought out the owner of the voice, the feminist and playwright Jane Arden. 'We just clicked, and I spent seven years with her, in a relationship of disciple and teacher. She was almost a guru – but I knew enough to know a guru ought to pray.' Saba came to feel that the power Arden exerted over young women, like herself, was dangerous as long as it lacked spiritual discipline. The clash between this fashionable, 'show-biz world' and the political concerns which made up the rest of her life became unbearable. By the time she was thirty she had reached the point of crisis. She fled.

The beauty of Ronda, in the south of Spain, had captured

her imagination on a visit the previous year. That is where she now went. The journey, she remembers, was 'a kind of death experience'. The tunnel through the Pyrenees was dark. Water dripped on moving figures, workmen with fluorescent stripes on their clothes – to her they looked like clambering skeletons.

She rented a cottage, with her boyfriend of the time. A memory started nudging her of something she had read, about certain men who spent their lives in prayer – she imagined them in caves on mountain tops. 'And I thought, I'll make, like phone calls. I'll send this message out into space and maybe one of these people will tune in to me here.'

There was a response. It began with a 'message': that once she knew herself, she need fear nothing. Then came an exorcism. Some gypsies, passing by with their guitars, stopped one night and played. Their music whirled into a Mexican tarantella – until Saba felt she had to get out, away from the intoxicating rhythm. A friend dragged her back. *Look!*, he said, and pointed. In the kitchen, two tarantulas had entered. To Saba they represented death, and 'the devouring web, the weaving self': all that was negative in the female psyche.

Now she waited, for the 'way' that she knew she would be shown. 'I got another instruction which said, "Go back to the source of your fear, return from where you ran." ' Shortly afterwards she was in the kitchen with some friends. One of them was caught in the evening sunlight 'and somebody said in a voice of absolute wonder, "Look, look!" I looked, and on the wall above this man's head was a gigantic praying mantis. It's not a beautiful insect, but it *shone* with this astonishing kind of light, it was effulgent. I said, "How beautiful!" And I knew that was the sign.'

They packed their bags for England. The tarantula had been a symbol of 'the dark, scheming feminine; the one who seeks to devour and control the other'. The praying mantis, she was sure, was the reverse. 'It was about *self*-annihilation, denying the self, death by something higher. It signified purification, a spiritual awakening – a promise of the high, spiritual feminine.'

Saba had fled from Jane Arden, so it was to her that she returned: 'I was afraid,' she confessed to her. 'Now I am on a spiritual search.' The next day Arden introduced her to an old friend of hers – the writer Ian Dallas, known to Muslims as Abdal Qadir al-Murabit. He had long been 'a presence in the background', but they had never coincided in Jane's drawing-room before. 'I knew he had knowledge of spiritual matters, because he was a Sufi, and I asked him if there was a science to prayer. He said "Yes", and gestured towards the south-eastern corner of the room, the direction of the holy city of Mecca. "You turn your face that way and you wash your face, hands and feet like this" '; he showed her what he meant. ' "You put your head on the ground. And you do this five times a day, at dawn, midday, mid-afternoon, sunset and at night. That's the science of it." '

Saba needed such precision. And there was something familiar in what he said. In Valencia, some months before, she had become aware of an 'all-surrounding consciousness' as she looked at the stars, something 'vast and alive'. Intrigued and very humbled, feeling 'small, ridiculous and blind', she went down on her knees in a prostration to express her awe. Now she understood why: 'There is a way you behave in the presence of God which makes it easier for you. *You* then feel you've done what is needed – it's *your* need, not His.'

Twenty-two years later, Islam permeates her life. We sat on the floor in a relaxed room. Saba wore trousers and a tunic top; she had her headscarf in her hand, and threw it loosely round her head if the doorbell rang, in case it was a male. Framed verses from the Qur'an hung on the wall. As she told the story of her life, she interwove the episodes with moral argument and explanations of linguistic roots. When the hour came to pray, she brought her mat into the room: 'Prayer is not a private thing in Islam.' She spread it out before the window: outside was a Birmingham garden; far beyond was Mecca.

Swift Arabic accompanied her prostrations. Several times she stood and then went down upon her knees again, touching her forehead to the ground. 'You first assert that God is greater,' she explained when she had finished, '. . . greater than any being or situation in front of you.' The opening *sura* (chapter) of the Qur'an must be recited next – seven lines which summarize the meaning of the whole Qur'an. Afterwards the person praying can choose which *suras* to repeat. 'Then, when you put your head on the ground, in the lowest position, it is part of exalting Allah in the highest. That is the great significance of the prostration.'

Sometimes, Saba says, she doesn't feel like doing the prayer, just as she does not always want to do the dishes, 'but you know you've got to, because if you don't you're going to feel like hell later. It's something you'd never give up, because it's like the core of your whole life.' When she is stressed or busy, just doing the movements fills her with relief; she feels washed clean. She loves the regular hours for prayer, which she says tune into 'cosmic times'. Within the ritual actions she perceives the 'sanity of Islam': the body performs the prayer, even if the mind, occasionally, refuses.

It was a 'tangible spiritual world' that Ian Dallas 'yanked' her into – pursuing her relentlessly, she laughs. He is a sheikh, a spiritual leader in the Sufic tradition of Islam: 'one who has passed through the barriers of phenomenal existence', Saba explains, 'and then returned to teach and guide others.' He was the representative in Britain of a Moroccan sheikh, the 'man of prayer' who responded, Saba says, to her cry for help in Spain. Ian Dallas was building up a group of Western converts, mostly young people like Saba from the political, theatrical and rock music worlds. 'We had no edges to our lives, and we were given definition and focus, brought back into a rhythm of life.' His 'spellbinding' words, everything she had ever yearned to hear, were poured out over plentiful meals served at regular hours. 'Tea-time has arrived in your life!' the sheikh said to Saba, and she smiles at the transformation of the Gitane-smoking coffee-drinker. She put on pounds, she laughs, but it was 'so joyful, in a way that wasn't to do with inspiration or adrenalin . . .'

To live together, the group squatted some dilapidated properties in Maida Vale. It was hard, 'but we were all in a state of being in love . . .' They stayed for seven years. Then, as they started to pair off and get married, they moved to Norfolk and tried setting up a village. It didn't work. They had little support from other Muslims, most of whom 'want the success story of the West', Saba says, and resented being told it was corrupt. The group, part of a wider movement called the Murabitun, has a particular interest in economic justice. It is known for its opposition to the apparatus of modern finance. It is now attracting younger Muslims, brought up in the West.

As a feminist, Saba had little time for marriage. 'The institution, divorced from God, had lost its meaning.' None of her relationships with men felt stable. Islam gave her a sense of order and direction, and her attitude changed. She married a man in the Murabitun – the father of her daughters, now in their teens and introduced with a flourish as 'the first generation of Anglo-Saxon Muslims'. A few years later she divorced her husband, and then spent a long time alone. Eventually, ten years ago, she decided she should marry again, and chose another man in the Murabitun, who she knew 'had the qualities necessary.'

One of her concerns was that her children should have a father-figure. Bringing them up, in an environment hostile to Islamic values, has not always been easy. At first they were taught at home and in the mosque, for 'the poison starts in schools'. The Murabitun tried to set up a school of its own, as it had in Spain, but lacked finance. Saba was forced to give way when they were ten and twelve, and now they go to the local comprehensive. 'I see the rubbish they get from it.

But you're fighting against the trend. All the other children are locked up in school, you don't see them on the streets any more.'

Her daughters sometimes sneak their headscarves off, she smiles, if they see their friends in town, but it's nothing very serious. They accept the teachings of Islam, moulded and supported by a community which, though scattered, is tight-knit. The Murabitun in Birmingham was started by Saba and her husband and is flourishing, she says. Several members were brought in to meet me during my short visit. One young Englishwoman was collecting her baby son, Muhammad; cared for at Saba's while she was out at work. This is an example of community life, Saba says. When she was young, she never dealt with children; now her daughters watch Muhammad's growth. She will be around when they in turn have babies. They are recreating a natural way of life, she believes: 'It's like replanting a rainforest, starting a new ecosystem.'

She is vehement in her criticisms of the modern State, which she believes deprives its citizens of liberty to live as they feel right. There is an 'orchestrated' campaign, she insists, by the government, banks and media: every aspect of life is being forced into conformity. 'All this multicultural rubbish means you can't be a Christian, a Muslim, a Buddhist – the atheist can't even be an atheist. Everyone has to be jammed together like a supermarket – stacked up, shelved up and not allowed to be authentic.' Even with their abhorrence of usury, Saba and her husband have to compromise, she says with annoyance: their house is mortgaged, because there is no other option.

She is actively involved in the Murabitun's efforts to challenge the system. Autumn 1992 saw the first 'Birmingham Fair', an attempt to restore the 'traditional market'. Until 250 years ago, the argument goes, the practices which now govern trading were outlawed by societies everywhere. Markets were set aside for people to exchange goods, without restriction or monopoly. Merchants travelled together in 'caravans' and nobody was allowed to go and meet them before they had arrived in town, in order to buy goods wholesale and at a lower price than they would have fetched on the open market. These are among the fair trading practices the Murabitun wishes to revive. In so doing, its members hope to bring about, ultimately, the collapse of what Ian Dallas has called the 'magical usury system'. This evil, he explains in a Murabitun pamphlet, 'is controlled by a dangerously irresponsible elite who . . . in their turn control the whole world's enslaved masses'.

Saba is concerned primarily for the freedom of her fellow-Muslims to live by God's law. She does believe that 'if you've really submitted and given up your brains, your ideas, your conditioning, you will find yourself in Islam. If you're somewhere else it's because you haven't made an all-or-nothing supplication.' But she says this lightly, with a laugh, and only when pressed. You do not coerce people into Islam, she adds, you invite them.

She does not smile much, however, when discussing the corruption and oppression of contemporary society, which regards itself as too enlightened to believe in God, yet allows people to live in cardboard boxes on the streets. She has always been militant, she says; ready to do battle when she believes it right. All Muslims are required to hold at bay the devil, and to oppose any system seen to have released his forces. The Qur'an teaches that the believer must fight for God, or territory will be lost to the enemies. 'There is' says Saba Khalid, 'no neutral, middle area.'

FOURTEEN

'It's the End of the World . . . and I Feel Fine'

'I remember giving a talk once, when I said, "Only one thing's certain, some time we're going to die." And somebody in the audience stood up and accused me of being a deathist!'

Malcolm Stern laughs. 'A lot of people give the New Age a bad name. Some of what goes on is very precious.' One of the founders and directors of 'Alternatives', the weekly lectures at St James's Church, Piccadilly, Malcolm is well known in New Age circles. He wrote the contribution on music in the resource book *A Seeker's Guide*, and is a member of Monkton Wyld community in Dorset.

'I think the New Age is a gold mine: about 5 per cent of what happens is fantastic, but the rest is very questionable. There are some great teachers around, there are some techniques for expansion and penetration into yourself that are wonderful. As with any other system, there are a lot of charlatans and glamorized types who've jumped on the bandwagon.'

When he first discovered New Age thinking Malcolm believed it all. He thought the millennium marked a transition from the strife-torn era ruled by Pisces into the Aquarian age of love, light and peace. 'I was quite naïve. "The world's about to change" – of course it is, because it's so terrible at the moment and now I've realized what's so wrong it must change!' He sees it a bit differently now. 'We *are* moving into a time of more heightened awareness and consciousness, but it is going to be gradual.' Evolution works where revolution fails: he points to the death throes of the old world in the breakdown of capitalism and collapse of communism. 'What's going to replace it? The Industrial Age is over, it's never going to be the same again. And that's good! "It's the end of the world as we know it, and I feel fine . . ." '

Malcolm found the New Age when he was forced to search for who he was. Legs flung over the arm of his chair, he talks with confidence. He is stocky, ebullient, dressed in a leather cardigan with zip and woollen sleeves. A black mass of hair curls about an energetic face. He gesticulates a lot.

He is forty-two, born into a middle-class Jewish family in the Orthodox tradition. At the age of five he read a book on his mother's shelf, called *The Scourge of the Swastika*. There were graphic illustrations. 'It had me totally paranoid about being Jewish. To me, membership of this club meant you go into concentration camps and you die. I spent the rest of my childhood and adolescence escaping from my identity as a Jew.'

He had little interest in religion. 'I went to public school, where I was taught to skilfully suppress my emotions and become a lord of the universe. And my ambition when I left was to make quite a lot of money, drive a fast car, have a number of beautiful women – basically, fantasy land.' At eighteen he became an articled clerk to a firm of accountants. 'It was the most boring thing I've ever done. I was good at it, I enjoy figures, but to do it all day long stretches one part of your being and leaves the rest completely untouched.' He swapped over to estate agency – rather a revolutionary move, he thought.

A pattern had settled in with women. He would embark on short affairs, which he abandoned when 'the real stuff' started to emerge. But at twenty-four he got into a relationship with someone he thought 'was a woman of real mystery'. For a few months he was madly in love, then decided to move on. This time, it didn't work. 'She used to sit outside my house all night long, beeping her horn, flashing her lights; she'd drive me off the road; she'd be at a cocktail party, come up and burn me with a cigarette; she'd find out where I was. She'd ring up a hundred times a day. She drove me crazy.' He lost one job, then another – and so it went on, for four years. 'It was the *weirdest* scene. I thought I was in hell.'

He tried everything, but if he was nice she wanted more; if he swore at her she wore him down. 'At the time I was smoking dope and just really confused, and from being quite confident and pretty all right with what life was presenting me, I became quite paranoid.' A job was advertised in Suffolk, as housefather in a home for adults with learning difficulties. He had never dreamed of doing such a thing before, but 'for three months I was in heaven. I was earning £20 a week and board and lodging, and I was as happy as I'd ever been. I was doing something useful and valuable, this woman didn't know where I was, and I was just able to be myself.'

She caught up with him. The phone calls began again. His boss sent him home to sort it out. 'On the way, I was in such a state, I was driving my car and I took the wrong road. I was seventy miles in the wrong direction and got more and more panicked, and more and more agitated, and I smashed the car up. I found myself sitting holding the steering wheel with my car a wreck around me, and I was completely unhurt. I thought, "This is crazy, I'm gonna die if this carries on." '

Well, crisis is often the opportunity for change, says Malcolm, and now he's glad. A few months later he developed a thrombo-phlebitis in the leg. The GP gave a prescription to thin the blood, but would not explain more: ' "Don't worry, I'm the doctor" '. Something inside Malcolm snapped. He was *furious* with the way life was turning out. Four years of stress! 'I thought, "I'm damned if I'm going to take some pill just because a doctor tells me to, to take away the symptoms of what I've caused!" ' He went to see the Queen's homeopath, since the recommendation seemed good. Here, he says, he finally got treated as a human being. He gave up dope and had a go at meditation. 'And from all the fighting I'd had to get rid of this woman, suddenly she wasn't on my case because I was no longer the person she'd been relating to. I was irrevocably changed. I had found something *religious* again – or something spiritual. A search was initiated.'

It was another woman who unwittingly led him to take the next step. His boss had a girlfriend, 'extremely beautiful and extremely seductive, and she practically said, "Come and see me." ' Malcolm spent a couple of nights with her. Then one evening, 'all of a sudden, I saw the face of the devil on her face – the horns, the jowls, the lot! I was having two conversations, one with her and one with this figure superimposed on her. It took me four hours to get out of the house. I was acting very weirdly, clapping my hands, trying to break the atmosphere, laying my hands on her head trying to exorcise her. I was very naïve . . .'

Malcolm, now 'very freaked out', went to see a Buddhist monk he had come across on Hampstead Heath some time before. For a year he took instruction from him. His life started to calm down, although he was still prone to extremes. 'I switched to a "macroneurotic" diet which I was completely fanatical about. I was pretty crazy in those days, but I was exploring and experimenting.'

He worked in an old people's day-centre, and then as an auxiliary nurse in a terminal cancer hospice. For two years he was on the staff of Greenpeace and sailed on the *Rainbow Warrior*. Not that his memories are heroic. He went to Norway to protest against a seal cull: 'We spent eight days at sea and I lost eight pounds in weight from puking up. When there was a volunteer needed to fly a film back to ITN my hand went up quicker than anything you've ever seen in your life!' But their actions did occasionally stop culls. He learned that people acting with integrity and energy can sometimes make a difference. 'We're not as powerless as we think we are.'

By now Malcolm was thirty. Most summers he went to meditation camps in the Alps run by New Age Sufis (not Muslims). The teacher used to give *darshan*: looking into people's eyes, he would tell them the next stage on their path. When it was Malcolm's turn, 'I really felt him penetrate, beyond the point where I was putting on my face. He said to me, "You can't reject life until you fully live life, you have to go into life before you can put it aside." I realized I'd been trying to run away – I'd escaped into a spiritual search.' So what next? A friend suggested he get married and have children.

At a yoga class Malcolm found himself sitting next to 'a very beautiful air stewardess. We started chatting. And there was a wonderful – you know, the chemistry sometimes happens between people . . .' Within a fortnight Malcolm had moved in; after a month they decided to have a child. 'I was suffering from delusions that this was my soul mate. We went off to India and it was all very blissful, until the masks started to peel away.' When their baby, Melissa, was ten months old they parted. For the first time, Malcolm had lost someone he loved – his daughter.

He had said the arguments were all his girlfriend's fault, because his meditation made him calm. It didn't wash any more, even with him. His spirituality seemed to lack something. Eager to examine his emotions and find out what made relationships work, he enrolled on a course in Humanistic Psychology. Therapy helped bring balance to his life. 'I used to dress in white before that, talk very softly, move very slowly, and it was just crap!'

In need of a job, Malcolm had returned to estate agency. He stayed there five years while he studied, started running his own counselling groups and 'tried to build a bridge away from it'. He had become involved with the 'Turning Points' series of lectures at St James's Church, forerunner of 'Alternatives'. 'I started to meet some very spiritually attuned people; and also to see a lot of the bullshit that's talked in the name of spirituality. Because you have to walk your talk. If you don't, you're just mouthing platitudes.'

Malcolm has 'a passion' for St James's. It needed a fundraiser – he applied and was appointed. At last, an 'alternative' job, where a tie was not compulsory and there were people he could talk to! He got to know one of the 'Turning Points' regulars: Amanda, a dancer and expert in 'body work', a teacher of healing and relaxation. They married in 1987 at St James's, in a wedding ceremony they devised from Jewish, Christian and Sufi sources; attended by a rabbi and a priest. Neither wanted to reject their origins; both felt they were on a spiritual search, transcending boundaries: 'all religions speak of one God'. That is what they wanted to express. Malcolm's father, who had threatened not to come, made an impromptu speech declaring it the best wedding he had ever been to.

It is hard for any two people to come together and build a life, says Malcolm. This time, 'there's a commitment to work at it and that's the difference. When the unconscious stuff comes up we'll explore it and talk about it. That's where I've landed relationship-wise.' He says his children are his spiritual teachers – can he change a nappy with love, as he puts it, after giving an uplifting workshop? Can he 'keep his centre' when they're having tantrums?

They moved to Monkton Wyld soon after they got married. London was not the best place for a family, they felt, and Amanda got a job in the Steiner-based kindergarten there. Like all residents, they get a room, board and pocket money in exchange for their work. Malcolm is responsible for the finances and the workshop programme, many of them run by outside facilitators. Courses offered range from psychosynthesis to dance, from women's weekends to basket making. Malcolm runs a year-long seminar called 'The art of loving', dealing with relationships, and has been developing his interest in counselling. 'What we're exploring here is a way of helping people find their potential – whether through their creativity or through a therapy group.'

The setting is an enormous Victorian rectory, with eleven acres given over to an organic vegetable garden, a small farm, a children's playground, lawns and woodland. There is a reed-bed sewage system, built by a former member. 'We're trying to live more harmoniously, to get more of a feel of living at one with nature.'

The residents of Monkton Wyld are bound together by 'a search for wholeness', but there is no single creed. People do not settle there for ever: the five years Malcolm and Amanda have remained is longer than most. It is an experimental lifestyle, Malcolm says, and it was not an easy adjustment to make after the relative affluence he was accustomed to. As a family, they have three rooms and, unusually, a bathroom of their own. The residents take turns to cook and the kitchen is shared: 'For me that's the hardest thing. I'm a foody and it's great being cooked for but I may not fancy pizza . . .'

Living with twelve other people – and coping with their families – can be a strain. Selection of members is careful. Even so, Malcolm describes fierce rows about 'Wheelies' (a breakfast cereal), hygiene (poohy nappies in the dining-room) and whether head lice should be treated with chemical lotions or essential oils 'that didn't work'. They have had to deal with all types, he says – the disturbed, the difficult, the manipulative. 'If someone's a pain, the odds are they're *in* pain. If we're honest about it we can work with it. But not if someone's in denial, saying, "This isn't happening". Everyone else is saying, "It bloody well is!" ' One of the most important disciplines in the house is not talking behind others' backs. All decisions are made by consensus, and this is one of the things he has valued most.

'It has been the most creative period of my life. Now, I can understand my talk. I deliberately didn't say "walk my talk", because I'm on the road to doing that. There are times when I really struggle.' He has been free to work the hours he chooses, and to explore his talents. There has been time to make three albums of New Age music with a group called Stairway. The last one, *Medicine Dance*, is an attempt to capture the essence of nine different animals in a dance piece.

'I'm interested in the possibilities of music and dance for generating change, and I use quite a lot of that in my workshops. I think you bypass the intellectual faculties when you do that, and it's a way in. Music can lift the spirits, can touch the soul and heal you.' This, he adds, is different from New Age Muzak, 'some whizz kid on a synthesizer, a computer specialist who's able to make plinky-plonk types of sounds'. New Age music must have *heart*, he says; be 'positive, and I don't mean no negativity and it's all wonderful and lovely.' He means Peter Gabriel and Yes, people 'with something to say'. Sting's song about the Chilean women widowed by the military junta 'captures the essence of what the New Age is all about'.

You have to put your own life right before you tackle the world, he says; but the New Age has been wrong to keep aloof from politics and poverty. He has no desire to be so heavenly-minded he's no earthly good, as the saying goes. Take money, for instance. Malcolm thinks therapy should be paid for, but has a problem with the people making fortunes from it. One woman he counsels is quite poor, so he charges her £5 to ensure there is still an *exchange*. 'I'm not talking psychobabble here. Money doesn't stop somewhere, money goes round, and I want to be part of what helps it circulate.' Monkton Wyld is an educational charity. Costs are low, and it has a system of subsidy, based on trust, for those whose means are limited. It does not seek to make a profit. Nevertheless, 'We are a business. We turn over £100,000 a year, running over 200 workshops. Money's an energy. You've got to learn to master it, make it work for you. For me it's a matter of fierce pride that it's commercial.'

Malcolm's father once lamented that his son had lost all his ambition, but 'I'm *very* ambitious. I want to find myself and be all of who I am.' Taking himself too seriously, however, is a temptation he tries to resist. 'A friend of mine – his wife left him for another woman. He was in a terrible state. He heard there was a guru in India, who helped you through problems. He didn't speak any English, but you went there and he would take away some of your pain. And my friend went and sat in front of the guru for two hours and unburdened himself of his problems, while the guru sat there very bravely. Right at the end, the guru picked up a feather, tapped him on the forehead, and said, "Lighten up, arsehole!" '

Postscript: Shortly afterwards, Malcolm started working part-time as a counsellor for the National Health Service. He and his family were planning to leave Monkton Wyld in summer 1993.

FIFTEEN

Findhorn

The Findhorn Foundation is thirty-something. It has grown from a couple of caravans to a miniature village; from a group of three to a community of 150, with many more associated and involved. The New Age has settled in.

At the beginning of the 1960s Eileen and Peter Caddy and Dorothy Maclean moved to a caravan site in north-east Scotland, unemployed and almost penniless. They listened hard for the inner 'guidance' they had learned to trust. God, they believed, had a plan. If they followed his instructions, however bizarre, they would be cared for in every aspect of their lives, from the sublime to the mundane. But meditation was not easy, so cramped were they for space and quiet. No one was more surprised than Eileen when her guidance directed her to the public toilet. Every night she spent long hours there, in joyous visions, receiving instructions for herself and for the group.

They became convinced that there was a global 'network of light', from Siberia to the Kalahari, and that they were connected in telepathy with 'magnetic centres' like their own. Humanity, Eileen was given to understand, was rushing from the 'source of good' towards darkness; and their task was similar to that of Noah in the Flood. 'My child,' her guidance said, 'this place is a fortress created by radiations from above and below and within. It is the most powerful fortress that can be built.'[1]

1 Eileen Caddy, *Flight into Freedom*, 1988

Dorothy, meanwhile, was also receiving guidance. She believed she was in touch with the *devas* or spirits of plants, and with the 'landscape angel' of the place. They told her how to grow vegetables in the barren, sandy soil. The results were startling, and word spread about the giant cabbages and copious beans of the Findhorn garden. People came to visit, some to stay; on travels round the country, Peter Caddy linked up with others in the nascent New Age movement.

Over Easter and Whitsun 1966 a number of people gathered at the caravan park. Many of them felt the destruction of the world was imminent. To their surprise, they experienced instead a sensation of love and light pouring into them, 'the power of the holy spirit'.[2] Convinced the tide had somehow turned, their gloom swung to optimism and they pledged themselves to work towards establishing 'the new kingdom of heaven on earth'. The following year, on Christmas Eve, Eileen was 'told' to go to a particular hill with her husband and a friend. Here, at midnight, she felt her body fill with light, trembled violently, collapsed and then came to, with an overwhelming sense of oneness with the universe. All three felt radiant, exhilarated. It was the beginning, Eileen's guidance told her, of a massive release of cosmic power that would soon be changing individuals everywhere.

* * *

'An evolutionary expansion of consciousness is taking place all over the world, creating a human culture infused with spiritual values.' This is the conviction, spelled out in the 1992 guest programme of the Findhorn Foundation, that unites its members. There is no formal doctrine, and some members are practising Christians or Buddhists. But the principle of the founders is retained: that God, or 'the source of life', is accessible to every person; and that nature (including

2 Ibid.

the planet itself) not only has intelligence, but is participating in a 'wider plan'.

Dianne Falasca has lived at Findhorn for seven years. Her shyness – the result of feeling rarely understood – has given way to talkative, if gentle, confidence. The community gave her the support she needed to 'discover' who she was. 'I was very impressed by what I found here. It was a place that was extremely practical . . . I just really believed in the principles they talked about: putting love into action, the spirit of unconditional love that's been my life . . .'

Dianne always had 'a very rich and active inner reality'. It gave her courage, while 'tragedy and insanity' unfolded around her. Alone of her family, neither drugs nor alcohol have claimed her. 'I prayed, without knowing I was praying. I always had the sense of being sustained or nurtured by something that wasn't physically present. And it was so natural to me I never questioned it or thought much about it.' She found few who understood. But an early 'soul sister' had a husband who was fond of gardening. 'One day he said to me, "You've got all these same strange ideas about love and community as . . ." and he handed me *The Findhorn Garden*. I remember looking through it and thinking, "I'm going to go there one day . . ." '

Dianne has a soft New Jersey accent, from the East Coast suburb she grew up in. She is tiny. Serenity and quiet gestures complement her mobile smiles. But it has not always been like this: 'I had a rough training.'

Her mother was an alcoholic, and the drinking got heavier as Dianne entered her teenage years. Childhood happiness degenerated into insecurity and struggle. 'In alcoholic families it's crazy – you never know from minute to minute what's happening or what you can rely on, or when you come home from school what's going to be on the other side of the door.' Dianne became the 'caretaker', and believes it stood her in good stead. At Findhorn she leads workshops and is involved in counselling, therapy and conflict resolution. She sits on the Core Group, which keeps an eye on the 'spiritual integrity' of the community. 'Most of the work I do here, why I'm in certain positions, is because I have an ability to see the larger picture. That was my training ground in the family – always having to reach beyond what was apparent to see what was actually going on.'

When Dianne was seventeen her sister was murdered – one of a series of unsolved killings of young girls that summer. The shock hastened a spiritual 'opening or deepening'; but her emotions took a long time to catch up. 'I moved out of home, and wandered around aimlessly . . . I was in a pretty lost space for quite a few years.' She set up house with a long-standing boyfriend. Then, in a parachute accident, he too was killed.

At the time, she was training as a nurse and working in a burns unit. The patients' injuries were terrible: most were on the point of death, the rest needed a year in hospital to mend. Again, her spirituality was roused: 'It's just a magnificent thing, working with people that die.' But she became disillusioned with hospitals. Shaken – and released – by her boyfriend's death, she left New Jersey. It had never felt like home: 'that feeling of, there's something else . . .'

She headed for Colorado – up into the mountains. Here she met a couple in a restaurant and moved into their geodesic dome. For two years she meditated and practised yoga with them, surviving by taking on any job that needed doing, from dry wall finishing to plumbing. Then, fired with ideals of community living, she set off with a group of friends towards Montana.

On the way, they drove over a hill into a breathtaking view of the Mission Mountains. 'We all got the hit at the same time – let's stop here!' In a little town called St Ignatius, on an Indian reserve, 'we got the education of our lives. Slowly our ideals had to ground with reality.' They began by renting rooms in the hotel, 'but little did we know that there was an invisible line in the town and we were on the wrong side of the track'. It was a flop-house, mainly used by down-and-out young Native Americans. One night the youngster in the room next to Dianne blew his head off with a shotgun.

Violent deaths and alcoholism were common in the Flathead reserve. It was deeply poor. Yet now began 'one of the grandest adventures of my life'. With a small – and diminishing – group of people, she ran a tofu factory and a wholefood distribution business. The hours were long, the work monotonous, but 'It was just one of those magical times.' She learned new skills, took on responsibility. And while she made the tofu she listened to a tape from Findhorn, the music of The New Troubadours.

Community life, eventually, became too much. 'I didn't have a very good self-identity. I could be a good world-server but I didn't know my limitations. So I burnt myself out very well!' She moved into a cabin in the woods, where bears came down to her backyard and there was wilderness. Weeks went by when she saw no one. 'My thought was, "Who am I, when I have nothing outside myself demanding that I move?" '

But she was not cut off. She sometimes worked as a midwife, and regularly attended the Unity Church in town. The minister ('my first spiritual teacher') and his wife became close friends. While they 'worked on their relationship', she helped by caring for their children. Though she had wrenched away from her family, in order to be purged of its malfunctions, the 'sense of family' remained. In Findhorn she has discovered she is 'a collective being'.

Sitting in her cabin one day, after four and a half years, Dianne realized, ' "My purpose for being here is over, now I need a new purpose . . ." ' Immediately, she thought of Findhorn; and made an 'invocation' to go there, reckoning it would take five years to earn the money. Later that week she visited the minister's family. His parents said they had been dreaming of Dianne, and felt they were meant to help her. As a mark of gratitude for all her 'giving', they provided her with sufficient money to stay at Findhorn for a summer, and paid her to work for them until she had the plane fare. A few months later she was on her way.

She was going for an 'Experience Week' and a gardening workshop – but '*knew* without knowing' that she must give everything she owned away. Sure enough, the week grew into years. She has only been back to the States for visits to her family. 'Everything went well. It was like the angel here, the Spirit of Findhorn, drew me in.'

We sat in one of the many light-filled, wooden buildings which are taking over from the caravans of Findhorn. This was the community centre, and children played noisily downstairs. Nearby a guesthouse was in the process of construction, with turf roof, triple glazing and cellulose insulation. Other 'ecological' buildings include three round houses made from whisky vats. The road to them is lined by tidy bungalows with twining flowers, and lit by knee-high street lamps. Cyclists pedal by. Beyond, the footpath to the beach passes a humming wind turbine, which produces 20 per cent of the site's electricity.

Findhorn has 9,000 visitors a year. The public relations officer, who acted as my guide, is busy. People frequently stopped to exchange a hug with her and gossip, for she was in the throes of managing a crisis. Some of the locals from the nearby village of Findhorn were alarmed by the scale of building at what had been, after all, a caravan park. That morning's local paper reported yet another fracas, and quoted a villager's ire at 'the usual arrogance' of the New Agers: 'the boil on our backside'. Anxiety shimmered in the sunny, smiling community at 'the park'. It was proving hard to stay calmly 'centred' in the face of such antagonism.

Findhorn soul-searching is often turbulent, Dianne explains – despite the neat contentment it presents to the casual eye. At the bottom of the original garden (long past its days of giantism) was an ancient, borrowed caravan: her solitary quarters. She was preparing to move into one of the new bungalows with her Norwegian boyfriend – and expressed some trepidation: 'I like living on my own. I like my independence and my solitude.' There had been plenty of relationships throughout her life, but her need to be 'conscious' had always prevented her from falling in love. Then Ulf, a young romantic, pursued her. 'I gave way to the tenderness, and I know this is my next adventure . . .'

Dianne patted her pregnant tummy with a smile. Their baby was due in the autumn – not long after her forty-first birthday. It had not been easy. 'I went through this whole process . . . I felt betrayed by God.' She had had an abortion at eighteen, and considered doing so again. But 'I finally asked what choice would bring me closer to God, and got very clearly "Say yes". And I trust that bit of me when it speaks. I'm so glad I accepted, because it's opening the door to another phase of me, of my life, of my potential for growth and wholeness; and it's been lovely and graceful and charming.'

Nesting instincts were afflicting, and amusing, her. Preparing the home was 'a mystery to me, part of my growing . . .' The Special Needs Fund had helped with carpets and paint, and the community always has spare furniture. But she longed to go to a shop, choose exactly what she wanted and *buy* it. For the first time, lack of money bothered her – 'How do I not go into disempowerment with that?'

Her experience is not unique in Findhorn. As new houses go up and families settle, the caravan park is being urbanized. 'The community used to be very self-fulfilling,' Dianne remarks, 'it satisfied a lot of needs. You didn't need to spend much money – it was so full, enriching and rewarding.' Now there is a shop, a cafe and a pizzeria – with menu and delivery costs on notice-boards and in guest caravans. 'The village energy is starting to come in. And the money doesn't stretch. We used to have community sharings all the time. Now there are shows, movies, which all cost. So it's all changing, it's evolving.'

Members pay for their first two years, on a sliding scale

from £1,800 to £5,000. They may then become a staff member, and receive a small allowance, food and board. Unfortunately, Dianne smiles, the system recently collapsed amid fights about who was entitled to eat in the community centre. Many people have moved into Findhorn without going through the formal membership procedure. They feel they belong, but others are not so sure. That is not the only sticking point. Members previously exchanged 'blue money' at a bulk food shed; now they have to use the shop, their buying power has diminished. It is very challenging, she comments ruminatively: 'More and more people are saying, "Just pay me!" And we're saying, "We don't want to go into an economy of employment." . . . But I think we are being asked to bring our consciousness into money now.'

A new system of 'governance' is also required: 'We've outgrown ourselves.' The numbers of residents, and guests, have increased vastly. A range of courses fills the summer. Some members feel the educational programme has got so big community life has been forgotten. Meanwhile, the small 'work departments' have grown into flourishing businesses, which include a magazine, computer consultancy and solar panels manufacturer. They function independently of the Foundation, but are closely linked. The need to cultivate efficiency and profit has started to collide with Findhorn's slow decision-making by consensus. Some members' trust is wavering under the onslaught of 'slick kind of business terms', Dianne says. But for her there is a challenge: how to ground commerce in the spiritual.

'What does it *mean* to love at a business meeting, to interact in a respectful way? Because for me, love isn't sweet, nice at all – it's a pretty intense force, it demands a lot of truth.' Much of her time and energy, on Core Group, is spent addressing questions such as this. Findhorn, she insists, is a 'school for transformation' – or it is nothing. If you live there, you are accepting a call 'to open up to the divinity within yourself and live it in relation to others, to become more of who you really are. There's nothing magical about it, or esoteric. It's just a lot of hard work.'

That individual process is sustained by communal effort. Group meditations take place at regular hours in the various 'sanctuaries' – though their importance is disputed. Some (like Eileen Caddy, still living at the Park) think daily attendance is essential; others do not see the point. 'Attunement' prepares the way for each decision and activity: 'We all hold hands, and the focalizer (someone holding the energy for that day) will say a few words to focus people in the silence. It's a way of becoming present in the moment, acknowledging both that something's about to begin, and the spiritual presence that's there.' Attunement could mean aligning with 'the angel of the kitchen' before a meal, or finding who should be on Core Group.

Every department and every meeting has a focalizer – who takes responsibility, but is not in charge. 'To keep awareness' of the whole there is a Foundation focalizer. Key positions, such as this, are filled by Attunement in the central meeting place, the Universal Hall – preceded by 'fishbowling'. Nominees sit on the floor in the middle, and anyone who wants to question or affirm them comes and does so publicly. This is gruelling, according to Dianne, but the result is unity: 'It's one of the times you really feel the spirit of this place.'

Such experiences wipe out her frustrations, and confirm her belief that Findhorn is a 'planetary centre', where new forms of relationship are being tried and demonstrated. She is content if the 'chaos and darkness' of the outside world are lived in miniature in the community – for it is a 'kidney', she says, where they are processed. She has been happy there, but one day she expects to move on – to continue elsewhere her 'adventure in consciousness'.

Postscript: In November 1992 Dianne gave birth to a baby boy, Tobias.

SIXTEEN

Forest Path

Ajahn Santacitto sits on a cushion, cross-legged before a statue of the Buddha. He is forty-five, but frail and slightly stooped, swathed in a robe of orange-brown. His head is shaved. New York sentences come slowly, so quietly it's hard to catch his words. This is the Jewish boy from Brooklyn, who became a Buddhist abbot.

He was concerned about the interview – misrepresentations had occurred before. In preparation, he sent me 'homework': newsletters, tapes and books. The printed word for Buddhists, he explained, was an 'offering, which may inspire and suggest ways in which people can be going forth and rising up in their lives. In being willing to do this interview with you, it's with a similar intent.'

Everyone had an inner call, he said – not 'the usual sort of natural curiosity which leads to the distracted mind' – and I should trust my own. He wanted me to be spontaneous. Nervously I began: 'I'd like to ask you about this room.' He nodded in the stillness. 'Yeah, right, I like the way you said "I'd *like* to".'

It was the shrine room, 'where people have brought and recharged their peace . . . a refuge, a sanctuary for the heart. We're all refugees in a certain kind of way. Meditation is done here, chanting, very skilful praise to wisdom, to truth, to virtue. As a result, each one of us has the opportunity to taste more deeply of our best qualities, to feel them resonating, wakening – to take the peacefulness beyond the monastery, back into life. So this room is a resource of emptiness, it clears the slate for us, we can empty our mind . . . it *is* the monastery, it's what the monastery's all about. It's available as an offering to those who feel mature enough to make use of it.'

Why, I asked, do the monks bow towards the statue of the Buddha, flanked by flowers and candles? 'I could fill your tapes for hours just on that topic! Because that's the best way to come in, in spirit as well as form . . . like bringing your hands to your heart: let all of your doing, all of your being, be going forth from the heart.' They bow to 'the *Buddha*, the *Dharma* and the *Sangha* – wisdom, truth and purity – bringing them forth in the act of bowing, humbling one's pride and foolishness'.

The rhythmic, nasal chanting of these three Pali words follows the monks' prostrations at the start of every meditation. The peaceful demeanour of the Buddha represents 'the potential for human perfection, for enlightenment, for finding ultimate reality and living that'. The Buddha needs nothing: in the bowing, the Ajahn said, 'I'm being given a chance to reawaken that which I'm bowing to in myself.' The *Dharma* is the Buddha's teaching; and also ultimate truth, to which the teaching points. The *Sangha* is the community of those who practise the Buddha's way: it usually refers specifically to monks and nuns.

Ajahn Santacitto expressed his approval of the way the interview was going, and our first session closed.

A few monks were sitting drinking tea in a little room between the shrine room and the kitchen. The Devon *vihara*, or 'monastery', is a whitewashed cottage with scattered *kutis* (monks' huts – which I did not see). Tort Pa Bah, the annual festival 'for the spread of generosity', had taken place a few days before and among the offerings was a sapling. I was whisked off to plant it with another laywoman – for the monks are not allowed to pierce the ground by digging. We lowered it into the earth, in bright autumn sunshine; around us scores of twig-like trees peeped from plastic tubes, an incipient, fragile forest.

The Devon monks follow Ajahn Chah, of the Forest tradition of Theravada Buddhism. Many of them spent years at Wat Pah Pong, the monastery which grew up around him in a malarial Thai forest. The first of the Westerners to join Ajahn Chah, in 1967, was a newly ordained American monk, the Venerable Sumedho. In 1975 he became abbot of a new monastery in Thailand for English-speaking monks. Two years later he visited England with Ajahn Chah – who left him, with a small group of his Western disciples, in Hampstead. Now he too was an Ajahn ('teacher', a monk who has spent ten rains, or yearly monsoon retreats, in robes), and responsible for the only community of Forest monks in Europe.

The monks transplanted every detail of their practice, including the daily almsround, which in London tended to be fruitless. But as they walked with their bowls one day on Hampstead Heath they encountered a jogger – who happened to own a forest. He gave it to them, and Chithurst, in Sussex, became the first of the Western Forest monasteries. England now has four such monasteries, and at Chithurst and Amaravati, the largest, there are also nuns. Interest has spread: France, Italy, Switzerland, New Zealand and Australia all have Theravada monks – or, more correctly, *bhikkhus* ('alms-mendicants').

I had arrived at the *vihara* in time for the weekly all-night vigil, set according to the phases of the moon. There were about ten people in the darkened shrine room – the monks, *anagarika* ('postulant'), and one or two lay visitors – sitting on cushions and wrapped in cloaks. Four and a half hours of chants and meditation took us up to midnight, and a break for cheese, chocolate and tea with sugar. The monks tucked in, relaxed and joked – not moving from their cushions.

Why, I later asked the Ajahn, when nothing may be eaten after noon, are they allowed this curious feast? He laughed. The Buddha permitted certain high-energy 'medicine foods' when the going was tough, so soya milk is allowed because it is 'bean juice', whereas dairy milk is not. The rules were made in India more than two millennia ago, but Theravadin monks are known for their strict adherence to tradition. They put great emphasis on 'keeping the *holistic* vibrancy between spirit and structure rather than just allowing the spirit to take on the form of a new culture; because the structure holds the secret of the potential to unfold human enlightenment'.

Dharma talks are part of the Theravada method: on this occasion a visiting monk stressed *seriousness*. This was surprising, as decorous banter seemed to be the Devon style. Over the washing up the *bhikkhus*, amused by the disparity, asked me my opinion. Carefully, I said I had found the talk *long*. 'Ah, well that's our style: rambling.'

The vigil went on till 3 a.m. but I was showing signs of strain. The Ajahn kindly suggested I go early to my caravan to sleep. Though the rising bell is usually at 4 a.m. a lie-in was allowed next morning. I arrived in the cottage as the *anagarika* was beginning to prepare the one meal of the day, served at 10.30 a.m.

'We are forced by the Buddha to be completely dependent materially for survival each day. I cannot store food to eat tomorrow,' the Ajahn explained. Monks never handle money or prepare a meal. Their dependence frees them, so they can devote themselves to 'the goal of awakening to the *Dharma*'. It reminds them of the uncertainty of life, and of the need to behave in a way that is worthy of the alms they receive.

In return for physical support, the *bhikkhus* offer 'nurturing from the depths', the Ajahn says. 'The lay people say they find us a great support in making spirituality part of their daily lives.' This mutual dependence 'helps ensure that Buddhism is a living tree: the laity are the branches and leaves, the monks the roots – neither can survive without the other. You can get very selfish about your spiritual life. *However*, if these are the people who are keeping you alive . . . maybe they're bringing their problems with them, but there's a greater sensitivity to their need, through gratitude. In responding to them you're learning the relevance of the teaching of the Buddha to our times.'

It is difficult for *bhikkhus* to survive in the West by touring local villages on almsrounds. When I was there the meal was prepared from food offered earlier and kept in the larder by the *anagarika*. He served the monks as they filed past the table with their bowls, and any visitors helped out. This was nerve-wracking: the monks take what they're given, but subtle gestures indicated preferences. There was a delay as I tried to serve tomatoes. 'You must stab them with a knife!' somebody whispered. (They are regarded as 'alive' because they can regenerate themselves, the Ajahn told me with amusement later.) Savoury and sweet all went into the bowl together: 'Apparently', one woman told me, 'the French guy finds it really hard.'

The meal over, the Ajahn and I went back to the shrine room to carry on our talk, accompanied, as always, by another *bhikkhu*. A Theravadin monk must never be alone with a woman; and I had been warned not to shake their hands or even give them anything. In fact the Ajahn himself handed me a sheet of paper, another monk a tea-towel: they wanted to be sensitive, the Ajahn later said, in case I did not know the rules. Once I'd settled in objects were slid along the floor between us; if a monk was left alone in a room with me, he discreetly opened the door. 'Living a celibate life one has to skilfully deal with masculine energy,' the Ajahn said, 'and these rules are ways of helping one to do that without being overwhelmed.'

He was yawning, and spoke with an exhausted drawl. The weekly vigils were demanding, he admitted, but they were a reminder that 'few of us are really using our full potential. Even though you're tired after an all-night sit, you feel a strong sense of well-being.' The following day is a day of rest, dedicated to conserving energy for spiritual purposes. The value lies in the routine: 'what it's like to be stretched, yet not feeling uncomfortable because it feels right. The first year there's a lot of resistance, but it's something you acquire a taste for.'

That evening there was *puja* (meditation and chanting), as usual; the next day we gathered at 4.45 a.m. After an hour of meditation each person went to walk outside, alone. Dawn was etched by the outlines of the trees; there was just enough light to glimpse the silent, pacing figures – robes covered in cloaks, shaven heads with woolly hats. The clarity of air, and motion, were reviving. At 6.30 there were chores. I was given the shrine room candlesticks to polish, so courteously little that I asked if I might also do the bell. At 7.15 there was gruel.

'The lifestyle of a monk or nun provides a structure, a form in which the spirit can deepen. It provides all the fertilizing and protection – the garden in which the rosebush can grow.' Meditation is not something you *do*, maintains the Ajahn, 'it's something you allow to happen'. The key to making routine come alive is awareness of what is experienced. And 'the enlightened mind' is one that is constantly aware, 'just simply at one with what is, continuously . . .'

Most people, he agrees, find the regime austere, and even strange. The *bhikkhus*, however, believe it counterbalances the 'sensual indulgence' which characterizes modern life. Yet after twenty-one years he is prepared to admit that it is often very hard: 'not "they lived happily ever after" '. Unexpected internal struggles can have devastating effect: 'It's quite incredible! People really healthy come into this way of life and fall apart physically! . . . But there's a kind of falling apart which is a reflection of things coming together.' The aim is not to become a 'perfected vegetable', but to achieve an equanimity which allows joy to be radiant, sadness to be sober – both accepted as part of the 'natural flow'.

I had been told of recent upsets in the Forest monasteries, with two senior monks departing to get married. This was where the interview grew tense. The Ajahn was concerned I might be seeking to sensationalize, from some misguided view of what might interest readers. Their disrobing had stirred things up a bit, he said, but the monastic code of discipline was honoured and no vows had been broken – the Buddhist monk is free to leave at any time. Everyone felt sad that the previous abbot's 'magnetism, his loving qualities' now reached fewer people, but it had been hardest for the laity, he thought, who had idealized the monks. It had reminded people they were human – this he valued.

A castrated man cannot become a monk, the Ajahn said. *Bhikkhus* are required not to suppress the sexual urge, but to transform the rawness of its energy and 'reinvest' it. Without the years of celibacy 'love was something which, if I knew it at all, would have been in a very small way, for individuals.'

Ajahn Santacitto's own acutest struggles occurred when he was just beginning as a monk. Talking of his personal history felt like a come-down, he said, but he would look at 'the evolutionary unfolding' of his path.

'There was something strange about me all along': he warmed to the drama, gathering threads. 'It's like, *I wasn't willing to play the game*.' At university there came a day when he suddenly couldn't bring himself to write another paper. He dropped out. After two years in Israel he travelled, heading for the East because a girl he had once loved was going there.

He was 'a mathematical genius', he smiles – and it unbalanced his character. 'It was abstract purity which fascinated . . . something beyond logic. I didn't know what it was: a pure system, which was beyond all the limitations of the human world . . . And one day on acid in Katmandu the vision formed! *Yes*, everything is connected with everything else!' He laughs, and then recollects himself: LSD has been a catalyst for many of the monks, but they do not recommend it. The truth you might see for a while on drugs, he says, is not easy to carry into life.

He picks out another thread. As a youth he scoured the New York libraries, searching for – he didn't know what.

'It just went on, a crazy obsession. Until one day, by some wonderful miracle, I actually found what I was looking for! It was a new book at the time, *Toward a Psychology of Being* by Maslow. He was talking about self-actualization. My heart, my guts knew, "*That's it!*" It became like a Bible to me.'

When he met Ajahn Chah 'the connection was made': this was a self-actualized being. They first met at a public ceremony – all the chanting and bowing, the dripping of wax into holy water, the curious antics with a large white cloth, were ridiculous to the American iconoclast. But Ajahn Chah's expression startled him: 'the grin of a mischievous lad having a grand old time'. In his voice 'the sound of compassion was unmistakable'. Steve Saslav was 'trapped'.

He decided to stay six months, and from then on 'it just happened day by day, in twenty-one years'. It was like a rebirth, the setting aside of a lifetime of accumulated habits. Though he struggled, still enticed by the life he had been leading ('I was in Bangkok, I was having fun!'), he could never bring himself to leave. 'There was nothing out there pulling me which I trusted. So it didn't have the power to convince, only to disturb.' In the *Dharma* he had found what he was looking for: 'the purity of mathematics allied to the humanity of psychology'.

He stayed for thirteen years in Thailand, with visits to the West; seven years ago he came to England. He has had to learn to be an abbot, with responsibilities he often feels unfitted for: he has no natural instinct for 'social dynamics' and is burdened by being 'somebody for others'. But since the age of thirty he has felt a need to serve.

The son who had been so hostile to his parents was transformed, and they were glad. When he visited, his mother tried hard to help him keep the discipline – the rules about women apply within the family as well. Once she forgot and slapped his knee to share her laughter at an anecdote: her apologies were profuse. But during her last illness, in hospital, he reached to help her when she slipped out of the bed –

and she was overwhelmed, his sister told him later. It was the last time he saw her.

His origins remain with him. The monks are his spiritual brothers; he respects them beyond measure. But 'at the level of personality, it doesn't feel like I'm in the right family'. In New York he once went to a gathering of some strictly Orthodox, Hasidic Jews. And though they were strangers and 'look weirder than we do . . . I walked into that meeting and I *knew* everybody . . . and weird as I looked to them I could be accepted there. They felt that's where I belonged.' If you're out in the desert, they told him, and a kind person offers you water, you may stop for a while – but it's not your home. ' "What you didn't realize was, your home was in your own backyard. It was there all along and you didn't know it." '

But it made no difference. 'Even though in a way *this* doesn't feel right and that does . . . in the way that counts, this is right.' The heart of the Buddha's teaching, he says, is the doctrine of 'no self'. Part of being a Forest monk is 'not being able to be who I'm comfortable to be, in order to go beyond being just that'.

SEVENTEEN

Iona

In late summer the sea looks kind, the cliffs majestic. The beach is sheltered by the great arms of the bay, and a few sheep graze on scattered tufts of grass. But when St Columba landed here in 563 he had sailed from Ireland in a coracle, with little hope of welcome.

His monks took Christianity through Scotland and as far as Europe. Iona, where he built his abbey, became a holy site. Columba made a prophecy: that though the voices of monks would give way to the lowing of cattle, Iona would one day be as it had been – honoured by foreign rulers and holy men.

To the Presbyterian, George MacLeod, Iona seemed 'a thin place – only a tissue paper separating earth from heaven'. In 1938 he started to rebuild the abbey and make an experiment in community life. He invited new Church of Scotland ministers to join him. His idea was that their stint there – building, worshipping, studying and living together – would prepare them for work with the poor in crowded cities. From this grew the Iona Community, which today is ecumenical: made up of men and women who regard the island as their spiritual home, although they rarely live there. The 200 members (there are many more friends and associates) commit themselves to pray and work with the Community for justice and peace around the world.

Margaret Legum went often to Iona as a student in the 1950s, because her boyfriend's father was the Community's deputy leader. Years later she wondered idly what it was really like – probably not as delightful and as 'child-sized' as she'd thought then, for after all she'd been in love. When her husband, a foreign correspondent with a Sunday paper, had to dash off yet again to Africa one Easter, she decided to take her two small children and revisit the island.

'And of course I *adored* it!' she says, dropping her voice to a dramatic whisper. It was ideal for the children, 'with those hills that felt like Everest and no traffic and cold sea so they weren't going to drown'. They began to go there regularly.

'I just felt, in a strange way, *this* is where I fit in', she says. First, because her grandmother came from that part of the world, 'real atavistic echoes of home: Grandma Mackenzie, this is how she talked!'; secondly, because in the Community 'there was *no* sense of hierarchy . . . And if there's one word that describes my belief system, it's egalitarian.'

Margaret had never been sure where she belonged. She grew up in 'an absolutely standard South African nuclear family' – yet with certain attitudes that set it apart and were decisive, she believes, in her conditioning. Her parents were 'bitterly opposed' to apartheid. 'We didn't see black people as below us . . . But we tended,' she chortles, 'to see the Afrikaaners as crummy.' When Margaret came to Britain its class-consciousness intimidated her, although 'I'm a *great* chameleon in terms of accent and I instinctively know what I have to bloody well do to be accepted.' Her voice now is 'Oxford', forcefully projected and peppered with emphasis.

Her mother was 'by *far*' the more intellectual of her parents and loved conceptualizing, but only about politics. In the 'appalling society' they lived in, she believed, there was no time for culture ('which is *rubbish*!' Margaret exclaims). She was also – unheard of in their circle – a socialist.

Politics, since then, has shaped Margaret's view of the world and offered a way into it. Unlike most women she knows, she has great confidence in her own intellect: 'extraordinary . . . I can feel *terribly* unconfident about *everything* else, but intellectually you can't put me down . . .' Her CV boasts a string of First Class degrees and other qualifications, as well as a long list of employment, skills and publications. Her confidence, she finds, is threatening to women, and even more to men. Yet because her mother saw her father – a highly successful civil engineer – as simply 'useful' because he brought in the money, Margaret always took it for granted she would be supported by a man.

When she was twelve her parents divorced. For some time her mother had been having an affair with an MP, one of the few other socialists in the country, 'who was *terribly* nice, a *wonderful* bloke, and I'm really sorry I didn't get to know him because I just *hated* him . . .'

Nevertheless, Margaret felt she had to marry a 'great man' like him. Colin Legum, fifteen years her senior, was already a well-known journalist when she met him through her mother: he seemed to fit the bill. Their marriage has been unusual, she remarks. Colin was a widower, with grandchildren the same age as the children of his second family. He and Margaret now live in different houses, though they are not separated. He enjoys a hermit's life, taming a 'wild acre' in Sussex; she travels, and loves entertaining friends in her London flat.

They had not been married long when they wrote a book together, calling for sanctions against South Africa. It led to their exile. They settled down in suburban Richmond, but 'not living the couples' life – 'I always felt I was a bit of an imposter'. She coped by joining the Labour Party and campaigning on issues of the day: comprehensive schooling, mental health and race relations.

It was politics, not religion, that drew her into the Iona Community. 'So they may be talking a lot of guff up there and I may not understand three-quarters of what they're saying: "by whom and with whom and in whom and the power and the glory . . ." But I *know* that what they're about is the same as me in social and political terms.' People at Iona believe in 'equality' too – and with just as much emotion.

Ecology, the Peace Movement and Celtic spirituality are some of the themes most frequently on offer in the annual programme at the abbey and Macleod Centre. Each week, Margaret explains, a new group of people turns up and 'forms a community'. That could just be sentimental, she admits, if the organizers were not clear about their aim: to create a situation 'where you're learning and sharing and doing things together'. The week opens with an act of worship, which is 'pretty quick, not lots of bowings and salaamings and "Dear God, look after me and I'm a terrible sinner" '. Chores follow and everybody – even, on one occasion, the 'top brass' of all the main denominations – joins in. Each evening 'there's something *hilarious* to do – dances till 2 a.m., concerts, ceilidhs.'

She offers to tell me 'a wonderful example' of the way it works. A couple of years ago, euphoric about the release of Nelson Mandela and the collapse of the Berlin Wall, she planned a political week on the island called 'Breaking the chains that bind us'. She persuaded her husband (who generally keeps away) to help her. When they arrived they found two-thirds of the group were people with severe learning difficulties '. . . like, "differently abled" as you've never met before . . . autistic, severe cerebral palsy, Down's Syndrome, you name it'.

Colin assumed the disabled people would 'muck about in the craft room', while the rest got on with their slides and lectures – 'he's absolutely out of order!' she laughs. He was told that was not how they did things on Iona. Instead, *everyone* went into the craft room and moulded their own 'chains': one woman made a kitchen sink; an autistic man beat and beat his piece of clay until it held the marks of his palms. Those who wished then went into the 'talking room', to listen to a woman who felt the chain binding her was the strife in Nicaragua. The tales told there were so gruelling for one or two that they slipped away to the craft room to paint, or outside for a walk: 'And we'd say, "Oh all right then, you take Alastair" (the very noisy autistic chap) – so Alastair galloped down the hill.'

The 'able-bodied' and 'disabled' mingled. 'And it was the most wonderful week,' Margaret sighs, 'marvellous. We *made* a community! Out of this lot, without dividing us . . .' Her husband thanked her, saying it had completely changed his outlook, and he had learned far more than he felt he had given. For Margaret, that is the essence of egalitarianism: 'It is about learning, and about the truth.'

She says she never laughs as much as she does with people from Iona, 'there's a lightness of spirit there, of experience . . . and it's *not* cynical.' It is due, she thinks, to people's faith.

The first time she went to a service in the abbey, she joined those who knelt at the front while the minister came round and recited over each of them some of Jesus' words. 'You didn't choose me; I chose you', were the ones that fell to her, evoking 'a huge sense of relief that was just marvellous. I felt also – this seems to be something about belonging.' It was even better when the minister whispered that they had once met in Malawi, and invited her to join the Community for coffee.

Her Christianity, at the time, was vague. Her mother had always written 'faith in human nature' in the religious slot on forms; and since Margaret had never had an 'old man in the sky' she never had to deconstruct him. At Cambridge University she suffered 'a *great* depression'. All the doctors could come up with were questions about her sex life: 'Just *hopeless!*' So she struggled on.

She started to browse among her boyfriend's books, curious about his attachment to Iona's Christianity. 'The Community's got a very sort of Liberation Theology approach, you know. Not at *all* evangelical. And I remember one of the books was about the life-changing character of the forty days in the wilderness. And I thought, *that's* me, that's what I'm going through . . . and thanks, that's what I needed.'

She went to a local clergyman, she chuckles, and said: 'I think I must be confirmed, because I've never had any of this stuff, baptism or anything.' After that, she occasionally went to church – and was still depressed, for a year or so. Some time later, stricken by appalling eczema, she took a course of steroids and entered analysis. A terrible fear of desertion came to light. Neither depression nor skin trouble has afflicted her since.

Margaret still wasn't sure about the Christianity. She found if she behaved as if it were all true it seemed to 'work', but she wasn't sure she 'believed' it. She still feels much the same. 'If you told me today that everything in the Bible is untrue – that there never was such a person as Jesus, it was a hoax, the book was written in the seventeenth century – I'd say, well, what a *wonderful* story! How extraordinary that someone could invent it!' For the gospels' implications, she argues, are undoubtedly true. She loves their use of paradox: if you try to preserve your life you lose it; if you cast your bread on the water you will gain a hundredfold. Prayer, for her, 'is about trying to understand those paradoxes . . . and acknowledging that I don't have to worry. To the extent that I worry, I'm an atheist.'

When she became an associate member of the Community, twenty years ago, she committed herself to study of the Bible. This was a novelty, especially as it required her to attach herself to a local congregation. The Richmond Anglicans, she found, were snobbish and sexist – although 'it's quite different now. I know, for example, they'll be celebrating like *mad* Wednesday's decision' – the Anglican vote to ordain women as priests. Margaret had heard the news on the radio while lying in her dentist's chair, 'and I *wept*'.

It took her sixteen years to move on to full membership of the Community and to accept its fivefold rule. This requires her to pray or read the Bible daily; to account for the use of her money in local 'family groups', including the payment of a tithe; and in the same groups to account for the use of her time. She is also expected to 'meet with and account to' other members of the Community, in regional meetings and plenaries – and must send an annual assessment to the leader of how she is keeping the rule.

Were these requirements difficult? She laughs in surprise: 'No!' – though they did involve radical change. 'Iona integrated my life, it's not challenged it in the sense of making me do something uphill.' It steadied her, she thinks, and helped her fit in elsewhere. And the most important part of the rule for her is still what attracted her at the start: the call to 'action for justice and peace'.

She answers this call in her professional life, as a trainer in 'gender awareness' in Third World countries and in the workshops she runs on 'Understanding Racism'. The workshops, especially, are dear to her heart. She and her black colleague take them to South Africa for four months of the year – to companies, universities and community groups – and to the Iona Community. She would do them even if she were not paid, she says gravely, and in a way she would prefer that 'because it's kind of only fair that those of us who've benefited so much from racism should give it back free.' The workshops reflect her own 'enlightenment' eight years ago. 'My heart would beat at understanding something I hadn't understood before of what racism is. It's about the *system*, the ideology, which says *we* are superior and *you* are inferior – and all the manifestations of that.' Earlier in our conversation she had only just stopped herself describing her depression as *black*: 'You see – that's the sort of language we've inherited.'

Margaret's home is a comfortable ex-council flat, looking over the River Thames, not far from Kew. She is not badly off, and lists among her hobbies horse-riding, opera, and running her own narrow boat. So it seems odd to hear her talk of Christianity as meaningless unless it is 'being *with* the poor'.

I say as much, and she nods: 'I used to think it had to

be literal, and then I met somebody who's living in Guguleto, a township in Cape Town. I just remember the sweet indulgent way the Africans talked about him – you know, "He doesn't fit in here, he can always get out again if he wants to, it's phoney." ' So she moved to being 'avowedly aware, and acknowledging in what I do, that my life is totally involved with those who are excluded. I can't make it a part-time thing. That's what Christianity means to me.'

Contemplative prayer is not her style. She is an extrovert who joined the Iona Community, in part, because of all the fun she thought she might be missing out on. She learns about God, she says, through other people. Like the man, at their new members' week, who admitted that the thing that put him off prayer was that he was terrified it might work: 'Maybe I'll actually *find God* . . . Aargh!'

'Quite *right!*' says Margaret, and roars with laughter at the memory.

EIGHTEEN

Corrymeela

'Why is Northern Ireland such an emotionally absorbing place?' Derick Wilson asked aloud the question he has asked himself a thousand times before, sitting forward in his chair intently. 'We are living in the predicament caused by the failure of two sovereign governments to resolve their difficulties. There are people here who have identified with London; there are others who have historically identified with Dublin. And so we are all caught up, like the tides outside the centre here: as they race through each other there's sometimes calm, sometimes waves, sometimes a huge upheaval and chaos.'

Derick is a busy man, and the time he gives is snatched between commitments. Yet he summons up reserves of thoughtfulness and warmth. Just when you think he has forgotten to fix up your accommodation as he promised, or to send you that report about his work, it's done. His face is kindly, deeply creased though he is only in his forties. And if he seemed distracted in the months we were in touch, he had good reason: one of his closest friends and colleagues was dying from a tumour of the brain, at the age of forty-four. Frank Wright's name came up each time we spoke; and in Northern Ireland that weekend, I heard it mentioned many times by others. The Corrymeela Community works for reconciliation from a cliff-top centre overlooking the Atlantic and in Belfast city; and its friendships obviously go deep.

Derick sighs. 'For me, the confusions that people experience here are not unique to Irish people; but they might illuminate the tensions and pulls that people meet in many situations where there's a clash of identities.' Northern Ireland, he says, is one of the unresolved areas of Europe, but with this difference: that it belonged to the winning side in both World Wars and Britain could not ditch it. Because it is a place where 'people have no common sense of who they are', the atmosphere is charged. 'To walk down the Mall in London or O'Connell Street in Dublin, if you feel British or Irish, is to celebrate belonging to something. You don't have that sense of free, unbridled celebration in a society such as Northern Ireland, because you don't know that everybody around you agrees with you.'

The nature of conflict is that everything is subordinated to it: 'that includes issues of gender, the environment, child welfare, religious belief. Everything is used only for you to beat the other. In a conflict you *imagine* you have the freedom to choose, but in reality you are caught up simply in choosing which issue, or theme, or instrument to use next to secure your position.'

Some people do opt out, and nearly everyone, at times, 'politely ignores there is a conflict here'. But Derick feels that anybody wanting 'something new' – not to live at the expense of others – has to face the issues. There are few opportunities for thinking in new ways, yet many make the effort. He stresses they are normal people, making simple choices, in extraordinary circumstances.

The Corrymeela Community is a grouping of such individuals, scattered over Ireland with a few abroad. For more than twenty-five years it has offered an alternative to division. In the early days, says Derick, he and other members fell into the liberal trap of criticizing those who disagreed, 'simply ensuring that they didn't look at what we did seriously, because they already felt condemned'. Now he prefers simply to say 'I choose to do things differently'. Because his upbringing did not leave him bitter, he feels he is freer than those whose emotional legacy is more severe. But that freedom carries with it an 'imperative to see if other ways are possible'.

He was born, an only child, into a working-class home in the centre of Belfast. His father was a pillar of the Presbyterian Church, not involved in politics at all. But he had sympathy with the unionist tradition, 'so Britain would have been his point of identity'. *Northern* Ireland, a province of the United Kingdom, was what Derick understood to be his home as he grew up. School trips went to Scotland rather than across the border; daily assembly, in infant days, was held in a hall which displayed a picture of the Queen. Catholic friends now swap notes with him, and remark the subtle variations of conditioning: they were taught to look to Dublin, and saw themselves as part of *Ireland*.

Derick's family lived on a dividing line between Catholic and Protestant districts, with both denominations represented in the street. So although his childhood church community 'was very staunchly Presbyterian without being staunchly Protestant or anti-Catholic', he was always aware of 'us and them'. Fear of 'the other' was instilled. Derick and his friends were warned about the local Catholic church: 'If you have to pass by the chapel at night, try to pass by on the other side. Strange things happen to young Protestant children if they're snatched behind the chapel walls . . .'

At grammar school he moved into a middle-class world each day, returning to his own at night. He was unable to swallow the stereotypes that either had about the other. The school was 'mixed' – which meant, at that time, that the pupils were both Protestant and Jewish. Again, it was 'us and them'; 'and again, we were in the vast majority, as we were in my street. We thought of ourselves as being very tolerant, because after all there were Jewish people in our midst, and look how well we treated them! Looking back, we were taught to be tolerant of people who were a lot less strong, numerically and politically, than us. So "tolerance" for me now has negative connotations, and I'd go so far as to say that you're tolerant of people who are no threat to you.'

During Derick's teenage years, in the 1960s, the Catholics'

voice grew louder, and Protestant 'tolerance' towards them correspondingly diminished. At around the same time the mistrustful world he had been introduced to was steadily 'punctured' by experience. He helped out at the church by doing Christian Aid collections, and was sent into Catholic districts such as the New Lodge Road, which is now a 'flashpoint' area. Year after year he was told he would get no money there; yet he was greeted with warmth, and always came back with the envelopes filled. 'The old images were being cut . . .'

There was an exciting 'atmosphere of change in the wider world' by the time Derick went to Queen's University, to study Physics and Mathematics. He got involved with the work-camp movement: 'people building walls, putting roofs on buildings and schools in Spain and Italy; working with immigrant labourers in Holland . . .' Meeting Germans, who were still 'thought of as being different, fearful and threatening by our parents', gave a heady sense of breaking down taboos.

He was one of a small group of students clustered around the chaplaincy at Queen's and eager for an alternative to confrontation. Difference, they felt, should be explored – not feared; and they were influenced by Christians who had challenged the bitterness and violence of the Second World War. 'We met all these people who had stood up against injustices and the things that divided the world, and who had been able to live through it and find some way forward. And it was Ray Davey, the chaplain, who brought us into this atmosphere.'

As a prisoner of war, Ray Davey had been one of a group who sustained morale, and built up mutual trust, by telling stories of their lives. Corrymeela was founded on this memory. He inspired the students, mainly Protestant, to form an ecumenical community dedicated to 'reconciliation'. 'If Christians cannot speak of reconciliation', he said at the opening, 'then they have nothing to say at all.' It was 1965, three years before the Northern Ireland Troubles started.

'So we ran youth clubs, adventure playgrounds, holiday schemes, and used this place as a resource for that. I would have hired not minibuses, but two trucks, and brought children here for a weekend together with twelve students. We'd have fed them, walked them miles and had ghost story-telling and sing-songs that went on into the night . . . We were creating a place here where there was a sense of vitality, energy; where people experienced *life*. Above all we tried not to be "religious people", but to say that if we came together and brought other people who were different together, that was one understanding of the Christian Gospel. And that if we *weren't* doing that, we were worth nothing.'

Corrymeela (the name means 'hill of honey') has always had two strands. It responds to the political and social issues of the day in Northern Ireland; and to developments in the world-wide Church. The events with which it opened set the tone. At a political conference the then Prime Minister of Northern Ireland called on unionists to involve the Catholics in government (these were the days of Stormont). 'Of course, within a few months he was deposed. But from our point of view it was an important way, to our surprise, to open a reconciliation centre, because no one had ever said that publicly before.' A religious service followed: Pastor Tullio Vinay (renowned for helping Jews escape war-time Turin, and for founding the Agape Community) declared Corrymeela open, and wished it well in its proclamation of the 'New World of Jesus Christ'. It was, he said, a meeting-place; and a question mark to churches everywhere.

Corrymeela stands for all that is inclusive and accepting: anyone is welcome who is prepared to talk. Mother Teresa of Calcutta and Allan Boesak from South Africa have visited in recent years. The Community has initiated conferences which have made it possible for Cabinet ministers to meet former paramilitaries. 'Hard-line Protestant kids' have made friendships with men they have later discovered, to their astonishment, were Catholic priests. Catholic mothers, bereaved through assassination, have made friends with the families of Loyalist prisoners.

But Corrymeela cannot give a platform to a political party, or to any dogmatist. 'It's always been a place where differences are visible – and valued,' Derick says. That has required 'hard dialogue', even danger, in a society where the fashion is to victimize. 'There's always the possibility it fails. Why this place works is that success isn't guaranteed. It depends on the extent to which people reach out and trust and risk relationship with each other. And that's what we feel the life of Jesus was about. Because the people he spent time with were the unexpected – a Roman centurion, a tax collector, or a woman accused of adultery. He broke the mechanism by which they were scapegoated.'

By the time the Troubles erupted, the Community was well-established and respected across both traditions. Members were able to evacuate 500 children overnight who were at risk, 'and the shooting stopped as our minibuses went in . . .' Now they handle things differently, recognizing that removing people from their homes is not the answer. Members of the Community work to bring teenagers from the two communities together, in Belfast as well as at the centre. It surprises the Catholic youngsters that when they say all they want is 'justice', the Protestants feel insecure; and the Protestants are amazed that their wish for 'more security' makes the Catholics get nervous. 'So reconciliation is moving across these lines; telling stories of your own life, hopes and fears in the presence of people from the other tradition. The telling of the stories changes people.'

A favourite example concerns 'Bernard Brett, a lovely man who was severely disabled and could only speak through a board and his finger and thumb – a magic person'. When a group of disabled children came to the centre at Ballycastle, he spoke at worship of how he coped with life in a wheelchair, and how he believed in a God of Love. 'There was almost a flood of tears just listening to this man; it was very moving.

Everyone entered into his story. And then he asked a young woman, who had had a very difficult time, to sing. And this large girl, who a lot of people in wider society may have written off, sang this most beautiful song – she was like a lark. She surprised everyone, including herself. She just radiated newness and difference.'

Corrymeela members – Derick among them – have been involved in a wide range of projects, from radical critiques of the Church to unemployment schemes; from setting up Gingerbread Groups for one-parent families, to starting integrated schools for Catholics and Protestants. A conference programme addresses the concerns of women, families and youngsters. There are connections with the Cross Group, for men and women in both communities whom assassination has bereaved. There are groups supporting long-term prisoners' families. Corrymeela is concerned with the humdrum divisions of poverty, and the extraordinary ones of conflict.

Eight thousand people are welcomed to the Ballycastle centre every year, by a varying group of staff and volunteers. But Corrymeela is a 'dispersed community' and the 150 members promise to further reconciliation in their daily lives. They also pray for one another – or *try* to, Derick smiles: it is 'a very human institution'. Worship and reflection form a focus of their gatherings, carefully structured so that no one feels excluded. At Ballycastle there is a small stone building called the *Croi* (the name means 'heart'), not quite a sanctuary or chapel. Once a year all the members who are able go to Belfast for a joint renewal of commitment. The service, in a tidy modern church, is remarkable for understatement. Even though the leader of a dozen years stood down in 1993, and was making his farewells, the fuss was minimal. 'That's typical of us', my neighbour whispered.

Derick's whole career has been bound up with the Community. In the late 1960s he was tempted to take up a scholarship for study in America, for it was difficult, then, to support civil rights within the Protestant tradition. At an early ecumenical service some Protestants were spat on as they stood. Derick had already rejected the idea of entering the Church: the institution, he felt, was buttressing traditions rather than accommodating difference. But, with Corrymeela as the antidote he needed to the shootings and the taste of fear, he stayed in Ireland, to do community work in one of the most difficult parts of Belfast, with youngsters who had been involved in violence.

Later, he worked full-time at the centre. It was an exhilarating and exhausting seven years, full of 'extraordinary meetings'. His wife, Dorothy, is also a member of the Community – which made things easier. But eventually, they and their four children needed time to themselves, removed a little from the fray. They moved away, and Derick took a post as Research Fellow at the University of Ulster: studying conflict, offering training to trades unions, district councils and church groups, and attempting to take some of what he had learned into the academic culture. The project, 'Understanding Conflict – and finding ways out of it', is separate from Corrymeela but associated.

Discipline and sacrifice are words that Derick does not like. He and his wife made a choice, he says, that's all. Reconciliation, he believes, is not an 'extra', it lies right at the Gospel's heart. Christianity is not about *opposing* evil, he has come to think; it is a call to live in 'contrast' to the prevailing moods of separation and despair. He was brought up in 'a religious tradition rather than a faith tradition; a code, a system of beliefs, a discipline'. To be religious meant to claim superiority, to be exclusive. Identity was the hallmark, rather than forgiveness and love.

But on the 'hill of honey', his experience was different: 'something about being accepted, regardless of what we've done before. A knowledge that change is possible, the possibility of fresh beginnings.' Without the ecumenical community of Corrymeela, Derick thinks he would have cast aside religion – and never known about 'faith'.

NINETEEN

The Question Mark

'You *don't* get rid of distractions – no, no, *no*!' Martine Batchelor exclaimed with Gallic vehemence. I had failed to understand what Zen Buddhist meditation was all about.

'You are aware of your thoughts, your feelings, the sensations in your body, your reactions, the way you look at people': her explanation rushed at me. 'You're very alive. It's not that you see something and cut it out. *Not* at *all*!'

Martine was twenty-one and travelling in Thailand when, through a fortuitous meeting with a monk and a mistake in her ticket, she ended up in Korea. She thought she would study meditation for a month and then find work in Japan. But after three days she decided to become a nun.

Ten years later her teacher, Master Kusan, died. That 'changed everything' – because of their loss, she and a young English monk got talking. 'And we realized we were in love. We wanted to still be Buddhists, but we could not be monk and nun because we wanted to live together.' They left the monastery, got married in Hong Kong and came to live in England. 'I have a tendency,' she says, 'to make decisions quickly.'

She was born in 1953 in Beziers, in southern France. Her accent is still strong and she tells her story rapidly, with sentences that swoop. Her life was 'different' from the start, she says, because her father worked as an engineer on hydro-electric dams and every few years they moved. Martine dreamed of travelling and read a lot of books.

In 1968, the year of student riots in Paris, 'I was fourteen, so I didn't do much – but I would have liked to have been there! My family was socialist, and by the time I was seventeen I started to have anarchic tendencies, and my desire was to make the world a better place to live.' She thought of being a journalist or MP. Religion did not come into it, for her parents were humanists who followed the French norm of only ever going to church three times: 'when you're baptized, when you're married and when you die'.

At eighteen she ran away from home to explore the world. Her first attempt to go to university ended after one week and three hours, the second after three months. 'I just thought it was so dreadfully boring, everybody was so grey; I was living with jazz musicians and I thought it was much more interesting.' Her mother and father found all this rather hard but eventually accepted her choices, as long as she was happy.

She spent a few years between France and England, doing clerical jobs and dabbling in spirituality: Taoism by correspondence, a bit of T'ai chi and a week practising Rajneesh meditation. She went to a talk by 'one of the greatest Tibetan masters', Kalu Rinpoche. But it was Chinese Buddhism that attracted her most: direct and not too complicated, she says, ideal for a 'very practical person' not much taken with philosophy.

Her boyfriend did a little meditation and, she chuckles, was in a band called *Dharma*. In his flat she found a book, 'and reading that book changed my life'. It shifted her outlook from social to spiritual, for its theme was that before you change other people you have to change yourself.

'I decided, "That's a good idea; I should really look into myself and try to transform myself." ' She had had three relationships in as many years and was tired of making the same mistakes; and she was beginning to realize that Free Love was a limited philosophy, as she certainly did not want to share her boyfriend with anybody else. She set out to travel and learn about meditation.

It was fortunate, she says, that her search landed her in

Korea. Nuns there are equal with monks and the people are 'like the Italians – vivacious, open, interested in life'. She arrived at the monastery of Songgwang Sa on the 'biggest day of the year' when there were a thousand people in the temple. She started to help in the kitchen, and shortly afterwards met the Master. To be a nun would be a challenge, she decided, for a year or two.

Fitting into a different culture was not easy. For the Koreans too it was 'a bit tricky' when the foreigners – five men and two women – kept making mistakes. Songgwang Sa was the only temple where English was spoken and which had a group of Westerners; it remained Martine's home even when she was fluent in Korean. But she often went to stay with nuns in Zen halls or nunneries to practise meditation, receive direction and share their life. One very old nun, Songyong Sunim, she especially loved – for her humility and kindness, strength and wisdom, which had developed through years of meditation. Martine translated her poetry and recorded and wrote up her life story: day-to-day dealings with fellow monks and nuns, and a picaresque spiritual journey of hardship, paradox and visions.

Some of Martine's time was eventually taken up by her work as secretary and translator for Master Kusan, accompanying him on visits to the West and guiding visitors round the monastery. But for the first five years she spent most of her days in meditation. 'The first thing you have to do is learn to sit on the floor. Sometimes, you know, your knees are painful, your back is painful; and one is so distracted.' At first, she would slip off after an hour because it hurt too much, but Master Kusan said, 'You must bear beyond strength.' So she decided she would – and very quickly found that though the distractions and pain continued, she could let them come and go.

For ten hours a day, six months of the year, she meditated. 'You stop and then you concentrate your mind on a certain object, which is a question – so that you don't become dull, but you really question and question, and so there is perplexity.' In Korean Zen, she explains, the question and the concentration are the same: 'The question is generally "What *is* it?" You don't think about it; it's not intellectual. In a way, you just become a question mark.' It is, she says, a return to wonderment about the world. She never felt bored but she used to daydream. Now, after eighteen years of practice, when she sits in meditation 'it is pretty quiet and clear . . . it's like resting in the body and the mind, and at the same time you're very aware of what's going on.'

Meditation brought her naturally to follow the Five Precepts: harmlessness, trustworthiness, fidelity, right speech, sobriety. She found she could no longer kill even a mosquito. Her family had been astounded that someone so independent should want to be a nun; but rules, she found, could be a help. 'To be a Buddhist is to have three things together – morality, which is based on compassion; concentration, which is meditation; and wisdom.' The three always go together, she says. The morality is not about rules one must not break, but guidelines to a skilful life. You do not kill, because meditation and wisdom have given you reverence for life.

She likes the absence of a deity in Buddhism: 'You don't depend on someone outside yourself, it's only you.' Her upbringing made her anti-clerical and she did not like 'all those nasty things' the missionaries did; but when she became a Buddhist she started to meet and respect Christians a great deal: 'they were speaking the same language'.

In a photograph from her Korean days Martine is grinning and youthful, with round glasses and a loose grey robe, dyed with charcoal and tied at the side with a bow. She is with two other young nuns, and in front of them stands the diminutive and quizzical figure of Songyong Sunim.

Their heads are shaved: 'Of course, it was great! I did not mind at all, it was very fresh in the summer.' A few years later and a snapshot shows her standing in Hong Kong with her husband after their two-minute civil wedding, grinning as much as ever, and wearing a slightly odd assortment of clothes – for she left the monastery with nothing of her own. A scarf is tied around her head to hide the stubbly growth of hair: this, she says, was for her husband's sake – 'I didn't mind at all!'

She had spent ten years 'sitting on the cushion, concentrating and questioning'; coming to England was 'trying to do it in everyday life, bringing that quietness and clarity into everything you do'. The monastery was her training, she says now; it was only when she started living in a community in Devon that she realized how little she knew.

'Suddenly I was landed with an emotional life, and I went back to being eighteen. All these feeling came up. The first nine months were a little difficult, and I was sticking to my husband like glue!' When you live with seven other people, she remarks, there is nowhere to hide or deceive yourself, and there is always someone you don't get on with. It is especially hard, she laughs, for someone with a Latin temperament: 'In my family the decibel is very 'igh! My 'usband is more placid.' But as a Buddhist 'the first thing you are aware of is your reactions, your suffering, the suffering you might be causing to someone else.'

She and her husband Stephen had only one small room of their own – although this was the least of her problems, since for a decade her corner of the nuns' room was only the size of a park bench. But even getting used to her relationship with him was hard: 'jealousy and not being sure; and loving and how do you love somebody; also how do you nurture love . . .'

Though eclectic in approach, the Sharpham North Community is inspired by the Buddhist traditions of the East. Its members live in a glorious Palladian mansion on a hill which looks across the River Dart, part of an estate bought in 1962 by Maurice Ash. His hope was that spiritual communities in the countryside would again become centres of learning and innovation – the focus of rural life, as the monasteries once were. A Trust set up in 1984 has the purpose of 'enspiriting the countryside'. On the estate there is a vineyard and a bio-dynamic farm; in the house, a programme of talks and retreats run by the Community.

The Community works, Martine believes, because every member is committed to the Precepts and to meditation. The members eat together, share domestic chores and meditate together every morning and evening. Twice a year they have a week of silent meditation. Competition is not a problem, she says, but there are always power struggles. The Community works by consensus – there is no Master, which is unusual in the Buddhist world. It is important, Martine insists, to be grounded in one tradition. She describes herself as 'a Buddhist with Korean tendencies'; other members of the Community had a different training.

Although people come from far afield to the conferences and talks – on shamanism, Tibetan medicine, the 'Way of Tao' and more – the Community is there above all to serve the local people, says Martine; and Totnes is famous as the 'alternative capital' of Britain. In the six years she and Stephen lived as members their door was always open to people seeking friendship and advice. In the end they got extremely tired. A self-contained flat in a spacious wing of the house fell vacant, and they moved in.

Martine had no experience of living out of community, and feared she and her husband would be lonely or get on each other's nerves. But 'at breakfast there was only one person to deal with. It was *very* nice!' It is quite easy being together, she says with some surprise. 'From time to time I flare up a little, but it's getting less and less.' Their flat is sparely decorated with Korean grace: an enormous scroll, bearing the Chinese character for the Buddha in the calligraphy of Master Kusan, hangs on the wall; the courtyard is at peace, with plants in great stone tubs, and palms. The reference point in their marriage as in everything, she says, is meditation, wisdom and compassion.

For Martine, the transition from monastic to lay life was made easier by the Community. Even now, she and Stephen are not far away – they go to the talks and people call in from the estate; Martine still works in the organic vegetable garden, because she likes to be connected with the earth. They teach and write and conduct retreats, and feel involved in the local community in its wider sense. They travel – last summer Martine was interviewing Buddhist nuns in Asia for a book, and the two of them spent the winter teaching in South Africa.

When she first went to Devon Martine got a cleaning job, since everyone in the Community earns their own keep. Her initial reaction was ' "This is really a fall" – my heart sinking, my ego sinking. But there was nothing else I could do, I had no qualifications and I was French on top of it.' But when she began, her Zen training helped her: 'It is about being mindful in whatever you do, being totally present, not judging what you do.' She found she was happy in the work, and her employers were sensitive: 'Every now and then I would be cleaning the toilets and somebody would come and say, "Oh, by the way, can we talk about Buddhist emptiness?" and for ten minutes we'd talk about emptiness and then I'd go back to my toilets.'

But mindfulness questions *any* disturbance, highs as well as lows. 'Recently I was doing my cleaning and then I came home for tea. And there was this letter which sent me overjoyed.' It told her she had won a grant, which meant she could go to Asia to research her book. 'For the next hour I was disturbed, physically. I was so excited I could not work properly. I had to catch myself, watch my breath for a few minutes, come back to being fully present to my actions.'

'Whenever I am quiet, I meditate,' Martine says, 'and whenever I am not quiet I try to be aware . . .' Since she left the monastery, she has moved from rigorous discipline to a fluid response to the moment. When she and Stephen started living in the wing they still joined the Community for meditation sessions. Now they stay at home, and sometimes their meditation is a walk together, in silence, before the working day begins. 'It seems to me the meditation becomes more and more integrated. It's not something I do, it's something I am.'

The Buddha taught that life is suffering – that pleasure always gives way to pain; and sickness, old age and death is the lot of the living. Meditation, Martine explains, is not a way of escaping the world, but of responding to it: you discover an innate wisdom, which helps you deal with even violent emotions.

'You become aware that your pattern is suffering; and once your really *feel* the suffering of your pattern, you can be ready to let go. You think, "Do I want to do this and suffer?" . . . But you can't do it in one day.'

TWENTY

The Swami

Swami Bhavyananda put his fingertips together and closed his eyes. He leant back in his chair and was silent for a long moment. He pondered the question about his origins.

'The Hindus in general believe the present birth is a continuation of the past. The way we use the opportunities of our life develop certain tendencies and those tendencies gradually lead into certain desires. They are to be fulfilled, and when we are not able to do it in this life we continue the journey to the next life. We are born into a particular family, particular circumstances, which will provide us with the opportunity to express ourselves and bring fulfilment to our desires and tendencies.'

Reflectively, he closed his introduction and began to talk of his most recent childhood, enjoying himself and smiling as the recollections came. 'I was born into a family very middle-class. Nothing affluent, but nothing is wanting . . . Five brothers and a sister. The family was all right, as middle-class families go. But the emphasis was always on education – we must all be educated, because that will provide better opportunities.' They lived in a small town twenty-five miles from Bangalore, where his father had gone to get a job and, in his spare time, run a business. He still had land back in his village and savings went into the children's schooling. The Swami (a title of respect, now used exclusively of Hindu monks) was born in 1917.

'There were twenty in a class, maximum, in middle school. Wonderful teachers. They took interest in each pupil, in their personal lives. One teacher I'll never forget. If you weren't good in any subject he'd take you home to help you. Even local shopkeepers, small people, they would take interest. All these people helped in shaping the destiny and character of the children.'

Most of the pupils in the school were of the Brahmin caste. Because society was poor, their parents knew they would not be able to survive as priests: they needed education to get jobs. But often, when the families had scraped together money for the lessons, they could not afford to pay for food. The Swami remembers the 'Brahmin poors' going round the local houses to beg their meals, and his own family feeding his friends. 'This is how mutual support and help was given for education in this small place.'

The secondary schools were in another town and the children stayed in hostels. The establishment the Swami went to had been influenced by Annie Besant and the Theosophical Society: it gave him 'great character', he says. Every month there was a celebration for a great man – a religious leader or scientist. The pupils studied the scriptures of all the major religions. 'That was something wonderful in that place. Many of my Bible quotations I learned in those days!'

The teacher of the Bhagavad Gita was a monk from the Ramakrishna order. The teenage boy began to visit the monastery, where he made some purchases with pennies he had saved. 'I've got still a paper with me I picked up in 1936 from that place: *The Song of the Sanyasin*. I read it, liked it. I bought several pictures.' He and the monk, now eighty-six, recently swapped stories about this time, laughingly testing each other's memories. One of the monk's recollections is of an occasion when he offered the young man some chocolate and observed him putting it in his pocket instead of his mouth. The monk asked why. 'I said, "Today is Monday, I don't eat." ' The monk was impressed by such voluntary fasting, ' "This fellow is capable of doing something!" ' he told himself. The Swami delights in the story, but says his behaviour was not unusual. 'Mahatma Gandhi used to go on a fast. He used to come and stay in our school. We used to go and serve him.'

Swami Bhavyananda was one of a number of young men who started to go to the Ramakrishna monastery every Saturday to study '*character*-forming books! – books that inspired a person to live an ideal life! Swami Vivekananda, his spontaneous lectures; and Ramakrishna, his talks, all recorded. And the Gita, the Upanishads. Even Einstein, Abraham Lincoln . . .' The boys also did physical work, and helped build a gymnasium. A few later became engineers and doctors, but most entered monasteries. 'Some were very brilliant but they renounced everything.' The Swami chuckles: 'Most of them are now retiring! Very few are active still, except me. A few have died.'

Swami Bhavyananda is getting on, and cataracts and diabetes have begun to cause him trouble. Now and then his kind politeness lapses into tetchiness, but it returns. Heavily jowled, bespectacled, he sits behind a solid desk beside a summer window. His crisp orange robes and sandalled feet seem incongruous, though he has been in Buckinghamshire for many years.

The house, now the Ramakrishna Vedanta Centre, used to belong to the writer Edgar Wallace. It is large and very English, with a glorious ten-acre garden. Everything is quiet, with just occasionally a peaceful figure slipping by. There is an airy room for meditation. Lunch is served in the dark-wooded dining-room, adorned with carvings. Monks and novices live on the first floor, where females generally do not go: if any come on a retreat, they stay in the lodge at the head of the drive. The exceptions are visitors (such as interviewers) and the local woman who has long helped out around the house. She brought us coffee, and embarked on a discussion with the Swami about the dyeing of the robes, which she wanted to get started on.

We sat in the study. Behind the Swami's chair was a semi-hidden cupboard in the wooden panelling. He reached into it to get his photographs, of early Indian days. Books filled shelves which faced his desk: Dickens, Tolstoy, various religious classics – and Shirley Maclaine. On the walls were pictures of Jesus and the Virgin Mary; on the side a framed photograph of a bearded man, cross-legged, with only a loose white cloth about his thinness: Ramakrishna.

'Why did you choose to join the Ramakrishna order?' I asked. He was impatient. 'Like you married somebody – I'm in love with him, that's all! And very satisfactory, and he doesn't fight!' The Swami laughed. 'I tell you, a very human relationship is possible with this ideal – wonderful even; such a harmonious, loving, peaceful relationship . . . In India we have this idea – anybody with extraordinary powers of that type, we consider him as an Incarnation. For us, he is that. Christ also. This man appeals to me . . . *Very* satisfactory!'

Sri Ramakrishna died in 1886, in agony from untreated cancer of the throat, at little more than fifty. A large group of disciples had gathered round him over the years, as word spread about his saintliness and wisdom.

He came from a poor village family and was barely educated. His mystic's nature showed itself as young as seven: absorbed in watching a flock of milk-white cranes against a beautiful black cloud, he collapsed and lost all ordinary consciousness. When he recovered, he said he had experienced a state of bliss. It was not a unique occurrence.

As a devotee of the Mother Goddess, Kali, he settled at a temple on the outskirts of Calcutta. For twelve years he survived with scarcely any sleep or food, often in the jungle, in mystical contemplation of the Mother but not knowing if she was reality or symbol. He grew so desperate that he one day seized the temple sword to take his life. And at that moment she appeared to him: 'The buildings vanished from my sight, leaving no trace whatsoever, and in their stead I saw a limitless, effulgent stream of consciousness . . .'[3]

3 See Barbara Foxe, *Harmony in Chaos.*

Ramakrishna spent the rest of his life at the temple. More than once he entered *nirvikalpa samadhi*, the 'superconscious state', a realization of oneness with *Brahman*, 'ultimate reality'. After that he saw God everywhere. In serving people, he felt he was serving God. His followers are still famous for their works of charity: hospitals, famine relief, orphanages and other such. They are also known as universalists, who accept his maxim: 'Truth is one. People call it by many names.' Ramakrishna not only studied all the great religions, he experienced each one. He followed in turn the disciplines and prayers of Zoroastrianism, Christianity, Islam and others, and found they led to the same end.

After Ramakrishna's death, a well-educated Bengali became his most famous disciple; it was Swami Vivekananda who brought Hinduism to the West. After several years as a wandering monk, tramping India, he went to the Parliament of Religions, in Chicago, in 1893. From there, on lecture tours across the States and Britain, he was received with rapt attention. Vedanta centres were set up in America and England.

Vedanta means 'the end of the Vedas', the oldest Hindu scriptures. The Vedantists, from the ninth century on, gave systematic form to the teaching of the Upanishads. But Swami Vivekananda used the word almost as a synonym for Hinduism, to highlight the doctrine of ultimate unity with *Brahman* which he believed formed the religion's essence. He presented Hinduism as the oldest and purest of the world faiths. Indian pride was rekindled; Westerners were inspired. Vivekananda's Vedantism has had great influence, not least through Gandhi and the Independence Movement.

So why, I asked, does it provoke such criticism from other Hindus, such as the followers of Shiva? 'The reason is, it's philosophical. So intellectuals go to it. They are able to put across this thought in a very acceptable and rational way. That's how that particular branch of Vedanta has dominated the world scene. The other schools, of 'devotion' and 'work', have a humbler role to play, as it were. They feel the Vedantists are highbrows.'

Swami Bhavyananda decided early on to join the Ramakrishna order, but was told to finish his education first. His five-year training as a doctor was enjoyable: 'Oh, that's my nature! . . . You can be helpful.' Then, as a novice in the order, he was sent to Karachi, 1,500 miles away. Here he practised prayer and meditation and was trained in scriptural studies. He also helped in an outdoor dispensary. It was 'a wonderful period . . .'

Partition came in 1948. There was 'a lot of confusion. The Hindus were fleeing, the Muslims were migrating into the area and creating problems. So for me it was a hell of a time.' Immigrants, newcomers to the town who did not know the monks, looted their monastery. Going into the streets was dangerous, so the monks stopped wearing the robes as they carried out relief work. Only two of them remained. Swami Bhavyananda was one of them. He helped the numerous young refugees from Sind, fearing they would become 'vagabonds, mischief-makers.'

Eventually he was sent to Assam, on India's mountainous north-eastern frontier. Here he developed medical work at the Ramakrishna centre, and set up schools that are still, he says, 'going on wonderfully'. Education, in territory the Chinese claimed as theirs, was politically sensitive. The monks' classes stopped local boys going away to Christian schools, where they would lose their loyalty to the Indian government. The Swami also made sure the girls were educated, otherwise they would marry Christians, who 'always make mischiefs there'. Missionaries, including Mother Teresa, have shown interest in the region. They would have to accept the same conditions as the Ramakrishna monks, the Swami says, who 'will not convert *one* of the local people into Hinduism. They will worship the gods the local people worship.'

The Swami describes the nineteen years in Assam as among his most creative. But in 1968 there was 'some crisis in

Calcutta. A lot of communists. Therefore all the big first-class education institutions, they were all going to dogs.' The order wanted to send him in as administrator, though he was reluctant. In the end, he was asked to take over the small Ramakrishna London Mission.

Swami Bhavyananda's quarter of a century in Britain has not utilized his medical skills. His work has been 'purely spiritual', though varied. Much of the time he has been involved in education, helping disseminate accurate information about Hinduism for teachers. He is well known in interfaith circles, and is often seen at public occasions with prominent figures. 'That's nothing! I go like this', he indicates his cotton robes. 'I'm not to become important for my dress. I meet the Queen, Pope, Prince Charles – *everybody* I have met. But I won't put on any pretences.'

London is no place for a spiritual life, the Swami says. A house in Holland Park had been donated by a benefactor and the Swami sold it when prices were high; bought and sold a country house with similar success; and raised funds through public work. The order bought the property in Buckinghamshire a dozen years ago.

One English monk has been with the Swami twenty-five years. But few of the five young men ('the boys') living in community are likely to commit themselves for ever. Many have come and gone, staying for three to five years. They take part in the routine of meditation, study and work which begins at 4 a.m. and ends at 9.30 p.m. They learn and move on, and the Swami is quite happy with this. 'We don't *make* them Hindus at all. If they go to church, I encourage them. If they are Christians, perfectly all right. I don't see anything wrong!' It does not even matter if they do not believe in God. 'What is religion? Religion is *be* good and *do* good – that's all. The discipline helps you to achieve this.' So does belief.

Swami Bhavyananda says the hardest thing in the ten-year noviceship is 'taming the ego'. At first he was attracted by the glamour of life outside, but that wore off. He became absorbed in the routine and 'building up a spiritual ideal: "If you know the truth, the truth shall set you free." All other things are props to help this ideal.' He has noticed it is not a life for geniuses (the super-intelligent do not last) because all gifts must be subordinated to the spiritual. It is difficult, in general, for Westerners. They are not brought up to crush the ego, but to cultivate it. To his amazement, they worry what their parents think. He says to them: 'Accept it! If you don't have the courage of your conviction, don't grumble about it!'

The ones who survive are the gentler sort, he says; often those who have struggled in the world and seek 'protection'. He tells me about 'the saint', one young man he expects to stay, who has already been through a broken marriage. This is the type – he tells me anecdotes – who goes the extra mile, returning good for evil. The Swami is evidently fond of him. Even 'the saint', though, can find community life hard. 'When I rub him on the wrong side for something, I say, "How many times have I stepped on your toes today?" He says, "Only twice!" ' The Swami laughs. 'Only twice! That's it! He is very open. He will tell me, "That was not right." I say, "I am sorry. I am the boss." '

Obedience, he tells me with amusement, is not a strong point in the order. The vows are poverty, purity and chastity. The Swami is in charge and treated with respect, but novices do answer back. When we return from lunch he grumbles because the hall light is on, and shuffles up the corridor with a reproach. When an explanation is offered, he apologizes. There are occasions, he admits, when tyranny is tempting. 'Power corrupts me, I must say . . . but absolute power corrupts absolutely – there, one can be spiritually introspective.' He has learned to compromise; after all, he says, the novices are adults.

The Swami will not return to India. 'These boys I have brought up and trained' will care for him with affection, as will friends he has spiritually sustained. He did not find it hard to settle in England: 'to the large-hearted, the whole world is his family!' Now he feels he is so accustomed to talking to Westerners, he lacks the vocabulary to present religion and philosophy to Indians. A senior monk has come from Calcutta, at his request, to help. It will be a long time before an English monk takes over, for the Ramakrishna Mission has not yet taken root and wants to keep its teaching free from syncretism. For now, Swami Bhavyananda is still in charge, and will remain so, 'even when I become disabled. The person who's come will take over – eventually, when I am no more!'

TWENTY ONE

A Faqir

'Shall I tell you the story of my birth? It is rather extraordinary.'

Gai Eaton leaned on the arm of his chair; his back upright, his eyes eager. At his neck was a cravat, worn comfortably with corduroy and Fair Isle; in his hand a cigarette holder. All around were photographs and portraits of beautiful women, his daughters and late wife. A computer and a dancing Shiva stood on an ornate desk. The Surrey sitting-room was dark; in the garden the sun drew out the colours of begonias, voluptuous and draped with rain.

'My mother', Gai began, 'was very modern for her time.' She spoke to him freely about sex, even when he was a child, and told him of her love affairs. He generally calls her by her Christian name, Ruth.

At the age of eighteen, at the turn of the century, she went to London to lead an independent life. A decade later a distinguished ecclesiastical barrister, Francis Errington, took her under his wing. He was thirty years her senior – to her, a second father. But he, unhappily married and haunted by a sense that everything worthwhile was over, fell desperately in love with her. 'One evening, he turns up in the tiny flat she's rented, produces a small pistol and says he'll shoot himself unless she becomes his mistress.'

For ten years they had a secret affair, and then she became pregnant. 'It could have destroyed him – so he thought of a wheeze.' Ruth was to go to Canada on the pretext of settling the affairs of Francis' son, a fruit farmer who had died in the

First World War. There she was supposedly to meet and marry his 'nephew'. Francis insisted she make no friends, in case they learned too much about her.

Ruth went. She looked through photographs of young men under Francis' command who had been killed in the war – and picking the most handsome as her 'fiancé', named him Charles. A Canadian store called Eaton provided a surname. But then she got cold feet. So 'with extraordinary speed' Francis got her a false passport as the wife of Charles Eaton – now announced to be a mining engineer, who had just been offered a wonderful job in Europe. Disguised in a hat with a thick veil, Ruth travelled to Liverpool, where Francis met her and took her on to Dover and then Switzerland. From there, her family received a tragic letter: her husband had succumbed to appendicitis, leaving her with a son, Charles le Gai Eaton; on his deathbed, the child's father had appointed a guardian – his beloved uncle, Francis.

Ruth told Gai the truth when he was sixteen: by then, Francis had become a widower and she had married him. Gai was never allowed to tell him that he knew he was his father.

When Francis died he left a strange will which all but cut Gai's mother out. She took this as proof that he had never loved her and contested it in court. She won: a 'splendid revenge' on a man held in awe by legal colleagues for his impeccable morals. 'It was deeply upsetting for me,' says Gai, 'though I didn't realize it at the time.' Only recently, through recording his dreams, has he come to believe that his father's concern was not solely for his own reputation. Francis had already settled a large fortune on Ruth. And he was a Victorian, to whom illegitimacy was a terrible stigma. By refusing to acknowledge his son, he was protecting him.

Ever since these curious beginnings, Gai Eaton has lived with parallel identities; never everything he seems. His birthday was false, for appearances' sake. His passport was inaccurate, and when he tried to put it right, a baffled civil servant classified him 'stateless' – although he had been working for the government for years. In his twenties, readers of his book *The Richest Vein* thought the author was a sage; when they met him, partying the Jamaican nights away, they were appalled. He continued the wild life for years – even after his conversion, at the age of twenty-nine, to Islam.

But to be a half-hearted Muslim is impossible, Gai says. One day he entered a small white mosque in south India, empty except for three old men. One of them motioned him to climb the minaret. From the top he surveyed the arid landscape, and on impulse raised his hands: 'Lord, here I am,' he said. 'Do with me as You will!' He knew he had taken an irreversible step.

He has been a dedicated Muslim ever since; a *faqir*, a 'poor person' – what is generally known as a Sufi. Such 'spiritual poverty' is inward, and does not require an overt transformation. He says he would have fallen to pieces without Islam, but the only outward change has been benevolence, and serenity in the face of life's uncertainties.

Gai's wife, Corah, was a Christian. His career, from the age of forty, was in the British Diplomatic Service – he had a family to support, and drifted into its smooth Establishment ways. His religion was known at the top (they were reassured, he smiles, by his partiality for gardening) and ensured he was never sent to an Islamic country; yet he never told his colleagues. Since early retirement he has worked part-time as a consultant at the Regent's Park Mosque. The Muslims are his people, he says, and he loves them. But he remains a convert, a Westerner – known more often as Gai than by his Muslim name, Hasan.

It was Sufism, the mystics' path, that drew him into Islam; not its puritanism, which is 'totally alien' to him. He has always felt a tension between the sexual and spiritual; but sexuality, he thinks, is too often oversimplified as a physical impulse. His mother brought him up on Wagner, and he remembers lying in her bed and listening to 'this intense erotic mysticism, bound up with death'. At school he had two pictures in his study: *A Landscape with St Jerome* by Patanir, 'one of the most powerful spiritual paintings I know of'; and Frans Hals' *La Bohémienne*, 'one of the most purely sensual portraits'. They hang now by his bed, 'exact opposites, side by side, that tension . . . and although I don't like getting old, it's extraordinarily interesting. It really is a case of all passion spent, and for the first time seeing all these things objectively.'

Gai grew up among adults, who talked only of the Great War, 'of sudden death, lurking just round the next corner'. His uncles had been killed and there were no young men left for his aunts to marry. He had no cousins of his age, and no friends until he went to school when he was nine. He always felt the 'poor relation' with his father's family; never sure what was known about his birth, and what suspected. There was nowhere to fit in and little security. Since the Germans, he thought, might extinguish him at any moment in another war, he wanted to live life to the full – and *now*.

But he also had a 'hunger' to know the meaning of his own existence: 'I did not see how I could put one foot in front of the other unless I knew where I was going, and why.' His mother had sacked any nursemaid who mentioned religion, determined he should be free to think for himself. She sent him to Charterhouse, where he was taught that the world had risen out of superstition to enlightened reason. The Bible was presented there in the same way as everything else, and therefore made no impact. If religion is not everything, he now says, it is nothing.

Faith in progress has replaced belief in God for people in the West, Gai argues – even Christians. But he discarded evolution of this kind when he was young. He had rushed through the Western philosophers before his teens were out, questing for purpose: but 'these men knew nothing'. The serenity of the writer L.H. Myers appealed much more, so Gai wrote to him and they became friends. When Myers killed himself Gai concluded that his wisdom had not reached his heart. Perhaps, he thought, scholarship was less profound than simple piety.

Myers had introduced him to Hindu Vedanta, which now became his passion. The sense it gave him that the world was a dream beside an 'ultimate Reality' has never left him. From there he moved to the works of René Guénon, a French Muslim who argued there was one 'primordial tradition' – expressed in symbolic form in ancient mythologies, and in the metaphysical doctrines underlying all religions. Far from going forward, Guénon said, humanity regresses: we live in the spiritual dark age which anticipates the End.

Gai began to feel a stranger in the twentieth century and learned to conceal his views. 'But the thing about René Guénon's writings is that either he convinces you so totally that from then on, intellectually, you think you know the answers; or else you find him absolutely intolerable and throw the book away. I was one of those who were convinced.' Although he came under pressure from Guénon's friends to practise what he preached, he was not ready.

Gai was twenty-nine. He had been married for six years to an actress and they had a son, who was being cared for by his in-laws. The marriage was not going well. When the opportunity arose for him to get a job with a friend in Jamaica, his wife suggested a break would give them a chance to work things out. But Jamaica had an extraordinary effect on young Englishmen, Gai says. He hints at glamour, and paints vague pictures of rum, women and song. Two years later he returned – to find his wife out at an audition and three passionate letters on the mantelpiece from his Jamaican lover: 'From that moment the marriage was dead.' Shortly afterwards he got a job teaching English in Cairo.

But he was still obsessed by his Jamaican. His students were astonished when he read love poetry aloud in class, with tears streaming down his face. A warm relationship grew up with these young people, and Gai came to love their Muslim faith. He also paid regular visits to a friend of Guénon – an English

Muslim, whom he refers to as 'ML' to preserve the anonymity the Sufis prefer.

Eventually, Gai decided he must go back to Jamaica, but he also feared it as 'a deep dark hole into which so many had fallen'. He went to ML and asked him to give him the *shahada*, the declaration of Unity from the Qur'an that frames the Muslim faith: 'I declare that there is no God but Allah, He is one and has no partner. I also declare that Muhammad is His servant and His messenger.' It was Ramadan, and next day he fasted. He was a Muslim.

Passivity was one of the reasons he took this step, Gai says. He was afraid both to enter the fray of Jamaica and to throw himself into Islam. He knew of others who had made a nominal conversion – perhaps for marriage – which had sooner or later got a grip on them, 'and from starting out insincerely as hypocrites, they ended up as really believing Muslims'. He rather liked that prospect.

It was some years later that he handed himself over to God at the top of the Indian minaret, and completed what he calls his 'predestined homecoming'. Muslims hate to be called fatalists, he explains, but 'all our destinies are reckoned from the beginning of time. We have free will because we don't know what's going to happen.' The idea suited him. He had always felt he was 'non-viable', not a survivor: 'I was convinced of this – I had simply to leave myself open to whatever happened. I never really made an effort to achieve things, and they just fell into my lap in the most extraordinary way.' Like leaving Cairo for a passion (his friends thought he was mad, or possessed) – just three months before the anti-British riots. Several of his former colleagues were killed, he ponders, the others stranded in a hostile city; he was sitting on a Jamaican beach.

His belief in destiny means there is little he regrets: Islam has helped him to accept whatever is. The test, he says, was the death eight years ago of Corah, his second wife. She was Jamaican, though he married her in London, and in nearly thirty years of happiness they spent only six weeks apart. 'We really were extraordinarily close. It was very much like losing a limb, and if I could accept that I could accept anything.' The next day he got up and said his prayers.

He meditates for a minimum of ten minutes, three times a day. The practice has become the basis of his life. Like all Sufis he belongs to a *tariqa*, a 'path', guided by a sheikh (which literally means 'old man' – but in this context, 'spiritual master'). And 'the whole spiritual method of this *tariqa* is the invocation of the name of Allah, because for us God is present in His name . . . If every other Islamic practice were impossible, it would be sufficient to invoke the name with the meditations he has given us.'

The Sheikh is of Swiss origin, a universalist, influenced by Guénon. He called the *tariqa* after Mary – *Maryamiyya* – because of his belief in 'the intervention of the Blessed Virgin'. It has been shrouded in secrecy, Gai said, for twenty years, but recent events make it possible to talk more openly.

He sketched in the story. 'One of the great spiritual masters of all time, Sheikh El-'Alawi, received the Swiss universalist in North Africa in the early 1930s, and gave him the authority to invoke the Divine Name. He came to understand he was predestined to be a sheikh himself after Sheikh El-'Alawi's death, and quickly gathered round him a group of followers'. These were mostly intellectuals in powerful positions, who kept their Islam quiet. The United States became his home, 'and all sort of difficulties have arisen. You can probably imagine, in the American atmosphere, what can happen to such a group . . .' There were disagreements, a scandal, a court case – and the *tariqa* shot from secrecy to unwelcome publicity.

The sheikh, a very old man, grew weary of these troubles and has now told his followers that they are independent. 'Everyone is puzzling as to what that means . . . it presents a problem, because there is a saying in Sufism that he who does not have a master has Satan for his master.' But Gai admits he enjoys independence and feels happy with the decision: 'I ask God's forgiveness if I'm wrong.'

Alone, and with friends, he hopes to carry on the invocation. It is, he explains, a powerful technique. 'But to say precisely how it works for me is extremely difficult. You see, the moment you try to verbalize these things you falsify them, that's the trouble.' It's like being in love, he adds – who can define that, even to their closest friend? 'It's now an automatic response, either to anything beautiful that I see – a landscape, a picture, even a person – or to fear or alarm or worry; my response is simply the Name, the Name in the heart, the Name which comes out as an affirmation . . .'

Originally the *tariqa* was mainly for Westerners, recently augmented by large numbers of young people who were born as Muslims but formed by the West. Life in America and Europe is so busy, the sheikh has told them, that they must concentrate on the essentials. Prayers are cut to the minimum, and while many traditional practices take over an hour, their method of saying the rosary takes minutes. But it is their universalism which some regard as dubious. 'Nobody is accepted into the *tariqa* if they deny that Christianity is a perfectly valid religion, that Hinduism is a valid path to God and so on. That, to "fundamentalist" Muslims, is horrifying.'

In Islam, Gai says, what you do is between you and your creator. If you commit a grave sin you cannot harm God, so it's up to you what risks you are prepared to take. But what you must not do is set a bad example to the Muslim community, the *ummah*. 'Now this is extremely practical. Modern people will call it hypocritical. They want to shout their sins from the housetops and encourage everybody else to do what they're doing. This, in Islam, is itself a kind of hypocrisy, because what they're really trying to do is justify themselves.' The last thing you should do, Gai says, if seeking to be 'normal', is copy other people: 'Normality relates to a norm which is not of human devising . . .'

For a believer, the deviser of the norm is God; for nonbelievers, he suggests it could be Nature. 'I might say God is the human and humanizing face of Reality . . . Because man is the *khalifah*, the representative of God on earth, that human element in Reality is very deep in it.' The word 'person' is too limiting for God, yet, 'He's there . . . He's for us and we can speak to Him.' Is he within us or totally separate from us? 'He's both.'

In Islam, God is called by different names and many contradict each other – Lifegiver, Slayer; the Merciful, the Wrathful. That too suits Gai, who long ago gave up trying to appear consistent. 'It is precisely in the invocation of the name that the opposites are reconciled – but that is why I cannot explain it in ordinary discourse. There is in the scientific age a conviction that everything can be explained up here', he taps his forehead. 'This is simply not true. Everybody I've known has been a mass of contradictions.'

TWENTY TWO

Skid Row

Perched on a chair, with one leg folded underneath her, Say Leddington seems thin and nervy. There is a quake in her pale voice. Dark hair strays from an attempted pony tail, and is continually tucked behind her ears. She wears black leggings and fidgets with a cardigan, clutching it to her and pushing up the sleeves. But such mannerisms are belied by her assurance. At twenty-three, Say is only the third woman to lead the Simon Community in London.

On 1 September 1963 a probation officer called Anton Wallich-Clifford made 'an act of faith'. He had been looking for a new way of working with the destitute, and in one 'fleeting, dazzling moment, I had the answer: to . . . throw all hopes, ideas, ambitions, plans and future in the lap of God. To get a place, and have nothing of one's own but debt and the conviction that the plan would succeed. This would be really to identify, really to take on the same insecurity – the same unpossessing, unbelonging, unsquare living as those whom one would gather together in a close-knit group . . . To be a beggar for beggars!'[4]

And so it was. The venture was named after Simon of Cyrene, who did not take the cross away from Christ but helped him carry it. From the beginning Wallich-Clifford and his friends set out to draw attention to their cause: Simon was a campaign as well as a community. In the last thirty years, it has inspired or spawned coutless other 'grassroots' social

4 Anton Wallich-Clifford, *No Fixed Abode*

projects. But the London-based Simon Community is the only one to retain and practise the philosophy intact.

Or almost. There have been two significant developments. First, whereas the original members were predominantly Roman Catholic (devout enough to worship together and place crucifixes on the walls) few of the current workers or residents are religious. The Community is still attached to a Catholic church and the founding principles, based on Christian teaching, remain strong. There is even a chapel, which is being renovated – but as a place of reflection, comfortable for those of all faiths and of none. Secondly, though Wallich-Clifford expected the workers to be in middle-age and eager to make long-term commitments, most of the volunteers today are young, taking time before or after college. There is a rapid turnover. Unusually, Say has stayed for over two years and has seen over a hundred fellow workers come and go.

Affectionate first impressions come to her mind: 'I remember arriving at St Joe's, the "second tier house". It was a *crazy* day! There was quite a lot of tension going on, and I just didn't know what it was all about. I remember listening to Nellie and Fred, two residents, bickering *all* afternoon about things I just didn't understand at all. I got fed up with them yapping and told them to bring it up at the next breakfast meeting. I feel quite proud that I knew to say that on my first day! But I remember thinking, "Gosh, if I have to live here how on earth will I cope with all this tension?" In the evening they had a very very intense house meeting. I was quite overwhelmed with the intensity of communication and the confrontation that went on – everybody talking about philosophy but also manipulating it to their advantage.'

It was a relief to hear she was to work at the King's Cross night shelter, where discussion took second place to practicalities. She remembers being frantically active there, endlessly running up and down stairs. The shelter is the beginning, for many, of their life with the Community. Simon does liaise with other organizations, but does not accept referrals. It aims to catch people who have fallen through the net. Every night of the year a street team roams the areas popular with those who sleep rough. 'The idea is to meet people on their own terms, and then build up that relationship by talking, offering tobacco . . .' If a bed is available they may be invited back to the shelter, where they may stay for up to five successive nights.

From there, some feel they want to spend more time with the Community, and move to the 'first tier house' at Hackney. This was where Say too was sent, after her first three months, and where she spent her happiest time. Up to nine residents can be squeezed in, though then 'the group gets incredibly intense and dynamic and it will blow up and people will leave . . .' The optimum number is five, who may stay for several months to learn the Simon ropes. The nature of homelessness had been Say's study at the shelter; here she grasped the philosophy of the Community. Its emphasis is more on working and caring *with* the homeless than *for* them, she explains. 'We accept people as they are and don't try to change them. We try to live in voluntary poverty together. It's all very well helping, but it's important to know what it *feels* like for these people. I'm sharing some of my life with them.'

Residents who want to stay move to one of two 'second tier houses'. If they settle in London's St Joseph's they will take part in the 'Mission of Caring on Skid Row', doing 'outreach' work on the streets, helping in the office or simply making cups of tea. If they choose to go to the farm, near Canterbury, they will cultivate the land. Commitment is essential in both houses, for 'we expect quite a lot from people, a willingness to live in a group and participate'. Many stay for years, and know more about the life than workers, who pass so rapidly through. There is a wide network, Say remarks, of people who once lived in Simon and moved on.

If they return, as they often do, only the residents who have been around for a decade or so will recognize them. The former homeless hold the Community's history.

Say lived briefly on the farm, and for almost a year at St Joseph's. For much of that period she also worked at Simon's administrative headquarters, a dilapidated Camden basement and ground floor. Here, as one of two Community leaders, she still spends much of her time. It was with some reluctance she took on the role. But she realized no one else had her experience. Well, she admits with a little laugh, perhaps she *did* quite want to give it a go.

The two leaders work closely together for a minimum of six months, and share a flat: 'the first time I had a room of my own for ages and ages! Even that felt like luxury. And so, yes, there's more personal space now that I've been here longer, and I also think it's needed more now. I need to be detached in some way from the everyday running, to make difficult decisions and see things more objectively.' The leaders are accountable to a management committee of which they are also members. They are responsible for everything from the recruitment and welfare of residents and workers to finance, campaigning and the maintenance of buildings. Say deals with accountants and solicitors, and manages vehicles which she cannot even drive.

At first she lost her nerve, she says, and her anxiety was constant. Over the months she gained in confidence and resilience to criticism. She now confronts and then laughs off the surprise occasionally voiced that a woman can do the job. She has acquired detachment. 'I've learned about putting myself first sometimes to survive, and about how I cope as an individual; what makes me happy and what doesn't. I'd felt confused about that, quite torn – whereas now I just say, well this is me, and that's fine.'

The office is accessible to every member of the Simon Community. She likes the communication that results. 'It's amazing, if people've just dropped in to get their money for the rest of the week, how you end up talking about a problem in the house that they didn't realize they wanted help for. Sometimes I will spend a whole day chatting and then think, "Gosh, I've got to get on!" and type away at night . . . It's quite important to me to get on and think. I find I'm surrounded by people all the time, and that does become quite intense.'

Knowing when to stop, to immerse herself less thoroughly – this has been one thing Say has had to learn in Simon. At first she thought she did not need time off, and the sense that her life has purpose still makes her jump from bed to start the day. But she lost weight, and often fell sick. A stomach complaint, which she forgets in the absorption of the work, is exacerbated by the stress and diet. Companionable smoking with the residents increased her cigarette consumption. She now takes regular breaks, but 'I'm not as fit as I used to be, and I'm always more tired . . . so it does wear you down.'

Workers are on duty all the time: 'though it doesn't feel like it – it feels like your home.' They share bedrooms, meals and all facilities with residents. The main difference, as Say remarks, is that workers have a home to go back to and plans for a different future. They also have one day off a week – a forty-hour period, which they are encouraged to spend in a separate workers' house. Pocket money is gauged to match the benefits that residents rely on. They have enough to go to a band or a pub on their day off, and get £250 each eleven weeks to pay for ten days' leave.

Say describes the workers as a catalyst: they enable others to participate and to communicate. The daily breakfast meetings provide an opportunity for discussion and support. There are only three rules in Simon: no drink, no drugs and no violence in the house. Anybody breaking these can be asked to go, by any member of the household. 'I remember asking a resident to leave because I thought he'd been *supporting* lots of the other residents' benders on the drink.

He got quite angry, but a few months later he was sending me Christmas cards, had got himself a place to stay and in a sense it had done him a favour. He respects me for ever!' She laughs, with slight embarrassment.

When Say first arrived at Simon she was trodden on, she thinks. 'I remember residents coming in drunk and demanding tea. I learned quite quickly the ways to say "No" nicely, and still be respected. I got very endeared to that group of people. They were hard to live with, but when the positive things came up they meant so much more. Like when one woman decided to go dry for a couple of days after me talking to her for four hours the night before; and then letting me wash and comb her hair. It felt like a real privilege.' That is still what Say loves about living at Simon: 'those little times when you're allowed some access to someone's life, and they let you "carry" them when normally they're too proud'.

Many of the residents have problems with mental health, which can disrupt community life. But when you live with people, Say remarks, you discover unexpected qualities and are able to forget their illness. 'One man who is quite ill and quite uneasy is one of the most perceptive people I know. It's always, "Are you all right, Say? You're looking pale today . . . Are you getting enough pocket money?" ' She relies on her friendships with the residents for support and invests far more in them than in her fellow workers. She knows they will not be moving on so fast – and anyway, 'I'm here for homeless people'.

When Say arrived at Simon she did make friends among the workers of the time. But she has not become attached to their successors: 'I always wanted to work harder than they did, ran around a lot more and would see different values. I always found it hard when people laughed at a particular resident, and I guess that's still true now . . .' There have been times when she has earned a reputation among her peers for being confrontational and 'giving off disinterested messages'.

When long-term residents leave, Say finds it difficult. Over the summer there had been a spate of deaths. She particularly mourned Fred, whom she had first encountered 'yapping' on the day that she arrived. He had lived in the Community for twenty-eight years and was 'quite an example of what we're here for'. His story has strands in common with many other people she has worked with.

'He had been incontinent since he was eight, and that gave him a weakness down one side from an unpronounceable disease. He'd been married quite young, had a child and divorced his wife. He was quite upset about that. Always involved in petty car thefts. His parents died when he was quite young and his brother, his only other contact, in 1984 . . . He was in and out of prison and had had a pre-frontal lobotomy, which was supposed to deal with these petty crimes. It was a disaster . . .' In a vain attempt to get compensation, he constantly fired off letters to MPs.

Fred became increasingly immobile, and Say would attempt to wheel all 17 stone of him down the road, to his muttered accompaniment of 'Weak as a kitten, weak as a kitten!' He was a cantankerous old man, she says, but always behaved as a father. Obsessed with matches, he 'was a bit of a pyromaniac' and regularly set fire to things. But he was 'mentally alert, very very perceptive, very aware. He always used to tell me exactly what was going on in the house whenever I came home.' Lectures about the values of Simon were delivered to residents and workers, and if anyone stepped over the bounds of correct behaviour Fred would tell them they would soon 'be down the farm' – by which he meant, in the form of ashes.

Most of Simon's residents are middle-aged or elderly men, of working-class origins. Their homelessness has complex sources, and they need the support the Community offers. Only rarely are there residents in their teens and twenties, because there is other provision in London for homeless people of that age. Anyway, Say remarks, they do not combine well with youthful workers. There can be 'quite a lot of role confusion' – they are liable to fall in love. Romantic entanglements of this kind are frowned on within the Community; even when Say started going out with a fellow worker she tried to be discreet. 'The group is always put before the individual.'

Long before Say came to Simon she had liked to be available when others were in need. She volunteered for the university nightline, and always listened to upset friends who knocked on her door in the early hours. Conflict had also been part of her life, from early years. The first time she threw someone out for difficult behaviour, it felt familiar. 'When I was eighteen, I actually asked my father to leave our house.' She has barely seen him since.

He had never shown real interest in her, or in her mother, she says. School work offered an escape and a way to prove herself. She was solitory, an only child until she was eleven, with scattered friends. The family was poor, but Say won a grant to an independent school in Bristol. It was difficult relating to the other pupils: 'I always felt quite embarrassed about bringing people home, whereas now I'm proud of the fact that I was brought up in a council house.' For several years she lived with her grandmother, sharing the 'simple life': an unheated cottage, chickens, ducks and jam-making – she sums up its appeal. Say misses the country.

At Durham University she did a dissertation, for her Geography degree, based on the village she grew up in. She was appalled to discover the scorn that people who had bought their council houses felt for neighbours who still rented. 'In society, I just feel that lots of people will do the best for themselves all the time, and forget that perhaps they were once in that situation themselves.'

It amuses her that she went to Durham, so pervaded by the public school ethos she dislikes. Every term she started with less money than others, and ended up with more. Frugality gives her pleasure: at Simon, she enjoys wearing clothes from the common store of cast-offs. 'Basic living' was one of the appeals of moving to Simon, while other students headed for accountancy. Her mother is proud, though concerned about her health; relatives wonder, she smiles, when she is going to get that 'proper job'.

There was another motive for Say's choice. As a child she was religious: 'I had lots of faith. I can't remember not praying.' After school she spent three months at Taizé, the ecumenical community in France, where she loved the raw conditions, connection with nature and hard work. Shortly before she started at Simon, she stopped praying or thinking about God. But she sees her life there as 'Christianity in action'.

When Say leaves the Community she wants time to think and to reflect on faith. 'To me, there's a spirituality which is of God; and there's the other, which is inside you, that can motivate you on. And I think that's quite big for me, otherwise I'd probably have left. Because it's not always easy.'

Postscript: In April 1993 Say Leddington left the Simon Community. She spent some time living at the Society of Christ the Sower, Little Gidding.

TWENTY THREE

A Hermit

Mount Tabor Hermitage was the address. When I asked a man where Sister Irene lived he directed me half a mile beyond the hamlet to a mobile home by the side of the road.

Snow-covered mountains crossed the skyline, the highest one Croagh Patrick. In the summer the setting must be charming ('anyone would pray!' Irene enthused); in the winter it was wild but beautiful. I could believe her when she said the weather sometimes kept her awake at night: all afternoon, the caravan was slashed by wind and rain and, though the turf fire kept it snug, she showed me the sodden piece of cloth blocking a gap where the rain came in.

She glowed with health – her cheeks were rosy, her complexion bright. She wore a fawn habit, with a Celtic cross sewn onto it, and a veil. Although her manner can be sharp, her gaze is calm. She says she is happier than she has ever been because she is at peace, doing God's will. The hardship does not bother her: 'I think I have a special grace . . . I always find that simplicity and poverty help my spirit.'

Nevertheless, there will be central heating and a shower in the hermitage she is building a little further down the road. The renovated cottage which will form its core was almost ready to move into. We went to have a look at it – struggling down a long track, right into the squall; across a stream bridged by rickety boards, which she is currently replacing with stone at a cost of several thousand pounds.

Much of the restoration work she has carried out alone: 'It's remarkable, I've never had any experience with building.

The knowledge comes as I'm doing it, and if that's not divine intervention, I don't know what you call it.' St Joseph, she believes, is helping her. A year ago she made a novena (a set of nine prayers) to him and after 1 May, the Feast of Joseph the Worker, 'everything started rolling – and I'm not exaggerating. People came, sacrificing holidays, lots of voluntary helpers . . .' She has also had steady assistance from a village man and has paid a labourer to do the more specialized jobs, with money donated for the hermitage's cause. When she looked back on 1992 at the end of the year, she was overwhelmed with gratitude. 'I feel so happy when I come home in the evening I can't pray, I can just say, "Thank you, Jesus, for everything! You're just giving me so much!" '

Sister Irene is hoping to be joined by other women who want to live the hermit life. Many have written, expressing their enthusiasm. It all sounds rather sociable, but hermits are not always isolated. What Irene visualizes is a cluster of individual huts or 'cells', one for each sister. Most of their time would be spent in solitary prayer, but twice a day they would gather in a chapel in the central building. Irene hopes to have a priest to say Mass, and a couple of 'brothers'. The hermits would generally eat and work in their cells; though there would also be goats to tend and wood to chop. 'Empty chatter' would be forbidden on their daily round; on Sundays 'we'll go up to the mountains, and stretch our legs and walk and chat and enjoy ourselves, hiking a bit.'

Across Europe and America there is a rising interest in the hermit life. But it is not always easy to pursue, for the hermit's vocation, while admired in the Orthodox Church, long ago dropped out of favour in the West. Sister Irene emphasizes the traditional nature of her plan: 'I'm not doing anything new. I'm just reintroducing an ancient way of life that the Irish monks used to live and that was very much part of our inheritance.' She is a devout Catholic: loyal to Rome, anxious to abide by the rules. Even so, it has been a long struggle and her desire for recognition as a hermit has often been regarded as impertinent. It took her years to find her own vocation. When she did, it was many months before she was finally allowed to make her vows before the Archbishop of Tuam in October 1990 – the first professed hermit in modern Ireland.

Irene Gibson was born thirty-five years ago, 'on the Feast of St Joseph', the fifth of eight children. She grew up in the country, a few miles out of Dublin. 'I used to love to go and wander off in the fields, and I think that's really where I got my contemplative vocation. And one time I saw this Capuchin friar. He had his brown habit on and just the sandals with no stockings and his head was cast down, and he was walking. He made such an impact on me! I remember standing still and thinking, "Gosh, he's like Jesus!" and saying to myself, "*I* want to be a monk . . ." I didn't want to be a nun because the nuns were teaching me and I *certainly* didn't want to be a teacher; and I didn't like them because they used to slap me.'

Irene's education fell behind because she suffered from *petit mal*, a mild form of epilepsy which causes bouts of unconsciousness. The medication made her 'go a little berserk, I was wild'. She irritated the neighbours and was thrown out of several schools. The fits, and the tablets, stopped at fourteen: 'It was like coming out of a black hole. I realized, "My God, I'm alive! My goodness, I know nothing!" ' She was determined to catch up.

But her suffering had left her bitter. She remembers sitting in the library of her school, with its glass walls surrounded by corridors, as the bell rang for a change of class. The boys left her indifferent, but as she watched the chattering girls she was filled, as always, with loathing. ' "Why do I hate all those girls?" ' she asked herself. 'And the answer was, "Because they have friends and you don't." ' She asked why that was, 'and the answer came back again, "Because of your attitude to other people, because you're jealous of them." ' The Holy Spirit, Irene believes, was prompting her to face the truth. She smiles with pleasure as she describes the 'inner glow of grace', the instantaneous change that she experienced. Next day she stood at the school gates and greeted her surprised contemporaries with warmth. 'I found people becoming beautiful instead of bad, which I saw in everybody before – which was in me, of course, projecting my badness onto others. And after that, everything became so different.'

For some time she had been 'searching for a meaning to life'. If all that was in store was marriage, a job, old age and death, she wasn't interested: there must be something else. Her upbringing, she says, was not especially religious. Yet her mother went to Mass every day and when the holy pictures were taken down, in response to the reforms of the Second Vatican Council, insisted on leaving the one that hung behind the kitchen door. When Irene had a chance she looked at it more closely. It was tattered, but the words beneath were legible: a prayer for a mother to recite while her child was having an epileptic fit. How many times, Irene thought with awe, that prayer must have been said.

On her teenage quest for meaning she sent her mother 'up the wall with worry' as she rummaged through 'Religion' in the library and brought home books on everybody from the Mormons to the Buddhists. Then, in an attic, she found an old family Bible: 'I took it down and devoured it. And everything I was looking for was in that'.

She started to spend the lunch hour at the local church, where a vision of the Sacred Heart 'neither interior nor exterior . . . it's hard to describe' left a powerful impression on her. A look of sternness crosses her face: 'Of course, I was only at the beginning of my fervour, so I had to have these experiences to get me going. I don't have anything like that now, I can assure you.'

Everything 'became God' to her; all that she encountered spoke to her of Christ, 'so that's a proof of when a person is in love'. Perhaps she would be a missionary, she thought, and channel her fondness for science into medicine. Contemplative orders were unknown to her, but she quickly found, when she visited convents, that the only thing she liked about them was the prayer.

The 'real turning-point' of Irene's life was imminent. She was preparing for a 'Life in the Spirit seminar', and was excited: 'people lay their hands on you and you receive a new life in the Spirit'. But first she felt she must be purified; the burden of 'a sin which for me was a mortal sin', committed at the age of eleven, weighed her down. One day she felt she *must* go to confession and 'all of a sudden something kind of carried me into town' – and on, to an obscure church down on Dublin Quays. Inside, 'the light was on in the confessional and it was just me and the priest; the whole church was there for me.'

She asked the priest to come and hear her confession face to face, 'a really cheeky thing to do!' He sat next to her on the bench. She struggled through the little sins until at last, 'when I got to that particular one, I broke down and I cried and I cried and cried. And he kept looking at me saying, "It's all right, it's all right." ' Reliving the scene, Irene leans closer, with shining eyes and shaking voice: 'I was so overcome! I didn't even wait for him to give me absolution, because I knew at that moment when I'd told my sin I was healed. I was walking on air! I've never looked back.' And Sister Irene laughs even now, amazed with joy.

A Dominican priest she knew had advised her to enter 'a jolly convent with lots of singing'. But Irene was convinced she ought to join the Carmelites. She tried them and was disappointed – in that particular house they didn't seem to keep their rule of silence. Then she joined one of the English Benedictine houses, moved by the 'deep, deep silence' and the sisters' *reverence* – a thing she hungered for. The singing delighted her and she became a chantress. But her three years there were the hardest of her life. There were rules about how to cut the bread, and how to sit at table. Almost out of her mind, she lost all sense of who she was. 'The system' got hold of her, she says, until she could hardly make the decision to leave.

But she was eventually granted a year away. By now she was sure that she was to be a hermit. In prayer, she had felt she was on a mountain top, but she could see her body at its foot: 'In other words my *spirit* was on the mountain . . . for me it was clear that God was calling me to live apart and alone.' A man in a Dublin library told her about the Carthusians in Italy; she went to join them for three months. Here she was doubly 'enclosed' – in her cell, and within the monastery walls – but 'the first thing I experienced was a tremendous freedom, an unbelievable freedom.' She could *be herself* at last, 'and I felt – if you'll forgive the expression – I could almost be "naked". Because it's just you and God, and he loves you *as you are*!'

Certain of her calling, Irene left the Benedictines and returned to Ireland, which she missed. But she knew there were no Carthusians there. For the next two years she wandered the country, trying to persuade every abbot she could find to allow her to park a caravan on the monastery land. They told her she would be a liability – what if she had a nervous breakdown? Some feared she might be a temptation to the monks. A vocation to be a hermit is rare, they all agreed, and it was unlikely she would have it.

'I felt a desperate loneliness at not being understood.' One day she broke down in tears and asked God what to do. 'An inner voice said to me, "You know, you don't have to live in a hermitage to be a hermit; you *are* a hermit." And I realized that the very fact I was a marginalized person – that was the essence of my vocation.' From then on she understood that 'the sky and everything was my hermitage; but the real hermit was within.'

She finally found stability on the Aran Islands, where she was welcomed by the Aisling network.[5] But while she was there a new restlessness began to trouble her. She wanted to make a lifelong commitment to her calling. In the 1980s

5 See Chapter 1.

a new Code of Canon Law was introduced, which allowed for hermits to be 'legalized' – if they made public vows of poverty, chastity and obedience, and presented their constitution to the bishop. Sister Irene had already made a vow of virginity, but she wanted to go further. She wrote letter after letter to the Archbishop of Tuam asking to take the hermit's vows, all to no avail, until the Aisling priest Dara Molloy had a quiet word in his ear . . .

And still it was not the end. Her vows attracted newspaper coverage, and letters started to arrive from women wanting to live like her. She decided she must build a hermitage. After a year, she left the Aran Islands. As an outsider she had felt unwelcomed by the islanders; though warmly accepted by the Aisling network, she wanted greater privacy to work out her future. For five months she lived in a mobile home at the back of a pub ('What a place to have a hermitage! I can tell you, I heard some things!'), while she looked for a house. She found the ideal: it was derelict, owned by the Forestry Commission. They said she could not have it; until she wrote to the Bishop, who rang the Chief Executive – who offered her instead the crumbling building in County Mayo she is now restoring. The landlord of the pub gave her the mobile home, which she lives in still. For money she relies on gifts, and encourages publicity partly because of her need for funds. She has settled at last, and enthuses about the welcome she has met among the villagers of Drummin.

Sister Irene's day is on the Benedictine pattern. She gets up at 4 a.m. and from then until she goes to bed the day is punctuated by the Divine Office. In the evening, tired after her labours, she relaxes; and 'I could be up to three hours praying and I don't even know. Just sitting with the Lord and trying to open my heart to his life and talking to him in my heart . . .' Her relationship with God started off as a romance, she says, but it has deepened. 'I don't have any feelings of God. My prayer is totally, totally dry, like a desert. I get no emotional satisfaction in prayer, no nice consolation feelings, no visions, nothing.'

She spends some of her time doing craft work. There is a small printing press in the caravan for making cards, and an unexpected, brightly painted Buddha sits on the table – 'yer man over there', an aid to peace.

Her door is never locked, for 'the person you turn away might be God himself. I mean *you* could be Jesus for all I know!' – for a minute, she was helpless with laughter. She rarely feels nervous, but 'memories come back, regrets, things like that. And also you get a lot of temptation. I mean, as a woman, one thing I find particularly difficult is chastity. It seems when you come into solitary places you see more beautiful men than any other place. And one particular face could haunt you for days, and you have to keep on remembering the commitment you made.'

She called her hermitage after Mount Tabor, the mountain where Jesus was transfigured before his disciples' eyes, while he was praying. It is an image of the contemplative life 'and the moment of total enlightenment that we must aspire to. That's what prayer does for you, it purifies you and makes you more like God; and that's what we are born for – to become like God.' And how does she think of God? 'He's the air that I breathe, he's everything; he's in everything and everything is in him.'

People often ask her what she *does*, and why she is not working for the poor. 'What I do,' she replies, 'is offer *myself* to God.' She has absolute faith in her vocation and 'a total belief in the power of prayer. You have to have that as a hermit. You have to believe that you don't need to be *doing* with your hands, but just being with God, and that is the important thing.'

Postscript: A few weeks later Sister Irene's mobile home was blown over in a storm and she moved into the hermitage.

TWENTY FOUR

The Green Monks

Anelog, Sebastien and Hereward live in a Victorian house in Kentish Town. They wear long robes of green, brown and off-white stripes, the 'dresses' of the Graigian Community, of which they are the only members. Some three hundred people, however, have joined the Graigian Society.

Sebastien and Hereward are 'brothers'; Anelog, the founder and leader of the Community, is 'the Venerable'. The house, their monastery, has a Bohemian air, reflecting their concern at the decline of Taste. The studio is filled with old pine furniture, strewn with sunlight. Pottery, drapes, paintings and masks tumble over tables and across the gallery floor, and plants cascade from shelves.

The 'Green Monks' laugh a lot, but take themselves very seriously. 'Our philosophy is completely new', Anelog says. They acknowledge no debt: 'We have understood or experienced all of it ourselves, or it has been revealed to us.' They claim their Community, founded in 1983, begins the third monastic movement in history, after those of the Buddhists and Christians. They are eager to expand, but 'people like ourselves don't grow on bushes; people with the same amount of dedication,' Anelog declaims. 'Most people want fun and superficiality. What you must understand is that we're miles away – or even further – from conventional life. It's so extraordinary and different, our life here, it's very enclosed and introspective. It's very serious.' Nobody has been able to stick it out since Hereward, who joined in his early twenties almost ten years ago.

It is the 'robotic' culture of modern Britain, particularly suburbia, which Graigianity abhors. 'Industry and Christianity have pushed aside the sensitive and poetic in humanity and have abused nature,' Anelog complains with rising anger: people have let fashion make them mechanical to the point where they no longer know what they feel. 'That's why hardly anyone has any *taste*,' he explodes. 'People don't even know what you're talking about when you say "taste", they think you mean fashion or gracious living. But it isn't that, it's the innate ability to *savour*.'

The Green Monks say they attempt to be true to themselves as few others are. Graigianity, they say, is not a religion, requiring adherence to a particular creed, but a spiritual path. 'Christianity is rather superficial', says Anelog, 'because it sees everything as external, whereas we're interested in liberating the unconscious, with all its devils and monsters.' They use 'a profound system of Natural Psychology' which Anelog developed: it is based on the ideas of Carl Jung, who he thinks simplified things too much. Religion so far, he adds, has all been too concerned with the head and opinions and nothing to do with feeling. 'It seems to us that feeling is what really matters. We call it the Watery Aspect.'

The Graigians maintain that they are the only organization in existence which reconciles this 'watery aspect' with the 'fiery' or political. They are involved in environmental campaigns in London and in North Wales, where they own a small farm called Y Graig, 'The Rock'. They claim to be the originators of the Green movement and still print copies of *The Original Green Manifesto* of 1965, which Anelog says was inspired by insights he received during a 'period of miracles and extraordinary events'.

These events took place by the sea in North Wales: all Anelog's 'mystical experiences' have been associated with water. He presents them as moments of revelation in an extraordinary life. Clasping his hands round his ample tummy or stroking his snow-white beard, he tells of his birth in 1927 to an English mother and Dutch father in the Netherlands, and the early influence of his 'prominent and artistic' relations. He rattles through his tale, punctuating it with fulminations against the ignorant and unjust. He was brought up 'to be very discriminating and critical; there was a terrific emphasis on good taste.' Until he was twenty-five he knew no one conventional and 'didn't know how conditioned and mechanical the rest of society was'.

He wanted to be an artist and studied at the Slade. Afterwards he scraped together a living by knocking on people's doors in Hampstead and offering to draw portraits – 'I did one of Jonathan Porritt as a baby', he says with some amusement. It was a restless life, and he never managed to keep a room for very long: 'The landlady would give me notice to quit because of my exuberance, and the fact I didn't have any money.'

Then one night he set out to return to London from Oxford and had 'a very strong religious experience, a sort of rebirth, an extraordinary, magical, mystery journey. I was taking mescaline at the time but it wasn't a result of that. It was probably a number of things. I was having Jungian analysis, and I started to see the fourfoldness of life; everything was very meaningful. It was a sort of bout of heightened consciousness, which I've had intermittently ever since.'

Feeling guided from within he came to Wargrave on the Thames at midnight, got into a canoe which happened to be there and went out to an island in the middle of the river. He took off all his clothes and went swimming, 'and at a certain moment I panicked because I didn't know where I was or what I was doing or why. I had the sense to shut off my mind, and as a result I found everything – the canoe with my clothes and my bag.' The experience shows, he feels, that we can be unconsciously guided, but that the moment we start thinking there is conflict. 'My life was saved! I was naked and if I had started panicking I could have been drowned or locked up as a lunatic, couldn't I?' And he adds, as an afterthought, 'I also saw the water sign, a ☋ sign in the sky. And when we were on a Community holiday in 1970 everyone there saw this sign in the sky on my birthday.'

Back in Hampstead, he and a group of friends pursued their interest in natural psychology. Anelog developed what he calls 'an intricate understanding' of the four elements (air, water, fire and earth) and their relationship to the archetypes; this interpretation is now used by the Graigians. Each person has an archetypal essence, he explains. The mother archetype, for example, 'is to do with earth and fire and the solid aspect, warmth and comfort'. These qualities will appeal to people who have the opposite characteristics: 'I have this as part of my nature, so whoever is attracted to me always looks for this motherliness in me – which is something I'd never have suspected.'

In 1965, he joined some people who were exploring the ideas of Gurdjieff while staying in a cottage on Mount Anelog in North Wales. 'And there I had a second very powerful experience – of complete *being*.' He went down to a cove with some friends and 'took all my clothes off and became totally inwardly free and forgot about the past entirely. I was just there, I didn't know who or what I was. It was kind of an ecstasy, like throwing everything off. And I received a name, the name I call myself by now. It was really very wonderful. I saw from the clifftop a "W" made by driftwood and I knew that meant "William". I walked back, climbing over earth walls covered in brambles in my bare feet, back to the cottage where we were staying, having picked lots of flowers. And that was how it all began.'

He returned to London and started the Positive Movement, which became the Green Movement, which became the Graigian Society. Sebastien, who had first met Anelog in 1957 when taken, as a child of seven, to a puppet show he was giving in the local library, joined him in 1970. Eventually, with the help of loans, they bought the house in Kentish Town, where Anelog was already living.

Here they set up their monastery as a 'fortress' which 'keeps all that prejudice out'; a secure environment where sensitive young men could develop the feminine sides of their natures – a task they believe awaits those who wish to evolve. In 1983 they bought Y Graig, which gave them their title; Anelog called himself after the 'holy mountain' it stands on, and also officially adopted the name William which he had 'kept on ice for eighteen years'. North Wales is their inspiration; they go there regularly for retreats, and have had battles with local farmers about ecology. 'Humanity must become more human,' says Anelog. 'Just as there were two nations, Rich and Poor, there will be two nations, Green and Plastic.'

Each of the monks is expected to commit himself completely to the monastery and the task of becoming 'fully conscious', and is allowed no personal possessions, no close friendships and no work outside the house. They live on donations and the money they earn from selling booklets and pottery. Anelog boasts of their frugal habits and shows me the rolls of stripy material they bought some years ago from Brick Lane, which will make their 'dresses' for the rest of their lives.

They get up every day at 6 a.m. and have breakfast together. Then they do housework and chores before the 'meditation session' at 10 a.m. Lunch at eleven is followed by a siesta, and the afternoons are given over to shopping, handicrafts, entertaining or correspondence. Sebastien, as secretary, writes exuberant letters with a lot of coloured underlining and decorations. They are proud of the flexibility of the regime – when I left at the end of my visit, a tousled Sebastien had to be woken from a late afternoon siesta to say goodbye. They eat at 7 p.m. and rest a little before they go to bed at ten.

They take only one vow, which they repeat every day: 'I vow to remember Lady Deeplake always as myself.' A representation of the Lady, all darkly swirling blues, dominates the *salubriat*, the basement room in which they meditate. The Lady is the depth of the unconscious, and the ritual words remind the monks to be true to themselves. 'A lot of men will say "I'm not at all queer",' offers Anelog as an example of the way in which most people get cut off from their true selves, 'but that's just rubbish.'

The Graigians believe their view of sexuality is so radically unconventional that most people cannot take it. That explains, they say, why the literary establishment rejected their story, the *Myth of Anelog*, and why they themselves dare make available only one chapter. They argue that people are a mixture of male and female; too many are forced by convention into 'mindless marriages' and into bringing offspring into an already over-populated world. Anelog will add little to this, except to say that people are too quick to assume a relationship should lead to sex. Their own rule does not forbid sexual relationships: 'It's like having a wet dream – you can't make a vow you're not going to have a wet dream, can you?' and he chuckles in delight.

'We don't hide *anything*,' Anelog says, 'not our sexuality, our sexual fantasies, nothing. We do express our feelings quite violently at times. It's like *poohing*, you've got to get rid of that kind of thing.' Their morning meditation session is designed to facilitate this process. There is at least one archetype for each day of the week: the clown, perhaps, the warrior or the mother. Whoever is leading the session anoints himself and later the others with oil, and gives a talk on the archetype. He may illustrate it by rearranging the objects on the altar, which include symbols of the elements: plate, wand, cup and sword. The three may use 'divination' to get in touch with the unconscious. I visited on Friday: 'Love Day'. On the cushion in front of the picture of Lady Deeplake lay bits of coloured paper and wool on top of tarot cards, which the monks had thrown down at random in the morning session and then interpreted. 'If you look you can see steps going up, and figures,' enthused Hereward.

The time came to leave. They all stood at the door to wave me off, with promises to invite me to their annual puppet show next year.

TWENTY FIVE

White Man's Dreaming

Eric Maddern was born at the desert's edge, on the south Australian coast. It was 1950. His parents were communists and his father had been sent to organize the workers in a shipbuilding town called Whyalla. The party was preparing to go underground. Life was perilous, exhilarating.

Eric's mother's father had emigrated to Adelaide after the First World War, with ulcers on his eyes and lungs from gas. He ran a people's bookshop, and was one of the founders of the Australian Communist Party. Eric got his name from him; and it goes back, he believes, to the north-east of Scotland and from there to the Norsemen.

His surname he traces to the village of Madron in Penzance. The story goes that his great-great-great-grandfather was a sea captain who apprehended pirates off the coast of Africa and followed the gold rush to Australia. 'So on my mother's side I have roots that stretch back to the Vikings, and on my father's side to the Cornish Celts.'

Eric Maddern is a story-teller, preoccupied with the 'ancient future'. Only by unravelling 'the patterns of the deep past', he says, can we prepare for times to come. Surrounded by legends and books of folklore, he talked in a study which looked across a Welsh hillside and down to a wintry lake. He wore a thick woollen jumper with a red scarf knotted at the neck; and to stop me shivering in my city clothes, lent me a Mexican poncho he had picked up on his travels.

Britain, 'the centre of politics and culture', lured his family to London when Eric was three. A few years later his mother died of polio: she was the most important person in his life, and he did not lay her ghost to rest for many years. His father married again, and Eric loved the holidays he spent with his stepmother's parents on their farm near Llanrwst: 'So began my relationship with North Wales.'

For seven years Eric's home has been Snowdonia. Here, on a five-acre smallholding, he has planted vegetables and a small wood – there are even eucalyptus trees. Stone walls await a roof of thatch: a Celtic roundhouse in the making. Nearby stands the wooden framework of a tepee; and a bender, bowed and twisted out of hazel twigs – a traditional tinkers' tent. Further on, a treehouse and a sweat-lodge overlook a rushing stream. This is the setting for Earthbound: camps for children to discover their environment and history, and for adults to venture into permaculture, psychodrama and clowning.

Eric bought his smallholding with the intention of sharing it with others. At the time, he was mulling over lessons he had learned in the Aboriginal communities of central Australia. Noting that Britain's highest crime rate is among fifteen-year-olds and that a lot of men in their thirties and forties suffer mid-life crises, he wondered whether the two things were connected. Some young Aboriginal men, he knew, were also afflicted by the 'industrial diseases' of depression, addiction and violence – mainly in communities where tradition had collapsed, and where they were no longer being initiated by the elders.

A rite of passage from childhood to adulthood, Aboriginal initiations conquer a boy's fear of death and of separation from his mother, Eric says. The ceremonies open the door to the 'Dreaming' – the layers of myth, knowledge, and value which underlie Aboriginal society. Responsibility, for the land and for others, is drummed in during 'a maelstrom of raw intensity'. Each indvidual emerges with a sense of his place in the cosmos and community. Above all, the ordeal is set up and sanctioned by society: when the boy who goes off to his initiation returns, he has the honour and the duties of a man.

For generations in the West, Eric believes, youths have not been taught to channel their passions and find their purpose in the world. The camps and other events which take place on his smallholding are a response – an experiment, to try to fill the gap. They include Rites of Passage for adult men. These are run by Everyman, founded by Alex Wildwood.

'It is a time-honoured tradition', Eric says, 'for men to meet in circles to witness, challenge and honour each other. Something important happens, which cannot happen in mixed groups.' The men who come range from company directors to gardeners. The group develops trust by doing movement together and singing, 'things that will open us up and make us feel more safe, more in touch with ourselves. Then, in turn, each man tells his story, and, when he is clear about it, describes the change – or passage – he feels he is on the threshold of right now. When he has been heard he leaves the group, which then creates for him his own personal ritual in an extraordinary creative collective process.'

Each ritual is unique. 'We had a fellow had a bath last time, with candles and incense and flowers. It was wonderful, because part of his thing was to do with the water babies.' This is as far as Eric will go in giving details of the rituals. 'Sometimes it's like throwing rocks off your stomach, if you feel you've got this heavy burden. Sometimes they involve the shedding of tears.' Everyone who has been on the event has left feeling 'more alive and aware; empowered and more of a man'.

Eric is working to establish an educational Trust, so that teenage Earthbound camps can also become regular events. Adolescents would learn about ecology by living close to nature; about history by retelling legends and visiting ancient sites. They would make bread, pots and baskets, and participate in rituals: dancing, singing and using masks.

Expeditions through the 'wild, natural landscape' would challenge their courage and teach survival.

In the meantime, Eric reaches children and teenagers through his work as a travelling story-teller and singer. He has also written children's books. He is an advocate of 'initiatory education . . . putting the growth of people, young people in particular, at the top of our cultural agenda rather than material growth'.

* * *

The wilderness north of the Arctic Circle, the PLO camps of the Middle East and the streets of Eastern Europe at the time of the Prague Spring gave Eric his own teenage initiation. He tasted freedom, fell in love and was politicized.

At university he studied Psychology and Sociology, to find out 'what it was to be a human being'. But the scientific style left him cold: 'The emphasis was on abnormal behaviour, the minimum human – I was interested in the *maximum* human.' In his spare time he found what he was looking for in Maslow and Perls, the prophets of self-actualization.

His father had taught him that the world could be bettered: 'that was my inheritance'. But for Eric, political change was not enough. At university he met some born-again Christians, and 'I found I couldn't really talk to them because they were so set in their one particular way of understanding things. But what did impress me was that they seemed to have been genuinely changed by some experience, an encounter with something they called "God". That made me curious.' He was brought up an atheist, but now he wanted to find out for himself what religion had to offer.

'In search of identity', he travelled. In America he took up movement and massage, danced professionally and did odd jobs. He went to Guatemala, which he loved: 'I thought, "I must have that again – it was so good I want more of it!" I went back and it was disastrous, and I found myself falling to pieces. In some ways I think this period was my "dark night of the soul".'

For a month he lived in a tiny hut at the top of a mountain pass. It was the rainy season, and the time he 'turned around'. Every day he spent in cloud – except for the first hour of the morning, when the skies would open up to show volcanic peaks and valleys extending to the plains of Mexico. 'I discovered I had a choice in my life. That if I accepted who I was, then I could take the first step to where I wanted to be. I could make myself feel good by singing and just walking and appreciating the beauty of the natural world.'

He spent five days alone in a Hawaiian valley, and there he thinks he may have experienced what other people call God: 'a deep sense of loving and being loved'. Sitting on the beach one sunset he had a sudden sense of the vastness of the universe. At the pinnacle of billions of years of evolution is the human mind, he thought, 'and I am a living human being . . . it's all there focusing on me . . . After that realization, I could never sink as low again.'

He had started to dream about his mother, and 'knew there was something unfinished'. He decided to go to Australia to find out what it was. On the way he had a premonition that he was to learn about death.

In Adelaide he got to know his cousin, six years older than himself, and discovered she was suicidal. She suffered from schizophrenia, and there was little he could do. A month after he arrived she drove 200 miles to a mountain, and shot herself. A rug of hers, patterned with lions, still lies on his study floor: 'the most important place'. Vowing that her death would not be wasted and that he would never be so impotent again, he spent the next two years as a psychologist, immersed in every kind of therapy.

He started to find out more about his mother. He was twenty-six; she was twenty-eight when she died. He looked at photographs and read her letters, he talked to people who had known her: 'One moment I had her – and then she was gone. That just triggered off grief.' For six months he wept. Then he did a psychodrama, at the end of which 'I took her to that mountain top in Guatemala, shrouded so often in mist, and there I was able to say my last words to her and she walked off and disappeared . . .'

Now he felt ready to get on with his life. It was a 'bread-making ceremony', with a community arts team and a group of teenagers, which began to draw the many threads of his experience together. The recipe, symbolically handed down the line of children, called for rain-water. 'We'd forgotten to put any on the table, but at the moment it was needed it rained for a couple of minutes and then stopped.' None of them knew how long to bake the bread, but they told a tale, sang and danced – and when they took the loaves out of the fire they were perfect. 'From that moment I thought, "*This* is what I want to do, the kind of ritual that creates magic." We let go, committed ourselves, trusted, and the universe co-operated.'

So now he went to work with Aborigines living in the dusty outback – performing shows, writing songs and learning the didgeridoo. Then, for a year he travelled round Aboriginal communities in the Northern Territory, with one other man. In each they spent a few days, putting on shows and using stories and art 'to overcome the language barriers, and affirm and celebrate the people's own experience'. They did not touch traditional Aboriginal themes; their subject matter was the experience the Aborigines had of the White Man – like the adventures of the store truck driver who takes provisions out to the remote communities, and on the way meets a trickster spirit. 'We went in as entertainers and good-timers.'

Only about 200 people lived in each of the communities, which were between fifty and a hundred miles apart. 'There was a lot of poverty, yet I found I was uplifted. I saw people still strong and proud and fiery and keen and wild and knowing, and I was humbled by that. I walked with them around their land and I realized they'd been there maybe

50,000 years. Modern humans have been in Europe only 35,000 years.'

It 'was like discovering my vocation. Everything I've done has followed from that.' Around that time, Eric came across a book called *White Man Got No Dreaming*, by the anthropologist W.E.H. Stanner. The title was the beginning of a quote from an Aboriginal man: '. . . him go 'nother way, him go way belong himself, White Man him go different.' To this man it seemed the Whites had left the land of their ancestors for a place where they had no roots, no connections, no spiritual practice.

The 'Dreaming', Eric says, is the way the origins of the world are explained. In the beginning the Spirit Ancestors were resting, waiting under the surface of the ground 'like a seed or a dream'. When the sun rose for the first time it caused the Spirit Ancestors to burst up through the ground. They made epic journeys across the landscape, moulding every gully, mountain, tree and lake. Their adventures caused the shape of things: the kangaroo's long tail, and the emu's loss of flight. When everything had assumed the form it has today, a part of each Spirit Ancestor became an animal or human, and a part sank back beneath the earth. Each person has a Dreaming, 'a sort of totemic connection with a particular animal or plant – someone I know has a Milky Way Dreaming'. The Dreaming gives identity, and provides the moral law – it tells people who they are, and where they fit in.

' "Well, if there was a White Man's Dreaming," Eric thought, "What would it be?" . . . And I realized, in order to find that out, I'd have to come back to Britain.'

He did, and toured a show based on his work with the Aborigines. But he knew it was not his own culture, not what he was looking for. Then he was asked to be educational co-ordinator for an exhibition on human origins at the Commonwealth Institute, with Richard Leakey as consultant. Called 'The Human Story', it started with the Big Bang and ended with the future.

'*This* was the new Creation story – the one based on hypothesis and experiment . . .' And once he'd delved into the story he found aspects of the moral law he sought. In evolutionary history 'to put it extremely simply, there seemed to be a pattern of crisis leading to opportunity. And I discovered this ratio of 1 per cent: 99 per cent. We share 99 per cent of our genes with chimps; 99 per cent of the bio-mass of the planet is plant; for 99 per cent of history humans were hunter-gatherers.' He put the two together: 'Now we're living in a time of *huge* crisis – yet this could be the crisis that leads to a new breakthrough, a new level of evolutionary being. And 1 per cent of the population – which is what the Aborigines are in Australia and what the Green Party used to be here – can make all the difference.'

Then he found his sacred sites. He became a story-teller, travelling to Britain's ruins and stone circles, finding the stories that might once have sounded there and telling them again to groups of children. 'In the beginning was the word . . . the spoken word . . . heard once and then gone, vanished into the air', he writes in his teachers' guide to story-telling at historic sites, produced last year for English Heritage. Since nowadays even the oral tradition is recorded, he made a tape to go with the book.

Researching the myths, legends and folk-tales, and retelling them to 'keep them alive' has been, he says, an 'amazing opportunity'. The sites range from Avebury to Rievaulx Abbey; from an Iron Age hill fort to a Celtic village. But Britain's oldest stories are already lost. So for 'hunter-gatherer' myths of Creation he went to the Tsimshian people of far western Canada, who tell how in the beginning 'there was nothing but Raven's piercing eyes peering into the soft darkness'.

Ever since he had his 'great awakening' in Hawaii, Eric says, he has felt in the right place at the right time doing the right thing, sustained by a belief that 'it's possible to do everything you want to do in this life, except you can't do it all at once'. He dreamed, for all his fifteen travelling years, that one day he would have a house in the country with some land. He bought his cottage in Snowdonia when he felt his 'hunter-gatherer' time was over. 'I wanted to settle down and be a farmer. My life seemed to be echoing human history.'

And there he continues to develop his understanding of the White Man's Dreaming: 'the story we tell ourselves about who we are, where we come from and what we must do – if our time to come is to be as long as our time past.'

TWENTY·SIX

Earthworm

'This place has got my head together a hell of a lot.' It is three years since Laura Kemp arrived at the Earthworm Housing Co-op, Wheatstone. She was eighteen and in a mess. 'This has been like the new start of my life. I've now become me.'

She was brought up on a council estate in Southeast London. When she was nine the family moved to East Grinstead in Sussex: 'I remember having tantrums about wanting to live on an estate with all my mates!' Affluence embarrassed her. Her father was a self-made man with a successful glazing company, who hoped his clever daughter would become a glazier or professional golfer. Laura giggles at the notion. 'I couldn't handle my mum and dad's philosophy: "Oh, we want to give you better than we had ourselves." They thought that was the be-all and end-all, to have a comfortable life, but I could never accept that. I wanted to be like I was before, dead working-class sort of thing.' Her desire was to be 'self-made' too: 'I wanted to do things for myself and not accept things from my dad; to start my life from scratch and build it up like he had.'

At school in East Grinstead they were educated, she says, to make money. Well-paid jobs, at Gatwick Airport and in office blocks, were plentiful; but no one she knows is happy with their work. They force themselves into 9–5 jobs to earn as much money as they can for the weekends, when 'all that built-up negativity comes out. It's quite abusive really.' Alcohol and drugs, like Ecstasy and Speed, keep them on a high till Monday morning. These, she says, are 'Thatcher's children, and how they're coming out. And it's frightening! They've got no real *care* about anything.'

When Laura went home for a recent visit her friends talked only about their next night out. 'It was so *boring*.' Drugs are the only 'alternative' they are familiar with; they had no interest in the political and spiritual activities which now absorb her. 'Oh, they think it's weird – a total waste of time, and I'm just a drippy hippy. My pace of living is slow, I'm much more mellower than them.' The frenetic pace left her longing for the relaxed atmosphere at Earthworm. 'One of the main feelings I had was that I'm really glad I'm poor, I'm really glad I haven't got this money to abuse.'

Laura's clothes are old and torn, her appearance grubby. Visiting her parents is not easy, because her mother worries that a neighbour might call in and see her. But they have been to Wheatstone several times, and enjoyed themselves. 'My mum and dad are really nice, actually. They're all right. And they're generally really happy about it, in a way.' She smiles at their ambivalence. 'They obviously think it's scruffy. The main thing they don't like about me is my hair, my dreadlocks. But they basically say, "As long as you're happy, then fine." And my dad's now saying to me, "I really do admire you." He goes, "I've never been able to be me", and a lot of people feel that. I think in a way they're envious.'

Laura was unhappy in East Grinstead, but did not know why. 'I didn't have a clue of what I was looking for. Thinking about it, in a way it's always been hard for me to be as smart as I should, to present myself and things.' Her teachers told her she was clever and should not hang around with the 'hard girls'; she was expected to follow a career. She left school at fifteen and went to art college, where 'I had a Mohican, I wore really scruffy clothes. I was, like, really into it.' The competitiveness put her off and she went to work in a supermarket, then a building society. With a groan, she remembers her struggles to act the part. In the end, she got the sack for falling asleep at her desk when drunk. 'It was just so *boring*! I knew it was a false life I was leading.'

On her eighteenth birthday she met a man a few years older, an ex-addict and alcoholic. She fell in love, moved in with him, and within a month was pregnant. It was a 'traumatic time'. He was violent and a womanizer, Laura says, and matters came to a head when she found him with somebody else. She lost the baby. Having another one became an obsession – she didn't care by whom. 'I went through this nervous breakdown of like passing out on the street; started drinking loads and loads and went down and down and down.' She turned to her friends 'and just poured out crying and things, and said, "*Please* help me, I need help." And they didn't understand. And that's what really cracked me up. I thought, "I've got *no one* to turn to." '

Laura decided she had two options. 'I thought, "That's it. I'm either going to top myself, or I'm going to do it all by myself, no one's going to help me." So I got on this train, and I thought, "Right, I'm going to go as far north as possible!" ' She gives a self-deprecating giggle, as she often does to modify her more dramatic statements.

A friend in Yorkshire put her up. On the train it had occurred to her that a commune might 'do for a laugh', so she had a browse in Wakefield library. The only suitable directory was twelve years old and 'they were mostly quite New Age, sort of religious communities. This was the only one that sounded pretty all right and normal. So I came here, I visited, and I fell in love with it straight away.'

The first Community at Wheatstone was established in 1975, and became well-known. About a decade later, Laura explains, it fell apart. Some members left and others lost enthusiasm. Various groups passed through. The building was squatted by 'The Brew Crew', who 'trashed it, totally vandalized the place. They took out anything that was saleable, mainly copper pipes, fireplaces – anything to get their Special Brew and smack. They were only here for eight months but the damage they caused was immense. All the windows were smashed, walls ripped through. Totally unliveable.'

They too moved on, and in January 1989 a new Community took over Wheatstone. Some members had experience of co-ops, some were travellers. They formed the Earthworm Housing Co-op, and registered it with the New Universities Network in Birmingham. Twelve of them made it through the first cold winter, huddled into the one small room which they cleared out. And then one by one they left; a few joined, some moved on. Laura thinks they were too idealistic and should have concentrated on simply living together, the hardest thing to do in a community. By the time she arrived, in 1990, only three remained.

'I'd never been to a place like this before. It was all very new, all very alien, and it was exciting.' She liked the house, with its numerous rooms and seven acres of land. The tattiness was a relief. Dirty, cold and damaged as it was, the prospect of restoring it enticed. She loved the setting, in a Shropshire valley. Above all, 'When I came here, people were just being themselves. I was able to talk loads and loads.' For a while she was reserved, but then felt sufficiently at ease to talk about the trauma she had been through. Later she started to explore ideas. Her parents find her rather too outspoken now, she laughs: feelings and philosophy were not discussed at home.

The very fact she had made the break on her own initiative gave her the courage to stay. As time went on, 'I saw a lot of ups and downs. This *felt* more real to me: real people with real emotions, people doing things themselves, taking on responsibility. And I thought, "Right, I've found this place by chance, I'll go for it." '

Security is important to her and at first she felt vulnerable. Now she is so ensconced she is keen to have a family, though there is no boyfriend at the moment. It is not that she is broody from her miscarriage any more, but 'you feel comfortable about bringing your child up here'. One of the curious aspects of East Grinstead life, she remarks, is that her contemporaries 'just can't handle the thought of settling down and having children'. When her younger sister had a baby she was despised. 'It's very strange, you know, because you can sleep around with loads of people but if you get pregnant you're a "slag". It's stupid!'

For the moment, Laura lavishes attention on her dogs ('my family') and kept dashing off to sort them out. We sat on a piece of large-meshed net, swung between trees like a hammock. The daughter of one of Wheatstone's residents, a beautiful two-year-old by the name of Sorrel, disrupted our conversation. Illustrating Laura's enthusiasm for this children's paradise, she wandered freely under the casual eye of various adults, examining twigs and insects with talkative absorption. Then she came to join us on the bouncing hammock, and became hilariously entangled in the holes.

All around and in the distance, trees wore autumn gold. Laura took me on a tour of the grounds and showed me the 'permaculture crescent', planted during a course. Earthworm hosts numerous groups throughout the year, and advertises as 'a resource centre for events, summer camps, meetings and workshops'. Laura feels much more in the thick of things in Wheatstone than East Grinstead. She meets all kinds of people. The first task she took on was to make the visitors' room and kitchen welcoming. Her dream is to establish a network of camps around the country with Wheatstone as a focus. 'I *don't* want the prices to go up. I want it to be open for any group to come.' Any money made will go into improving the facilities and making them ecologically sound. They are in the process of building an elaborate new compost toilet, and dream of wind generators and other alternative high-tech.

Many of the visitors come to learn about their lifestyle, Laura says. The house now has a form of central heating from wood-burning stoves (it is perishing if they are not lit). She points out recently planted trees, which will eventually provide their fuel and save them £50 a week. They recycle waste and purchase relatively little. We walked round the garden, cultivated without animal products as part of their veganic discipline. But, I asked, you smoke and drink? – remembering the ashy beer-can debris of the sitting-room. She rolled her eyes and lit another, saying she was glad I'd brought that up. They are not puritans and she still refers to non-organic purchases as 'treats'. But she feels they live closer to the land than most and are guilty of relatively little exploitation.

Laura loves meat, though she refuses to eat it in protest at factory farming. The Community is vegan and she has been healthier on that diet. But when she found a dead pheasant one day, she knew where the challenge lay. She took it back to the campers' outdoor kitchen (where vegan rules do not apply) plucked, gutted, cooked and ate it. Living in harmony with the earth, for her, includes 'survival'.

'We've called ourselves "eco-anarchists" ', Laura laughs. In order to be listed in *Diggers and Dreamers*, the communes directory, Earthworm had to label its 'ideological focus'. But Laura does not really think she is an anarchist. She is aware of her dependency on the authorities, and does not feel she can ignore 'the way capitalism is showing its fascism'. Much as she might dream of living in the woods with dogs, kids and goats, 'I feel it's my responsibility as a human and a pagan to fight . . .'

The Earthworm members belong to a co-op of co-ops called Radical Routes, which is helping them raise the money they need to buy the house and land. Anybody anxious about supporting capitalistic institutions can invest in Earthworm through this secondary co-op. Most people in the Community draw Housing Benefit, which goes to the Co-op: they are both tenants and landlords. They hope to get a mortgage from the Ecology Building Society, to renovate the property. Much of the house is in an awful state. The Brew Crew's graffiti still deface walls and the air is pervaded by a smell of damp decay. But it is a vast improvement, Laura says: they have worked hard. As she takes me round, she enthusiastically details their ambitious plans.

The Community's legal status means providing housing is their primary task. 'We are the homeless. We are being housed,' Laura asserts. They now have twelve rentable rooms and two more which will be fine when they have floors instead of woodworm. All residents are members, and ages range from twenty-one to forty, with three children. Life together 'is not all peace and love. It's very hard, it's a big responsibility. I love this place and want to see it work. It really gets us down sometimes because there's a lot of pressure, especially about buying it and dealing with solicitors and bureaucrats. It's all too new and confusing and rushed.'

There is no leadership 'technically – but some people are a bit more forward, dominant than others'. Decisions are made jointly, by consensus. Most people meet to eat and chat in the evening and there are rotas for the housework, but there is no binding schedule. Laura has 'found herself' through the relationship with others, and has had to learn to cope with criticism. Emotional problems have to be ironed out, or they get the Community down. Only the other day she and another member had had to resolve a row, by getting to grips with it at a 'feelings meeting'.

'I think I've been so *lucky* to find my destiny,' Laura says. Much of her energy goes into her work as secretary of Radical Routes and co-ordinator of 'Skills and Knowledge-Sharing Workshops'. She is involved in political campaigns, but whereas others 'are fighting against negative things, I'd like to fight *for* positive things, and produce an alternative, getting people together. Because the planet in general is in such a chaotic mess, people are just cracking up.'

At Wheatstone, close to the earth, 'I've got quite into paganism. People here, some are spiritual, some aren't, it's not a collective thing.' The Community often has 'sweat-lodges' based on the American Indian model. Sometimes they are 'ritual', which she finds uplifting; 'other times, we just go in there for a good laugh, you know, it's really good fun doing it. Some people are really totally uncosmic about it all!' There are regular visitors from Pagan Link, many of them glad to get away from their city lives for a few days on the land. Wheatstone has a reputation as an 'energy centre' because it is said to be at the crossing of several ley lines. When Laura organized a gathering for the Celtic festival of Beltane, to which some 150 people came, her sense of achievement was enormous.

'The best thing with paganism is it's very vague.' Religion did not feature in Laura's upbringing, and she is glad: its absence left her free to find a spirituality that suited her, in Nature. She is not atttracted by the personal nature of the Christian God. 'I worship Mother Earth; I think she is very beautiful. That's where a lot of my politics come from, because she is being abused . . . I have a lot of real *love* for her, for what she has given.' The human race is destroying the earth, Laura says: 'We've caused all this shit. If we left all these other animals alone, they'd all live *totally* in tune with the earth. They are innocent.'

Laura is eager to talk about her politics and spirituality, recently discovered answers to the crisis she believes is imminent. The Government, she is convinced, is trying to shut people up. Look, she says, at the restrictions they are placing on travellers and squatters; observe the police's failure to bust dealers in drugs like smack, which keep suburbia quiet. Three years ago she too was 'ignorant'. Now she is fired by zeal to enlighten people and show them how they are controlled. Attempts to 'divide and rule' will fail, she claims. Pushed to the brink, communards and others will join and fight for 'housing without landlords, work without bosses, education without teachers. Actually doing things for yourself!'

TWENTY SEVEN

The Toad's Eye

There are a lot of toads in Gordon MacLellan's house. Some are ornaments; the others are poisonous, living in a tank in the back room. On the sitting-room wall are three sheep skulls hung with strings of beads and animal bones, and on one of them sits Erwilian Frite, the household goblin. Together, the skulls and the goblin make up the spell of the house, Gordon explains, which had recently 'cracked' for the first time in eight years – he had been burgled twice. Perhaps, he mused, it was because he was already thinking of leaving.

Gordon told his story sitting cross-legged on a floor cushion in his terraced house in Manchester, surrounded by cardboard boxes. He was moving to Surrey, to take up a post as Lecturer in Countryside Recreation, training the next generation of rangers and National Park wardens. He wondered, with a grin, what they would make of him. Gordon stands out: straight hair, tufted short on top and then drawn into a pony tail reaching down his back; a brightly coloured cotton jacket, 'Save the Rainforest' T-shirt and an array of earrings, one a silver toad climbing up his outer ear.

Gordon became a pagan at the age of ten. Catweazle, 'the demented Anglo-Saxon magician from the television series', was his role model. Later, he bought a do-it-yourself witchcraft book. But the turning-point was a children's tale by Alan Garner: 'I thought, "This is it, this is it, *this* is how it works!" '

The Moon of Gomrath has not yet been packed, and Gordon reads out the passage which he says set him free. A boy runs down the 'old straight track' at full moon and feels it flowing through him, '. . . and the bells and the music and the voices were all of him, and the Old Magic sang to him from the depths of the earth and the caverns of the night-blue sky.' Gordon had heard that singing, but the book encouraged him to listen to it: 'My head worked in that sort of space – the atmosphere of the book was perfectly right. You're out on a moonlit night and you know the world's alive.'

All that exists lives – that's all you need to know, Gordon says. The pagans have no dogma or creed but he thinks every one of them would say the life of the earth is sacred, and the earth as a whole a living force. 'Everything has the energy we might call spirit,' he elaborates. 'It doesn't necessarily have conscious expression the way we do – or maybe it's on a completely different scale. Like you can't sit down very easily and have a conversation with a mountain, because your whole life, to a mountain, is a breath.'

Everything is interconnected, Gordon says: 'Think of the complexity of ecosystems – if you affect any one thing you will change everything. Practical paganism is spiritual ecology.' The goal, he says, is to live in harmony with the world around us. 'Everything I do works towards that end.'

He studied Zoology at university and is an ecologist by profession. For five years he worked for the Mersey Valley Countryside Warden Service, 'managing land for people and for wildlife', and dealing with thousands of schoolchildren. Environmental education, for him, is 'a totally pagan occupation', a day-to-day expression of his spiritual beliefs and role. But he does not teach paganism. 'The individual never surrenders his or her choices. Your job as a teacher is to help individuals choose who they want to be.' All religions, he believes, are expressions of the universe; he is wary when one claims to be better than another.

He has not always received the same tolerance himself. At an interfaith festival of Nature, organized by a wildlife charity with one of Britain's largest cathedrals, Gordon was due to run children's workshops as a member of the Warden Service. The cathedral and the charity were upset when they discovered he was a pagan and asked for someone else. 'I was furious. They were suggesting I couldn't operate as a professional without preaching my religion, and I object to that really strongly.' His employers and others backed him: it was pointed out that nobody would have dared complain if he had been for example, an Aborigine. The cathedral and the charity backed down.

'I'm certainly not going to take on board anyone else's problems with who I am,' Gordon says. It has taken him a long time to reach that point. He is now thirty-three, and told no one of his paganism until his early twenties. But even harder than growing up pagan, was growing up gay.

He finally accepted he was homosexual when he was sixteen: 'I thought – enjoy it, that's what life's about, not getting uptight.' He was brought up in 'the small-town mentality' of Cumbernauld, just outside Glasgow. 'It's very difficult to say to your best friend, "It's not her I fancy, it's you." It's to risk everything. And it was the same spiritually. You could have said you were a Buddhist or a communist atheist – we had a lot of those – but to say you were a magician or a witch . . .' He had a lot of friends but he was never part of groups: he was a loner, writing poetry, going for long walks in the woods, sitting in ponds.

He has come to be very impressed by his Scottish father and English mother. They produced four children who are totally different, he says, and fully supported each of them. He told them he was gay seven years ago 'and they were great'. They had brought him up in the Church of Scoland, and he did not tell them he was pagan until his sister died, just short of her thirtieth birthday. He went to her funeral in a top hat and tails, camping it up in the way she would have loved. Whenever he saw anything that would have made his sister laugh, he told his mother, 'I pick it up and throw it up and say, "Jane, wherever you are, I hope this reaches you and you have a smile." And my mum said, "I do the same!" ' He laughs as he remembers. 'I said, "I didn't think you did things like that – you're a Christian!" '

After university he taught in a 'bizarre institute' in Malawi, where he covered the English A level Science syllabuses. 'As a teaching situation it was a dream', but socially, it was awkward: 'very straight and conservative. A white male wearing earrings and funny clothes did not go down at all well!' The experience shook up his emotions and confirmed his spirituality. He realized he had become 'tuned in' to Britain as a pagan when it took him two years to stop working to British seasons. 'And I thought, "That's that, nothing's going to be hidden." So I came back as out, pagan and gay.' He lost a few friends – and that was when they found out he was gay. 'I mean, what they'd have done if they'd discovered I was pagan. They'd probably have burned me at the stake!'

He had, however, other more lasting relationships, which had been developing since childhood. He is a 'shaman', who works closely with the spirit world: 'We've got a small group, a little family of us. I'm the only one of us that's got a physical shape.' Associated with him, he explains, there's a toad, his totem, 'who's my balance, if you like. Toad and I together are a composite entity, we give each other what the other lacks. Toad's been with me for years and years, and I've *known* Toad's been there.' There is also Erwilian, the household goblin, and Manchu, 'a seven foot furry ogre, like a renegade from the Muppets. She'd be very offended by that description!' He made the doll of Erwilian when he was sixteen. There are a few others 'who come and go'. Some have moved on: 'people who needed me or I needed them. And then the relationship ended and they went off. But the core of five has been together really strongly for a while now, and that falls into traditional shamanic patterns from tribal cultures.'

The evidence of their reality, he says, is that they are not there at his beck and call. 'There's a big cat, a lynx-type thing called Llyan, who came about five years ago. And she just prowls in and out. You can be doing something else, and it can be like a ghost walks right through you – Lynx has arrived. She's said, "What're you doing?" and wandered off again.' Sometimes his friends ring him after he has visited them and say Lynx is in their house, he's left her behind. He tells them she'll leave in her own good time. He does not own his spirit friends.

Erwilian 'holds the home together, and sometimes you find he's done something totally bizarre'. A couple of years ago Gordon was thinking of leaving, but didn't feel quite right about it. He meditated and 'approached the home to say, "Are we meant to be moving on?" And then – Erwilian had packed his bags and was sitting on a pile of books and the skull with a little bag of runes in the middle of my head, saying, "I'm ready, I'll go!" So we all work with each other. They're very loving, positive relationships.'

A shaman is a mediator between the community and the spirit world. 'The problem of human existence', Gordon says, quoting from a Siberian tradition, 'is that all food consists of souls.' The shamans tell the spirit world what the human community is doing, and report back the reaction; they are counsellors and magicians. Today, a shaman's task is not to find game or work the magic that will hold it in place, but 'to make sure your community always acts in harmony with the world around it'.

In the world of the spirit, Gordon explains, 'you exist as a spiritual being, and you will also meet things which don't have a physical existence. You meet the fairies, the goblins and the hobgoblins, all the characters in English folklore.' They are often, he says, the spiritual personalities of places, and you might meet them as an energy vortex or as a shape – each one is a consciousness and together you agree on a form so that you can meet in 'the Otherworld'. It's the same with the universe itself, which 'for us, isn't the product of a single masculine deity, it's almost the product of itself. It has its own, total awareness. And that is the infinite, that is deity.'

Deity usually manifests itself as a dual force, Gordon says. The 'masculine' is a sword-edge, precise and finely focused; the 'feminine' is wisdom, intuitive and enveloping. These are traditional terms for 'energy flows', not sexualities: the masculine is not the province of the male. Every type of being thinks in different ways, he says – if we're thinking in straight lines and something else in pyramids, it's hard to communicate. The figures of god and goddess are convenient, because 'you can't talk to the infinite, you can't have a heart to heart with the space between the stars.'

Some pagans worship these figures, but for Gordon they are deeply loved beings with whom he has an intimate relationship. 'They come and walk with me; I don't sit down and pray to them.' Organized groups, such as the witches' covens, have set mythologies and rituals – but he, like other shamans, acts independently, in response to the environment. A few months earlier the Manchester pagans had worked a fox ritual, to help the local foxes develop their cunning in response to increased baiting. 'Then, during the year, I'm always engaged on some toad things, keeping tabs on toads in this area.' The toad life cycle has some delicate moments, he says; when toadlets are looking for food before they go into hibernation, he diverts some energy to give them a boost. As a naturalist he helps them physically, and then supports his actions magically: 'I dance – my magic, my energy, my power comes with dancing, drumming and singing. We can work with the toad spirits to dance that ball of energy up, to empower toads in this area.'

Magic, Gordon says, is 'moving energy along the web of life'. Some people work money spells, which he says he can't get his head round – his are for the environment. Blocking nature, and manipulating events for private ends, is 'black magic'; human beings, he suggests, do that all the time, and call it ambition. But he thinks most people regard all magic, including his, as 'black' – and from their point of view, perhaps they are right. He is concerned about the planet, not Western society. He works as a magician to heal the disruption caused by humanity, which has become 'a big lump on the evolutionary web'. If his environmental magic works, it might well be 'the end of civilization as we know it'.

Being a shaman, Gordon says, is an ecstatic and delightful way of living in love with the world and everything that crosses his path. Every morning when he goes to work he stops to salute the sun, acknowledging the rising warmth and feeling the earth beneath his feet. In the evening he lights a candle or incense to 'centre again and tune back into myself'; and later does a half-hour dance or meditation to express his relationship with the two worlds, the physical and spiritual.

His spirituality is bound up with Britain. The Dakota Sioux in the United States, with whom he has been working closely for some time, trust him precisely because he has no interest in becoming an Indian. 'Their beliefs have really evolved out of the land they're on and it's the same with me. It belongs to these hills and forests and not to these strange wide open spaces.' They were, he adds, intrigued by the campaign for gay rights, which for them is not an issue. 'In Indian culture you are who you want to be, and who your vision says you are.'

Gordon's year keeps the rhythm of death and rebirth, revolving round the solar and seasonal festivals. The first is Salwen, the festival the Christians changed to Hallowe'en. The Celts believed it was one of the nights when time and forever are one – 'so the dead are there', says Gordon. It is the summer's end, a time to reflect and let go. At Yule, the winter solstice, he watches 'the sun come back' at dawn. In February and at the spring equinox, as the new growth begins, the celebrations are of birth, nest-building and the inspiration of the poet. Beltane, or May Day, is a time of joy: signalled by the first flowering of the hawthorn, sacred to the Great Goddess, it is 'the most ecstatic – richness and fecundity, champagne and effusion. It's wonderful.' At Midsummer, things are past their peak and the festivities are tinged with silence. In the autumn there is thanksgiving: at the September equinox the community becomes 'perfectly still for one night' and reflects on wholeness.

Gordon celebrates the festivals alone, 'exploring the changing energy, so I stop thinking summer and start thinking autumn'. Then he is ready to join the big community parties and help others sort out what the change means for them. He is a local teacher, leading ceremonies and running 'pagan picnics', and serving as religious contact for those in hospital. He recently gave up co-ordinating the Gay Pagan Network and was glad, he laughs, to stop getting phone calls in the middle of the night from 'distraught, if wonderful, weirdies'. He also has two apprentices, trainee shamans. For none of this work does he charge. You cannot take money for magic, he says; it is one of the oldest principles.

There are those who come into paganism for 'a mellow time' or an ego trip – you do, he smiles, come across a lot of witch kings and queens. But 'the people deep inside the pagan faith are hard, there's an edge to them. They're warriors.' It is rare to find 'far-in' shamans in long-term relationships, he says, 'we're too disturbed!' Following a pagan life is not always easy – he found his way alone, and would not wish on anyone the struggles he endured. Problems, both for the individual and the community, are contained by counselling, training and support.

If, for example, somebody living in Manchester ends up with Rat as their totem, Gordon tells them not to give themselves a hard time. 'Think about rats in the city – they're success stories! They're adaptable, versatile . . .' The symbolism is not intrinsic to the animals, it is attached to them by human beings.

So what is the symbolism of Gordon's totem, the toad? First, he says, the toad is a leaper and changer. 'If you're involved with an amphibian you have changed, and what you touch changes.' Second, the toad is earth-based, because it sits flat on the ground: 'For someone who's quite airy and fiery and explosive, it's really good to grab onto Toad, and I'm grounded. He's the earth grown up and walking.'

And third, traditionally, inside the head of a toad there is a gem. 'You have this brown, grumpy lump of mud and it opens its eye, this gorgeous golden eye. He's enchantment, the unexpected.'

TWENTY EIGHT

The Princess

Satya Kaur, formerly Isabel Cepěda, is a Portuguese Sikh – the only one she knows of. Converts to Sikhism are unusual, for it is in principle a tolerant religion which recognizes other faiths and does not proselytize. Its homeland is the Punjab, the land of five rivers now divided between India and Pakistan, and most of the Sikhs around the world have Punjabi roots.

The Punjabi Sikhs in London regard Satya and her Scottish husband, Shiv Charan Singh, with amazement, which takes one of two forms. Some think they are 'wierdoes' and wonder what their families must be like; others think they are wonderful and holy and want to fall at their feet. The response of non-Sikhs varies too. Satya used to be mocked and abused as she walked down the street – it happens less now, perhaps because she has relaxed into her Sikh identity and her elegant turban is taken for fashion. Her husband, however, stands out: 'with a big orange beard down to here', she indicates her midriff, laughing, 'and a big turban and blue eyes and a pale face, and he often looks scruffy anyway. He arouses a lot of antagonism,' she adds mildly.

Most of Satya's friends are non-Sikhs and they and her large, supportive family accept her chosen faith but show little interest. Occasionally, there is an amiable protest. When she was at home in Portugal this summer she washed her long, uncut hair one day and combed it out to dry. 'Oh Isabel, leave it down!' cried her mother when she saw her. But Satya wound on her turban as usual and no more was said. Another day, her mother said, 'Let me buy you some new clothes!'

and Satya agreed. But in town the grim absorption of the shoppers upset her, and their hedonism horrified her. What should have been a treat turned sour.

She was born in Lisbon in 1958, one of four daughters. Her father, an army officer, was a devout Catholic; her mother, a doctor, was an atheist. Satya was taken to church every Sunday, and confirmed, and recognizes now how the 'discipline and devotion' of her father's side of the family took root in her. But so did her mother's 'progressivism' – her refusal to go to church, and her enthusiasm for the latest ideas in science and psychology.

Because of the upheaval caused by the Portuguese revolution in 1974, Satya decided to go to university in London. She was 'more or less an atheist then, just exploring life and finding out about things'. But in her early twenties she began to feel dissatisfied. 'Everything was all right, and you could just go on having friends and going on holiday and drinking and going to parties, but it was all meaningless, there was no depth to it.' She began to search and read, and liked especially the books of Gudjieff, which encouraged her to look for a radical lifestyle to challenge the habits acquired over years. She no longer wanted to live 'unconsciously, without purpose.'

She started to go to yoga classes run by Tibetan Buddhists, but did not feel at home. Nearby, a health food shop called the Golden Temple opened, which was run by a group of Western Sikhs. They were members of 3HO, the Healthy-Happy-Holy Organization of Harbhajan Singh Khalsa Yogiji, who achieved a great following in the United States during the 1970s. Upstairs from the shop classes were offered in his method of Kundalini yoga, and Satya went along.

She loved the yoga exercises and, still more, the chanting and meditation which followed: 'it awakened and stimulated my soul'. She loved the grace of the teachers, all dressed in white, and the clarity and peace they carried with them. 'I thought, "This is lovely, this is amazing." ' She saw that the yoga they practised every day made them lithe and fit; she was vegetarian and liked the fact that they were too. She liked their straightforward, natural lifestyle and she was interested when they told her they did not cut their hair out of respect for God and in obedience to the natural law.

She had long been alienated by Western ways, feeling sure there must be an alternative to the pollution they caused. For a year or two she had floundered in a foreign country with no rules to live by; she had not known who she was, what to believe, how to live. If she had remained in Portugal she might have found another answer; but in Kilburn, it lay in the Golden Temple health food shop. She started to go to the yoga classes twice a week, and felt pulled not only to the lifestyle but also to the ideal: she too wanted to live 'as a saint and a warrior'.

'I thought, "I don't want to resist any more, there's no point in keeping away from it if that's where I feel I belong." ' She started to wear an occasional turban and to grow her hair long. In 1980 she married and later that year had a child. Her husband did not like her new interests and her persistence added further strain to an already failing marriage. In 1986 she divorced him. In 1987 she took *Amrit*, Sikh initiation, and later that year she married her present husband, who had converted while working in Holland as a chef in a Sikh restaurant – called the Golden Temple.

The word *sikh* means 'disciple' – a follower of the teachings of the Ten Gurus. The last Guru died in 1708, having ordained that from then on the ultimate spiritual authority for the Sikhs would rest in the Guru Granth Sahib. This, their holy book, contains the writings of the Gurus, as well as poetry by Sufi saints and others. It is built around the 974 hymns of Guru Nanak, the First Guru, who was born into a Hindu family in 1469. 'India at the time was under the Moghuls and in a rocky state. There were forced conversions to Islam, and the Hindus were caught up in rituals,' Satya says. 'It needed a kind of cleansing, so that people could come back to the realities of spiritual life.'

Guru Nanak worked as an accountant as a young man, but was preoccupied with God. 'There is no Hindu or Muslim, so whose path shall I follow?' he declared after an experience which he described as being taken to the court of God and into his presence. 'I shall follow God's path.' From then on he lived as an itinerant preacher, seeking to remind people of the underlying truth of religion and warning them away from the increasing emphasis on ritual. Ironically, he became the founder of a new religion.

'Sikhs believe in one God', says Satya. 'He's the Creator of everything and he pervades everybody. He's inside us, outside us, he's before us and he's after us; he's got no name, no form . . . it's there and it's everything, it's just an almighty force.' The Guru Granth Sahib, she says, was written by men in a state of bliss and inspiration, with the light of God inside them. 'By chanting it, reading it, absorbing it, you get into the same state.' She brings down one of the eight volumes from the top room of the house, where it must always be kept, and opens the white cloth it is wrapped in as a sign of respect. The pages are printed in the original Gurmukhi, with translations in English and in the thick black characters of modern Punjabi. 'Whenever I am stuck or confused I say a prayer and open it and read whatever is there, and it usually uplifts me.'

For those who take *Amrit* (and this is a sign of commitment not made by all) there is a strict code of conduct. Every day they must get up early, have a bath, and meditate on God's name. Five prayers a day are required – three in the morning and two at night. Satya usually says hers on the train, on the way to the hospital where she is training as a midwife.

They must never cut their hair or shave or change their form in any way – 'Well, my ears were already pierced and I sometimes wear earrings, but I shouldn't,' Satya says. They should be householders, not celibates; they should earn their own living and give a tenth of it away. They are vegetarian (although some Sikhs simply avoid meat that is *halal*, slaughtered according to Muslim ritual), and do not drink or smoke or take any other intoxicants that alter the state of the mind.

They should wear the 'Five Ks', the symbols of the Sikhs, at all times. Satya holds out her wrist for me to see the *kara*, a steel bracelet: 'It's to remind you of your actions, you're handcuffed to God. It's a circle, and being in a circle is supposed to protect you. And being iron it's magnetic and adds power to you.' At her waist she wears a *kirpan*, a mini-sword, as a symbol of justice and the requirement to fight, if necessary, for freedom – to be a soldier-saint. The *kacha*, a sort of loose underwear rather like boxer shorts, is worn 'for modesty and to remind you not to indulge in lust. And they're hygienic and healthy.'

The *keshas*, the long, unshorn hair, is 'to keep God's form, and also because it's got a lot of energy. In the East, holy men have always had long hair.' It should be kept under a turban when in public, 'to distinguish you from other people, and also to protect your head from knocks and from the elements'. In the evening, Satya takes off her turban if she is at home – unless visitors are expected, she smiles, especially if they are Sikhs. Underneath it she wears the *kangha*, a wooden comb, 'to keep a discipline and the hair tidy. And since hair tends to be very etheric the wood balances the energy.'

At night Satya puts the *kirpan* under her pillow, but takes the *kangha* out of her hair. 'Since I've taken *Amrit* I should do everything by the book. But it's better to be more relaxed rather than be so strict that in the end you say, "I can't do it any more", and go the other way.' Being a Sikh, for her, is about living practically, effectively. Her concern with 'energies' and being natural is typical of her, rather than of the religion. She describes the ideal, but also how it comes down to earth. It will be her duty, she says gravely, to facilitate the marriage of her sons, and if they have several different partners, to make her disapproval known. And then she throws back her head and laughs: 'Having done it myself!'

Her youngest son is four, and already very conscious, she thinks, of his Sikh identity. He hates to take off the little head covering which he wears until he is old enough to manage a turban. Certainly it doesn't seem to get in the way of headstands and other armchair gymnastics. He has a Sikh name, Kirit, which means 'God's Work', which Satya decided in the traditional way: through prayer, random opening of the Guru Granth Sahib, and reflection on the text for the day. His surname, like that of all male Sikhs is Singh, 'lion'. All women are called Kaur, 'princess'. Plumstead estate agents find this hard to grasp, so Satya allows them to call her 'Mrs Singh'. Her first name means 'Truth' (the 'energy of truth', she expands); it was given her by Yogiji, when she wrote to him with her date of birth and original name. A Sikh name, she explains, give you a direction in your life.

The 'princess of truth' smiles and tells me of her dreams. The nuclear family is impractical and ineffective, she says, and she would like to live in some sort of communal set-up, either in a big house or in a close-knit neighbourhood. She would like to live closer to other Sikhs, because she needs their support and inspiration, and for Kirit's sake. Community is important to Sikhs: the reason they share the same name is that a Sikh is expected to regard every woman of the same age as a sister, and every man as a brother; those younger as daughters and sons, those older as mothers and fathers.

But she cannot share the concerns and political passions of Asian Sikhs, many of whom have been stirred by anger since the Golden Temple massacre in 1984, and are pressing for an independent Punjab, a homeland. She sympathizes, but that is all. She misses having her own blood-family around her, but if she went back home to Portugal there would be no Sikhs at all. She still lives between two cultures, supported in different ways by both but fully by neither.

Yet it is plain she has found the identity and meaning she

was so desperate for a dozen years ago in Kilburn. She has an exuberant dignity, an easy grace. Her vivid pink and black dress fits well but loosely and sets off her turban of brilliant white. There is a lightness with constraints, which pervades her style and her philosophy. She rarely talks of darkness. 'It's normal to keep breaking your vows, nobody's perfect, God is forgiving. You've just got to keep doing your best.'

TWENTY NINE

The Asylum

At each end of the monastery's main room, an enormous diamond window floods the space with light and almost draws within it the trees outside. One end is a library; the other is a kitchen, with worktops of salvaged slate and a great oval table carved from an Ampleforth cherry tree. The room peaks into a v of pitch pine timbers from the Liverpool docks; the tiles on the roof outside come from demolished flats in Kirby.

It took six years to build the monastery. Sometimes Thomas Cullinan was alone; often he was helped by friends and neighbours, and his brother is an architect. The Mersey shipyards, eight miles away, were disappearing then, so Thomas bought materials at knock-down rates and built a house of prayer. But the connection with Liverpool means more to him than that: the monastery belongs, he says, at the edge of the city, and needs to keep in touch with the places where 'modern poverty, material and spiritual, wounds people'. God sees to it, he adds, that 'front-liners' working in the city come often to the monastery.

Building fascinated Thomas. But he came to see it as 'demoniacally dangerous', because it can become its own end. For this reason he and his helpers always kept to the Benedictine discipline, with its regular hours of prayer five times a day and its close at 9 p.m. for the 'great silence of the night'. He was often tempted to continue work and make the praying wait so he could finish off a job – especially if someone was there to help who might be gone tomorrow – but resisted. And now, though he may not feel like going outside to the chapel for Matins in the chill dawn, he says he always *wants* to, because he has chosen the Benedictine life as a way of doing the will of God. He knows the monastery could become 'a colossal ego trip in the name of God', and he is vigilant.

Four monks set off to build the monastery, eleven years ago. One died, one fell in love and left, one was sent away to be a convent chaplain, and only Thomas remained. 'So we had a crisis.' He went away for a while, his dreams broken, and wrote a full report for his abbot at Ampleforth. The two of them decided the project should go ahead. After the crisis he had a peace his friends had never seen in him before. He says it was because although no venture can start without a strong idea, the idea becomes an ideology and 'even ideas about God must give way to God himself'. The disintegration of what he and his companions had planned felt like a loss of faith; but it also collapsed in him his ideology. 'It was a shift from "I come to do your will" (where there's always a slight sense of "Gosh, God *is* lucky to have me") to "Let your will be done in me." '

And so he has carried on alone, though he says he would not be there without the 'extended family' of friends who work and pray with him. He has many visitors and is sometimes asked to give retreats and talks. But he would be glad if other monks joined him, and some have shown interest. Solitude, Thomas says, warps the mind; he has often felt morose, circling round in his own thoughts. It is also dangerous, 'laying you bare and vulnerable before darkness and spiritual powers which we usually don't have to confront'. He compares it to going into a cave: once you get accustomed to the dark you are able to see things you would never glimpse elsewhere. Initially it feels like the loss of everything, and great loneliness; later 'all sorts of things open up in the darkness'.

In his solitude he feels his connection with the world. Monastic poverty, he says, means nothing if it is not 'in communion' with those who suffer outside. This is, for him, the paradox at the heart of Christianity. How can the death of one man 2,000 years ago affect anybody at all, he asks? Because we are 'existentially bonded. We are not individuals before God, we are members of a body before God, and what God blesses in one member blesses the whole.' Some years ago friends joined him for the Easter Vigil at the monastery. As they sat in the depths of the night, they had the idea they should tell stories about the people they wanted to pray for all around the world. But it was not necessary, one woman said, 'because it is palpably evident that the entire world is present in this place tonight, and that we are in communion with everybody on God's planet.'

Thomas never intended to live alone. The very idea of a solitary monk is 'a nonsense', he admits – unless you feel called to be a hermit, which he does not. A Benedictine joins a particular Community, which then becomes his or her 'family' for life. Thomas was educated at Ampleforth, and the decision to join the Community there 'made itself' when he was very young. When he did his National Service in the Navy the other sailors found his plans mysterious; but for him to be a monk was normal, and he thought it would be easy.

1960, though, was World Refugee Year and Thomas – by then a novice and a student of Mathematics at Oxford – got involved, with consequences he could never have foreseen. He became closely connected with Oxfam and in later years was on its Council of Management. These interests took him onto the new Justice and Peace Commission in the British Isles – one of the results of the Second Vatican Council, which threw open the windows of change in the Roman Catholic Church. Back in Ampleforth, studying Theology, he asked himself what it meant to live in a world in which most people are not only poor, but dispossessed: 'They're not simply hungry; they're part of processes which deny them a share in their planet's bounty.'

He saw now that the poor were not a problem that the

rich should try to solve; 'we are all the problem'. He did not know what to do. What was the meaning of the Gospel, what was the function of monastic life in a world unjustly structured? 'It ate into me in an unhealthy way. But I don't regret it. It was an agony, and I think people have to pass through that agony.'

The powers which cause injustice in the world are getting worse, he says, and in the face of them he has felt impotent despair. But solidarity with those who suffer is the essence of the gospels, he believes, in a way that 'doing good', perhaps, is not. 'The heart of the Christian message is that the most salvific moment in the history of the world was when one man was pinned to a cross unable to do anything for anybody about anything. Until we can come to the point of living in the presence of that unbearable inability to do, I don't think we've really entered into the mystery of a crucified God.'

Thomas felt pulled to go to the Third World, to work alongside the poor. Perhaps his novice master was right when he said he should have been a Jesuit; but he was a Benedictine and they stay at home. He struggled, and he and others pondered what it was that Benedictines in particular could offer to the modern world.

Benedict's aim was not to do good works, but to set up a 'school of the Lord's service', where monks would learn to find God in everyday life. This is the reasoning that lies behind the ordered pattern of work, prayer and silence. But since the fifth century, when the Rule was written, Ampleforth and other Benedictine houses have also undertaken 'apostolic' tasks, such as parish work and teaching.

Such apostolic work makes great demands. There has always been a need, some have felt, for a monastic life free of its burdens. Thomas was one such. He came to believe that Christians are called first to be disciples – pupils, followers of their master's teaching; and that only some of them are also called to be apostles – preachers and public witnesses, workers with those in need.

Thomas and two other monks were given permission to set up a small house, where prayer would shape the day and where manual work would be as significant as work of the intellect. They wanted a place where the details of daily life 'would be the place of God's calling and blessing, as they are for most people'.

They were given the loan of a house at Little Crosby, on the outskirts of Liverpool, but after four years they had to leave. They were offered an island off Scotland, some stables near Leeds, part of a miners' village near Durham and a house in the Lake District, 'which would have been dreamy'. But they were not looking for a holiday home and they now had roots, they realized, by the Mersey. When they were out for a walk one day, in some woods not far from home, they came across a gate which led into a walled kitchen garden, large and gone to seed. The land belonged to a convent, and the nuns were glad to come to an arrangement which meant their woodlands would be managed. It was there that the monks started to build eleven years ago, and there Thomas lives still.

They decided to spend only what they had, since 'indebtedness is a spiritual issue', and the drive to indebtedness in modern society a major cause of evil. They laughingly decided to be wise in their 'economics' (in the original sense of the word – they would manage their household) and see how the finances worked out. And each Advent they would give any surplus away. 'I mentioned this to one of our other monks and he said, "Well, you've had it. You'll always have more than you need. The Lord can't but supply if you keep giving it away." I thought it was just a pious joke, but it's absolutely true.' Thomas travels by bicycle and recycles everything; friends and guests gather wood for the stoves and grow most of what they eat in the monastery garden; there is no telephone. He does not live austerely, but in simplicity. He has never run out of money.

He is there for no other reason than to seek God. Every day he puts on his long black robe for Matins, Lauds, midday prayers or Mass, Vespers and Compline: a daily rhythm of repentance and praise. Sometimes he is alone, often he is joined by villagers or visitors. The stillness of the chapel mingles with the smell of paraffin from the sanctuary lamp and the meditative chanting of psalms.

When Thomas joined Ampleforth he took the usual Benedictine vows. With the vow of obedience he freely placed himself under his abbot as mediator of God's will. Sometimes his own will called him more insistently, but 'conscience is not the way I am true to myself,' he says, 'it is the way I am true to God.' The vow of stability means he is for ever a member of the Ampleforth Community (even when his '*imagination* goes walkabout' and wonders if the grass is greener somewhere else); and calls him to be content in the here and now. The vow of *conversio morum* requires him to be in constant readiness for change when it would be pleasant to slide into habits of ease. The traditional vows of poverty and chastity are included in these three: 'Benedict had tough things to say about one's bodily self not being one's own as a possession.'

When he made his vows, he says, it was like writing a blank cheque, asking God to make him reasonably obedient, stable and flexible before he died. He did not realize then what they would mean. He has railed against them, but he has never considered leaving them behind. The vows are not, he says, 'a static thing; they're entry into a history which you're going to journey through with the Community.' He sees them as keys to freedom.

Without such structured freedom, he believes, human beings fracture. When the psychiatrist R. D. Laing visited Thomas some years ago, he commented that people need security in order to discover themselves; they need safety, boundaries and a sense of belonging in order to be sane. 'Your monastery,' he said, 'is an asylum.'

The wood beyond the garden wall is a pleasant place to walk. In the very early morning, after Matins, the trees stir into life after the 'great silence' of the night. The leaves flicker with the first warmth of the sun. Conversation is forbidden for another hour; but the psalms have already touched the air.

THIRTY

The Engineer

A military plane flew low with deafening noise, 'practising to kill someone', as Clive Newman put it. 'It's quite interesting,' he mused as he rolled another cigarette, 'they probably use more fuel driving up and down this valley than we do in a year.'

The Centre for Alternative Technology produces all its own electricity and could, if necessary, run on the power equivalent of a large electric kettle. It is not connected to the national grid, and most of its energy comes from renewable resources. If the breeze is too light to turn the windmills, or clouds keep the sun's rays back from the solar panels, a diesel generator fills the gap: what would normally be waste heat is recovered, which makes this one of the most efficient methods of converting fossil fuels into electricity.

'In small ways, very particular ways, we've lessened our impact on the rest of the world,' says Clive. But low consumption is the aim – not self-sufficiency, which he dismisses as ' a dead idea'. Using water, wind and sun to generate power would work better on a national, even international scale, he argues; but 'we're caught in a trap . . . while we demonstrate its possibility by living off it in a very isolated, self-contained unit – basically that isn't the way to deal with it.'

He was cosseting a cold and the sitting-room was cosy, with heat belting out from a small metal stove fed by local wood. The Powys sawmills benefit from selling CAT the fuel; still more from its decision to use the Welsh green oak and larch for building, which raised their value. 'It's silly shipping timber half way round the world when there are trees all around us,' Clive remarks. 'We try to stimulate the local economy . . . and there are global implications.'

Interconnections are what interest CAT; its message is about relationships, not self-reliance. Our use of energy, they say, cannot be divorced from our lifestyle, our consumption or even how we grow our food: local action travels far in its political effects. CAT does do some training courses for aid workers in the Third World, but 'getting the Africans to grow their grain better isn't going to make any difference, because we're still ripping them off,' says Clive. 'It's *here* that the problem is. Until we can lower our consumption in Western Europe everything we tell everyone else is just cant.'

CAT attracts over 70,000 visitors each year and responds to enquiries from hundreds more. Its role as a tourist attraction and educational resource developed gradually. Its origins go back to the early 1970s, when a 'visonary idealist' had the idea of establishing a village that was ecologically sound. The ruined slate quarry near Machynlleth was chosen as a suitable site and a community evolved, 'marching to a slightly different drum', Clive says, to other communes of the day. Others were into spirituality, politics and ecology, but the Quarry 'got stuck with its techno-kick'.

Increasing numbers came to look at its experiments in 'sustainable' living. It became an educational charity, regarded, Clive smiles, as 'cute but crazy'. Nobody believed that wind power was a serious option and the attitude to organic growing was 'yes we *know* you can gather all your shit and put it on your garden, but come *on* . . .'

Then suddenly the world changed its mind. The energy crisis and global warming made a fashion out of Green living and 'we realized we'd got to move in quick to keep in front, if you like, still have things to say.' In 1989, after agonized deliberation, the Quarry's permanent staff acknowledged that day visitors had become their 'core business'.

They decided they needed capital to improve the layout of the site; and changes in the way they thought of money precipitated a debate about their structure. The organization was split in two. Alongside the charity they created a public limited company, 'like the big wide world'. There was a share launch, which raised £1 million, 'and we used that primarily to build a big figurehead display, the cliff railway, and to improve our access . . . to increase our number of visitors, so we could increase our cash, so we could do more of the things we wanted to do . . .'

The water-powered cliff railway is the first thing you see when you arrive at CAT. Clive was one of the two engineers in charge. He took me for a ride in it and explained, with obvious delight, its system of computerized hydraulics. Water from a lake at the top was pumped into a tank beneath our carriage, until the balance tipped and we descended while the other carriage rose. At the bottom of the 197 foot track we watched the tank open and the water gushing out – some of it to be pumped back to the top, using energy reclaimed from the braking system.

The Quarry used to be invisible until you got up close. Now the railway shouts its presence to people on the road. It is symbolic, Clive says, of all the other changes on the site. The arguments of 1989 were bitter and the people who opposed the 'sell-out to capitalism' were right, he says, in their fear that it would change their lives. It was 'a big emotional shift', but one that he pushed hard for. Radicals become conservative, he says, clinging to their 'radical' ideas. A reluctant convert, he started to believe in commerce.

The success of the Visitors' Centre, run as a business by the plc, helps fund research; its 'respectability' has led to more and more consultancy work. CAT only has a small part to play, Clive admits, in raising consciousness about ecology and offering ideas, but 'it seemed there was an obligation to do it well – and openly, in a way that allows other people to see what you are doing.' The difficulty, he says, is learning to modify your message to ensure it gets across. He cannot bear it if the site gets scruffy – and not just because 'I'm anal retentive when it comes to gardening', as he grumbled on our saunter through a riot of organic herbs – but because '*that's* what people notice: all sorts of very simple, visual things . . .'

Clive is fifty but looks younger. He has a spiky haircut, and a casual smartness. His grin is easy and he *loves* to talk: 'You'll have to stop me or I'll go on and on, ' he said shortly after I arrived, when he had already covered the structure, tensions and meal system of CAT, 'I'm just incredibly garrulous.'

His Birmingham accent is a good vehicle for his wit. He's a city kid, he says, and waves his arm at the rolling tree-lined valley – 'Who'd live here?' His family was working-class, though he says he didn't know it till his thirties. His father was a 'rabid Tory', but neither politics nor religion featured in his 'totally normal, ordinary' upbringing. He served an engineering apprenticeship with a large electrical manufacturer and worked there for sixteen years – a job he enjoyed because of its technical interest. He was a shop steward, a trades union collectivist; he describes himself now as an old-fashioned socialist.

He was in his late twenties, married and living in a semi-detached suburban house, when he saw a picture in the colour supplement one day of some Buddhist monks setting fire to themselves in protest at the Vietnam War. This was 'the only real road to Damascus thing' in his life, he says with some embarrassment, reluctant to make anything of it. 'Being unusually reflective for me, I started thinking about what does a person have to *see*, how do they understand the world, when their only way of doing anything about it is to kill themselves in the most painful way you can imagine?'

He joined a group campaigning against the Vietnam War, his interest less in protest than 'construction' and change. He discovered the counter-culture – communes, anti-psychiatry, wholefood and the Peace Movement. 'I used to drop in to meetings in my suit and shirt and tie, and everybody else would be wearing tie-dye kaftans . . . Those sorts of movements didn't have a lot of industrial workers.'

The thread connecting his two lives was collectivity, and when he and his wife bought a larger house it quickly turned into a commune. They bought the house next door as well and 'it became fuller and fuller of stranger and more interesting people.' There were all the usual traumas about washing up and child-care; 'It was bedlam and a few people had breakdowns; it got exciting, lots of tensions and a certain amount of sexual activity, the demolishing and construction of relationships . . . I probably cried more tears than I've ever done in my life before or since. I wouldn't have missed it for the world.'

He left his job, which had started to seem meaningless: 'I saw a bigger world, a freer world.' Security and a proper salary were life's essentials in the poverty he had grown up in; now he lost his fear. He worked as a builder, and in a community press. 'I'm a bit of a romantic about the written word. I thought that we, the people, deserved high-quality printed material, and I'd spent a lot of my life handing out duplicated broadsheets on fuzzy pink paper, full of wrinkly lines with all the Os blocked. I'm quite evangelical about it; I've got a thing about quality.' He came across the Women's Movement, which taught him 'amongst other things, that what you did at home was also part of the political process. It brought the local onto my agenda.'

His relationship with his wife 'moved into a different mode' – he laughs at his own turn of phrase. At a commune in Scotland he met his current partner, June, 'and we've been together ever since . . . That doesn't really describe my sexual history very accurately, but it's about all you're going to get!' He and his wife had lived together for twenty years, through startling changes; she remains his best friend, a fact they are both proud of.

When they parted he felt he must leave Birmingham. He

moved to the capital – partly because he has a passion for modern dance and ballet, and wanted to be near Sadler's Wells. But he was head-hunted by CAT, and agreed to go there for six months. Six years later he has still not had enough.

Despite his gripes he loves it. 'It's hard to imagine a job that would be more satisfying. It's my hobby as well as my work.' Engineers have high status at CAT, he says, which makes a nice change. He suspects some people think they have too much autonomy – especially since the cliff railway, when they spent £½ million much as they pleased, hiring and firing and making decisions. There are three engineers; they have outspoken personalities and are seen as awkward. 'I mean *we* think we're pussy-cats! We don't have any real power; we're just Bolshy people.'

It would be very hard for anyone to take over at CAT, he says. Each of the work areas – restaurant, shop, education, building, engineering, information – is autonomous; issues such as personnel and finance are dealt with by elected groups. New proposals and budgets are submitted to an overview group and ratified by an assembly of all the staff. Decisions are made by consensus: there is a voting system, but the threat of using it has always been enough.

The system works harmoniously but encourages conservatism, he thinks: 'It's easier to stay where you are . . .' As an example, he tells me of a recent struggle about wages. All the staff earn £6,000 a year before tax and deductions, to cover rent and food; those with children have allowances which raise the figure quite a bit. Clive is one of the only five childless people, an 'underpaid minority' which is unhappy and wants change. 'I think I work harder and put more thought into what I do than some members of staff who earn considerably more than me,' he says, 'and that's past the limit of what I consider fair.' He is not seeking riches: he was happy when a provisional agreement was reached to 'move towards' paying everyone £12,000 a year, 'a sensible wage for the area'.

His partner does a 'proper job' in Newtown, so he can afford to go on holiday and run a car – 'diesel, so it's not *terrible*!' He has tired of austerity; like others in CAT, he says, he has lost interest in the puritan ethic. This is partly due to members' children, who have reached their teens and want TVs and trainers like their friends; partly for practicality. In the beginning they had no fridges and drank raw milk 'because it was thought of to be a groovy thing to do. Of course, it went off like mad. We tend to buy milk in bottles now like the rest of the world.'

Clive is one of a small, and diminishing, number of workers who live at the Centre. This used to be seen as an advantage: you weren't part of the in-crowd if you lived off-site; there weren't so many visitors, it was fun, and you could ensure your home was energy-efficient. But there were drawbacks: all the lights went out at nine o'clock, and the power was so ropey it was hard to make your hi-fi run at the right speed. Although things have improved, most people now prefer to rent or buy in the neighbourhood.

The staff who do live in form a small community with their own finance and meetings. They share chores and cooking, which some find hard. But Clive likes the collective life. 'I'm terribly institutionalized. I don't find that it inhibits my individuality very much – rather, it thrives within that framework. I've *always* eaten at Formica-topped tables with loads of other people.' He doesn't mind that he cannot choose his meals or when he eats them: once a fortnight he concentrates on cooking and enjoys it; the rest of the time someone else does that for him. The system provides '*lots* more time to do the things I want to do as an individual'.

'You get more for your money in the end, more for your work' if you collectivize, he says. The danger comes when you do it with the wrong things, from ideological notions of what is essential and what is luxury. Communes have always been dominated by middle-class graduates (and he confesses to 'various weights of chips' on his shoulder because he is not one of them) – the 'chattering classes', whose scorn of television banished it to the shared room. But televisions use little power and last for ages; watching them, he argues, is an individualistic activity: 'and all the stress and negotiating that goes into it! You may as well have one each.'

What he is happy to share is his bathroom. After all, he points out, he only uses it for an hour in the evening. When he built the house he lives in, he and his neighbour agreed that within the confines of their budgets they could either have two poky bathrooms or one – a separate building – that was relatively luxurious, 'a pleasant place to be after a hard day on the slate tip'. They also share a compost toilet, adorned with instructions as to use. And at the bottom of his tiny garden Clive has constructed a sauna.

Building his house 'was a little trip all of its own'. He tended to dismiss romantic notions about the profundity of providing your own shelter, he says, but then discovered they were true. 'I feel it's mine in a complex sort of way – except that I could walk away from it tomorrow . . . the bit of it I own is inside me.' All his life he has made things for other people; he designed his home so the next person who moves in can adapt it to their needs.

He has vague yearnings to settle down more permanently and does not intend to stay at CAT for ever. But his lifestyle suits the 'enlightened self-interest' which he describes as 'not a very earth-shattering philosophy, but probably the only one I've got'. He has relaxed his idealism and does a lot of what he fancies; occasionally he skimps on the recycling, he jokes, and gives himself a thrill by throwing away a jam jar. But he is convinced that 'you don't actually get anywhere unless you take everybody with you.'

He is an atheist, who finds 'having a belief-system as some internal thing a cop-out, just a lack of mental rigour. Religious people seem to make some funny choices, because they're working to another script.' Heaven isn't to look forward to, he says, we have to build it.

'We live longer and better quality lives than anybody has ever done in the whole history of the human race. We have more leisure, more freedom, better health, more opportunities. And what do we do with it? We watch *Neighbours*.' If we have any obligation at all, it is to think about what we're doing with our wealth, he says, and that is what they do at CAT.

He is 'an industrialist, a great believer in factories'. Their ownership is wrong, he grants; they should be in the workers' hands. But without them the great mass of people will never get the goodies: 'You can't all go for New Age Greeny little cottages in the country, *and* have CDs.' Technology holds the future.

THIRTY ONE

Taking Refuge

In the Scottish countryside is a Tibetan temple – the only indication a small wooden arrow, pointing down a drive to 'Samye Ling'. Brightly coloured prayer flags flutter between trees; at the bottom is an old stone house with window frames of green and red.

There were people everywhere in wellingtons, and a lot of mud. My first glimpse of the temple, side-on through heavy rain, was drab – just breeze block and a bit of a pagoda roof. But from the front it is impressive. Neary 40 metres wide, it takes up one side of a square and is reached by a flight of steps. The square will be the courtyard of a Buddhist college, to be built around the three remaining sides. For the moment the space is open, and it is natural to stand back to view the building as a whole.

The top tier is the reliquary: according to tradition, religious objects placed in a temple's highest point will radiate their benefits around the world. The middle tier has an audience chamber and rooms for visiting patriarchs. At the bottom is the temple with its massive doors (in Tibet there would be one; in Scotland, regulations call for several, marked 'Exit' as in cinemas). They open to a dazzle of colour.

Along the walls are *thangkas*, scrolls depicting scenes from Buddhist legend: each the work of several people who have steeped themselves in the tradition. Mythological animals, intricately carved, twine around the thrones and fourteen pillars. The ceiling has 400 panels of a dragon and a phoenix, silk-screened in seventeen colours. Everything is lavish; but the eye is drawn to the shrine, where a golden statue of the Buddha sits with volumes of his teachings, bound in brocade.

The imagery at Samye Ling, and all its crafting, is supervized by Sherab Palden Beru – one of the finest of Tibetan artists, with a long monastic training. One of the hopes of Samye Ling is that it will help preserve and carry on the culture of Tibet. Since Chinese forces occupied the country more than thirty years ago, its literature, philosophy and art have faced extinction.

Among those who fled the occupation were two young abbots, Akong Rinpoche and Trungpa Rinpoche, who ended up in Britain. The old stone house in Eskdalemuir was then the home of a small community with leanings towards Buddhism, and the abbots often went to teach there. Eventually the house was sold to them, at token cost. That was Samye Ling's beginnings; the first Tibetan Buddhist centre in the West, named after the very first Tibetan monastery. It grew fast. Twenty-one years later the temple was publicly inaugurated on a date regarded as auspicious – 8 August 1988 (8.8.88).

Marjan Wieringa first went to Samye Ling seven years ago, when the temple building was a shell, and helped to paint it. She went for a fortnight to sort out a relationship; she returned to visit twice within a few months, and then stayed for six years. Now she is preparing for the Long Retreat, which starts at the end of 1993 and finishes in 1997. She will be cloistered from the world, and will be forty-two when she comes out. 'It would be silly to have any plans for afterwards.'

To save up for the retreat she got a job in Edinburgh. Samye Ling still feels like home and she has a boyfriend there, so she makes regular visits. She has never been good at keeping up her meditation and now, she says, does less than ever – but that has made her more aware of the benefits of the retreat, and more determined to go on it. 'I need that sort of structured set-up, because if I don't have it my meditation falls to bits.'

At five o'clock we went to the temple, summoned by a gong. People, mostly young, entered and prostrated themselves three times before the shrine; then they settled all around the floor, cross-legged on cushions. A rhythmical Tibetan prayer rose and faded into silence to begin – its chanter a middle-aged Scot in maroon robes, who had a wife and children before he went to be a monk. Half-way through the hour, a girl went out in tears; one or two stretched limbs; most sat absolutely still until the beauty of the chanting filled the room again at six o'clock.

'I find just sitting in that position helps so much,' said Marjan as we came away, 'it clears out your system.' In a gap between the scheduled sessions of prayer and meditation she showed me round the temple. Sitting on a bench at the back – all dressed in black with silver-wire earrings, her fair hair falling round her shoulders and her hands thrust deep into her jacket pockets – she pointed out the Tibetan way with primary colours, so different from the European fear of 'clash'. Tibetan art insists on balance: red, symbolizing fire, must be counterpoised by green for air; yellow is earth, and not complete without a streak of blue for space, or white for water. The colours in Samye Ling are especially bright because the Western pigments used are powerful and have not had time to fade.

Marjan likes symbolism of this kind; but ritual and religious imagery mean little to her. She is technically an atheist; in meditation 'I'm focusing on mind itself rather than an external God'. She is sure there is an 'ultimate reality' – something that cannot be described; and that Tibetan Buddhism is a 'container' that has been used to bring an understanding of that reality to the West in a time of transition. 'The container was Tibetan; the content, I think, is universal.'

Her upbringing, in Holland, was not religious in the least. Her mother was a humanist, her father an engineer whose passionate belief in science extended to a fervent atheism. Her childhood was pervaded by the differences between them:

'this fairly stable, orderly existence of going to school and coming back home to a mum with a cup of tea . . . And my dad brought a lot of ups and downs and confusion, but also unusual liberal attitudes like sex education, and if I didn't want to go to school I didn't have to.'

There was a divorce, when Marjan was in her teens, and her parents never saw each other again. She took on, she thinks, the male role at home. 'My dad more or less disappeared. He went into a great cloud of being unavailable, and being drunk and being on the road . . .' Ten years ago, 'too old to be so wild', he settled down and Marjan went to see him often, to rebuild the relationship. He died last year, but she still describes him in the present tense.

To her he represents, 'in archetypal words,' (she stresses this) 'the alcoholic genius'. She sees him as brilliant and sensitive, ahead of his times and with a global view of things; but 'a disaster area in relationships'. He had invented machines, yet he lived as a down-and-out. He read voraciously – in the farming world he came from no one went to college.

'All religion is a rip-off,' he said to her; 'how can you be so stupid?' She bought him Jung's autobiography and Capra's books on the 'new physics', as a way of getting him to understand what she was doing. And it worked. 'He knew somehow inside himself that what I was doing was right, and I did feel his respect, *genuine* respect.' Her mother accepts what Marjan is doing simply because it is her choice; her father, she is sure, came to appreciate the Buddhist path itself.

Ever since her parents separated, Marjan believes, she has felt the urge to reconcile within herself their split. She recognized her mother and her father in her personality – and she needed to unite her 'normal' side, anxious for a steady boyfriend and a salary, with the 'wild guy' who goes to the very depths and very heights, and never fits in.

She hitch-hiked on her own round Europe; and then set out to study Child Psychology. She liked her course, but only did the bits that took her fancy. At twenty-one she met a man on holiday in London, and moved in. He was Turkish and needed a residence permit, so she married him.

After a while, she left the man behind and went back to Holland. 'By then I'd totally forgotten about studying,' she says with laughter. 'In a sense I'd got past that stage.' For the next few years there was 'some sort of journey of self-discovery – but I never thought of it like that'. She worked with heroin addicts from Surinam, and as a social worker. For a while, she was unemployed. She smoked a lot of dope, drank a lot of beer and hung around in pubs. There was always a man in her life, sometimes more than one. She looked into yoga, therapeutic drama and astrology. Then, she says, 'I was twenty-nine: Saturn's Return.'

At around that age, she says, 'people realize what they are . . . and become clear what they're about.' Two things happened to her then. First, she got a job in a crisis centre for adolescents: the beginning 'of a tremendous learning process . . .' The focus was people, the structure democratic; it was 'not theoretical' – nor is she.

And she fell in love with a South African: 'totally and ridiculously, head over heels, madly infatuated'. It was, she thinks, a '*Dharmic* connection'; nothing else explains her frenzied attachment to a man who jilted her within a month. Seething with jealousy because he had told her he was sleeping with another woman, she yet soaked up his eager tales of 'taking refuge' – becoming a Buddhist, as he had recently done with Akong Rinpoche at Samye Ling.

She was fascinated by the process going on within her. She needed to be free of her passion, but she also vaguely sensed it was 'about something else as well'. So when the man returned to Samye Ling, she followed him.

Within a few days, the obsession was gone; in its place she had a sense of 'coming home'. She was there a fortnight, but can still remember every day of it. 'You know how sometimes you suddenly understand the whole of something, rather than the various bits you've been digesting? That's what happened to me.' For an hour a day she listened to classes on Tibetan texts, 'and I used to think "God, they know everything!" I mean, in the shrine room they have several hundred "texts" (they're really books) and every one more or less explains the universe – it's ridiculous!' Above all she 'circumambulated' Akong Rinpoche. 'I was sort of looking at this guy thinking, "Hang on a sec., are you enlightened or not?" After the fortnight, I was totally convinced he was.'

So what *is* an enlightened being? Good question, she says. She didn't know what she was looking for, but she felt sure it would be obvious. 'Enlightenment means you have freed your own mind from all karmic obstacles. I knew it had something to do with not being conditioned, being free of fixed ideas about good and bad – to have liberated yourself from feeling attracted to things, or repulsed by things. To be open to anything that arises, and to deal with it totally spontaneously and also totally adequately, because you don't judge things on the basis of the past or ideas of the future.'

She listened to what people said of Akong Rinpoche; she watched him. She asked for an interview – which she expected to be formal, but which turned out to be an easy five-minute chat. One day, she saw light coming out of him ('it sounds very dramatic, but it's what I experienced'), and she knew there was something for her in Buddhism, or between her and this teacher.

She went back home with a sense of meaning. 'Not that I all of a sudden behaved differently or anything, but inside me everything had fallen into place. It felt like clearing your head, taking a mental shower, all the black fuzzy things disappeared . . .' It was as if she suddenly saw something very simple which she had always known. 'That insight changed my life.'

Her head was too full of other things to meditate, but a few months later she felt strongly she wanted to return to Samye Ling. With a sense she was going into danger, and yet wanted to, she put all her holidays and days in lieu together and went back for seven weeks. Akong Rinpoche was away. On his return, in a little ceremony, she 'took refuge'. He gave her a Buddhist name, to sum up the essence of her character, so she can strive to liberate it. 'That's a fancy way of putting it. You could say he gives you any old name, y'know.' She is 'Glorious Quality': all the Buddhist names, she adds, are *very* nice.

Marjan says she tends to be afraid of taking anything the whole way. Being a Buddhist meant she was required to do her best for all beings, 'including yourself; it's not martyrdom or anything'. Though she felt aware of great inner development, she carried on in Amsterdam much as she had before – not even turning vegetarian. But eventually, she gave up her job and left her boyfriend of the time to settle down in Samye Ling.

And the richness of life is there, she says, in all its aspects. People have affairs and quarrels; they gossip and negotiate. Because the jobs – running the office, building, book-keeping – are done on a voluntary basis, they seldom accumulate power. Some people spend all day in the temple; some, like Marjan, work very hard and find their karma – as she puts it – lands them yet again in pressurized activity.

She showed me round the workshops, where Westerners turn their hands to temple art. They weren't around, but they had left behind them pots of resin and gold paint, and scattered statues of the Buddha, incomplete. Further on a 'sculpture park', of jokes made out of junk and rags, bobbed and creaked beside the River Esk. Going back for lunch, we passed the houses people built who wanted to make it their permanent home – Samye Ling has grown into a tiny village.

The dining-room is cheerful and chaotic. On the notice-board outside there is a message on behalf of Akong Rinpoche, requesting that no music should be played, except at certain hours – so that the old stone house can still be quiet for residents and visitors. The request will be enough: though not everyone at Samye Ling has 'taken refuge', they are united in respect for Akong Rinpoche.

When Marjan went away, to prepare for her retreat, it was as liberating to leave as it had been to arrive: 'part of me quite likes this shedding . . .' Running the office at Samye Ling had become exhausting, but it had given her experience in managing volunteers, which she used to get her present job: setting up a respite care project for people with mental health problems. It has reassured her she has skills to offer to society. She loves having a house to herself, watching television and buying what she wants to eat in supermarkets. But though her Tibetan and meditation often go by the board, she is still set on her plan.

Saving up is easy – she was used to having very little money. In Samye Ling she could live for a month on £30, and her work in the office covered her keep – so saving up is not a problem. The fee for the retreat is £8,000, which covers living and tuition costs for four years. But Akong Rinpoche told her to save what she could manage and that would be enough: it gave her the incentive, without the pressure.

She is vague about what the retreat will entail – though its pattern is largely traditional, details are revised from time to time to make it more fruitful for Westerners. There is a daily programme, from 4 a.m. to eleven at night. Some of that is theory but most is 'practice'. There will be about twenty other women, and at first they will do most things together – later it becomes more individualized. She will regularly see the Lama in charge: 'It's very important it is supervised; it's strong stuff.'

At the end of her first year the retreatants will come out for a month or two, to decide whether they want to continue. This is a concession to the Western mentality, and it makes it easier, she says, to take the plunge. Other than that they will see no one apart from the caretakers who do the shopping and cooking; they are segregated from the men who are doing the retreat at the same time. 'Basically, I just think I don't know what I'm letting myself in for,' she says. 'It is realistic to just go in with faith.'

Of the last group who emerged from the retreat, a good proportion went straight back in to do another. She feels that four years of the sort of intensity she is expecting will be the equivalent of many years' experience outside. She knows it will be hard to leave behind the boyfriend she has been with many years, to go to the retreat house up the road; and she has faced the fact that because of her age, 'I think the decision has been made I won't have children'.

The aim of life, she says, is to liberate yourself and others from suffering and the cycle of life and death – to achieve enlightenment. There is no 'meaning' beyond that. 'As long as beings suffer, there is some sort of purpose. But ultimately there's no purpose at all.'